Cambridge Studies in Social and Cultural Anthropology

Editors: Jack Goody, Stephen Gudeman, Michael Herzfeld, Jonathan Parry

71

STEALING PEOPLE'S NAMES

A list of books in the series will be found at the end of the volume

Stealing people's names

History and politics in a
Sepik river cosmology

SIMON J. HARRISON

Department of Sociology University of Ulster

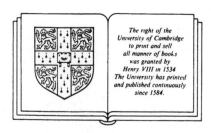

The right of the
University of Cambridge
to print and sell
all manner of books
was granted by
Henry VIII in 1534
The University has printed
and published continuously
since 1584.

CAMBRIDGE UNIVERSITY PRESS

Cambridge
New York   Port Chester Melbourne Sydney

CAMBRIDGE UNIVERSITY PRESS
Cambridge, New York, Melbourne, Madrid, Cape Town, Singapore, São Paulo

Cambridge University Press
The Edinburgh Building, Cambridge CB2 2RU, UK

Published in the United States of America by Cambridge University Press, New York

www.cambridge.org
Information on this title: www.cambridge.org/9780521385046

First published 1990
This digitally printed first paperback version 2006

A catalogue record for this publication is available from the British Library

Library of Congress Cataloguing in Publication data

Harrison, Simon J.
Stealing people's names: history and politics in a Sepik River
cosmology / Simon J. Harrison.
    p.   cm. – (Cambridge studies in social anthropology; 71)
Includes bibliographical references
ISBN 0 521 38504 0 (U.S.)
1. Manambu (Papua New Guinea people) – Politics and government.
2. Manambu (Papua New Guinea people) – Social life and customs.
3. Avatip (Papua New Guinea) – Social life and customs.   I. Title.
II. Series.
DU740.42.H375   1990
995.3-dc20   89-29679
                                                                          CIP

ISBN-13 978-0-521-38504-6 hardback
ISBN-10 0-521-38504-0 hardback

ISBN-13 978-0-521-02647-5 paperback
ISBN-10 0-521-02647-4 paperback

Dedicated to my mother
and to my father

Contents

Illustrations

Tables

Acknowledgements

This book is based on fieldwork carried out under a scholarship in the Department of Prehistory and Anthropology of the Australian National University, and on a thesis written while I was a postgraduate student there. I am grateful to that institution for the financial support and stimulating environment it provided.

Before my fieldwork, Donald Laycock helped me invaluably by making available his field notes and tapes on the Manambu language. I would like to thank Anthony Forge, Alfred Gell and Robert Tonkinson for their academic supervision; Michael Young for the encouraging, and very generous, interest he took in my work; and my fellow graduate students, especially Jon Altman and Jadran Mimica, for much academic inspiration. Andrew Strathern, Donald Tuzin and the late Ralph Bulmer all made insightful and constructive criticisms of my thesis.

I am grateful to Kilian McDaid, of the Department of Environmental Studies of the University of Ulster, for preparing the maps and figures for this book, and to the Royal Anthropological Institute and the American Ethnological Society for permission to use material from the following articles:

1987. Cultural Efflorescence and Political Evolution on the Sepik River. *American Ethnologist* 14 (3): 491–507. Copyright © 1987 American Anthropological Association. All rights reserved.

1988. Magical Exchange of the Preconditions of Production in a Sepik River Village. *Man (N.S.)* 23 (2): 319–33.

1989. Magical and Material Polities in Melanesia. *Man (N.S.)* 24 (1): 1–20.

In Papua New Guinea, Micah Kalinoe and Ambrose Vakinap gave me my first introduction to Manambu culture. At Ambunti, I should like to thank the Assistant District Officer, Ray Bray, Horst and Eugenie Schmidt of the Summer Institute of Linguistics, and Alan Gallagher of Las Kampani for their hospitality and practical help. My greatest debt is to my hosts at Avatip, of whom I must especially mention Narwanggən, Wapikas, Francis Kamimeli, Kamatəp, Wawiandu, Sunggwarwakən, Tapi, Mandjikəmban, Gabriel

Acknowledgements

Kənggətəndu, Lapakawi, Mbərakwundi and Lumeli. Above all, I should like to record my gratitude to Kwulanawi Yuakaw, his wives Manum and Ndumwiwaləp, and all their children, for their hospitality and many kindnesses.

The ward of the subclan Maliyaw at Yentshanggai.

Debating the ownership of the name Kərekəndawai, Malu village, April 1978.

Introduction

Introduction

This is a study of cosmology and political life among the Manambu, a people of the Sepik River in northwestern Papua New Guinea. When I was planning my fieldwork early in 1977, there was little published material on the Manambu apart from an outline of their language (Laycock 1965) and a brief but fascinating ethnographic sketch by Newton (1971). These suggested close cultural links between the Manambu and their downriver neighbours, the Iatmul, whose culture had been the subject of one of the most original monographs in the ethnographic literature (Bateson 1958).

Before I had ever been to Papua New Guinea, I had been intrigued by Bateson's references to ceremonial debates, in which Iatmul descent groups disputed the ownership of ancestral names and totems, and by his characterisation of the Iatmul as a people among whom personal names formed 'a theoretical image of the whole culture' (Bateson 1958: 228). But I had no plans to make such matters the focus of my own research. I hoped to study a more familiar theme in Melanesian ethnography: the ceremonial wealth-exchanges which tend to be an important feature of traditional Melanesian politics, and the self-made leaders, or Big Men, who earn their status and influence in these transactions.

But it was clear from the start of my stay among the Manambu that the villagers had an intense, and highly disputatious, preoccupation with the ownership of personal names. I arrived at the settlement of Avatip, where I later established my home, to find the community in the throes of a major dispute between two of its largest descent groups. A few years earlier, both of these groups had apparently given one of their infant children the same name, Manggalaman. It was explained to me that it was anomalous and highly offensive for children of different descent groups to be namesakes. The two groups had since then quarrelled bitterly over which of them owned the name, each accusing the other of having 'stolen' it. Preparations were under way for what my younger English-speaking informants described as a debate, in which the elders of the two sides would compete and the winners (by some obscure means described to me only as 'like a school examination') would force the

1

losers to relinquish the name. The atmosphere in the village was very tense. My rather rash attempts to enquire into the dispute at this stage were met with a good deal of suspicion. As I only learned much later, the senior men of each side were closely guarding certain secret mythological lore crucial to the dispute, and were very apprehensive that it might fall into the hands of their opponents and enable them to win the debate.

The debate took place: a big, elaborate event which lasted for about twenty hours and involved the whole population of the village. Before many more months passed, a number of similar disputes broke out between other descent groups, and more debates were staged. Much time and energy was being spent on these affairs; the important political figures in the community were men expert in debating, and these oratorical contests seemed to be the key political institution of the society. The villagers did not make competitive or otherwise overtly 'political' gift exchanges with each other, and wealth seemed to have little political significance. I felt that I would be giving the rather low-key bridewealth and mortuary payments, which I witnessed in the meantime, an artificial importance if I made them the focus of my research. I also began to feel quite disoriented, as the months went by and I established personal relationships, by what appeared to me a completely unintelligible obsession with the ownership of names on the part of my friends and informants, who seemed in all other respects people of exemplary good sense and sanity. It became a personal necessity to discover the reasons for it, a way of surviving what is wholly inadequately called culture shock.

Altogether I spent a little under twenty-two months among the Manambu, between July 1977 and December 1978, and between July and December 1979, and the 'ethnographic present' of this study refers to those years. I made my home at Avatip because it was the largest of the three Manambu settlements, and seemed therefore to offer the best opportunities for research. The questions in which I became interested called for an intensive familiarity with a single community, and I carried out most of my research at Avatip except for short visits made to the two other communities for purposes of comparison. I was quickly incorporated into the clan system and given a Manambu name, though I suspect this was done in a spirit of systematisation rather than for sentimental reasons. The Manambu are relentless 'totemic' classifiers and insist on including virtually everything in the world, even stray Englishmen, into their totemic categories. The Manambu language is not an especially difficult one and in time I was able to understand it reasonably well. But throughout my fieldwork I remained a mediocre speaker of it and often had to resort to the *lingua franca* of Melanesian pidgin, in which most of the villagers were fluent. The language of Avatip oratory uses a specialised, archaic and heavily 'Iatmulised' lexicon and a difficult, esoteric imagery; I found debates impossible to follow without extensive help.

Introduction

Realism and nominalism

The immediate ethnographic aims of this book are to explain why rights in personal names are the most important strategic resource for which political actors at Avatip compete; to describe the processes by which these conflicts over names are carried out and resolved; and to examine their implications for the political history of the society. But more broadly, my theme is the relation between the symbolic order and the order of political action and power. In Avatip society, power consists in knowledge and rests on the most insubstantial yet refractory of bases: an intersubjective, shared world of meaning. In the early chapters of this book, I discuss Avatip religion, cosmology and ritual, because it is these which define, for men, the goals of all political action and form the universe of means and ends within which they compete. This discussion lays the groundwork for an analysis, in the later chapters, of the politics of debating and of the key processes of conflict in the community, which I shall call name-disputes.

Avatip descent groups have specialised hereditary functions in magic and ritual. These groups, or rather the senior men who represent them, are conceived as collaborating in this way to maintain the total world order. To the villagers, their society is held together and made into a politically organised totality, a 'polity', by the organic interlocking of all their descent groups' cosmological powers. At one level, the early chapters form an extended exegesis of a fundamental concept, *ndja'am*, which encapsulates the idea of a 'total' reciprocity between groups, involving exchanges of women, wealth, magical and ritual services, and esoteric knowledge.

Ever since Durkheim's critique of Spencer's sociology, a long-standing question of theory in social science has concerned the opposed perspectives of holism and individualism: the question whether society is to be understood as a supraindividual reality or as just a collection of transacting individuals (Andreski 1984: 37–41; Barth 1966; Durkheim 1933; Gellner 1973: 1–17; Leach 1961a; Peel 1971: 185–191; Popper 1957; Spencer 1876; Tuzin 1976). What has made this question a difficult one to settle is that it is not only a question for the observer. The peoples that we study may themselves often be faced with making similar choices about how to represent their social worlds, and may implicitly use theories resembling nominalism and realism. As Gellner (1973: 5) notes, individuals may themselves 'have holistic concepts and often act in terms of them.' A folk model of this sort may perhaps only be an ideology, a politically motivated misrepresentation of the way the society in some sense actually works. But even though it may be only an ideology, it will feed back upon action and have real effects.

Avatip social theory, as expressed in ritual, is very much a realist one: in ritual, men portray their society as a transcendent, relational totality, with the subclans and their funds of ritual power having a timeless reality quite independent of the existence of their members. All the processes of political action that I analyse in this book are oriented wholly toward that image and are impossible to understand without reference to it.

I try to identify the conditions – social, economic, historical and so forth – that have predisposed Avatip men toward adopting realist conceptions of this sort in their ritual representations. But more importantly, I wish to examine the consequences which the use of this model have for long-term processes of political action.

The most basic consequences are first, that cosmology and ritual are conceived to form a closed, finite universe of personal names, ritual powers and other forms of immaterial property that men treat as having a reality transcending themselves; and second, that men compete politically on the basic assumption that those resources, and the status they confer, are limited and of scarce value.

Avatip realism is implicitly a political ideology because the division of ceremonial powers in the society creates hereditary inequalities in status between groups and between individuals. These inequalities operate beyond the sphere of ritual only in limited and indirect ways. But they are an important organising principle of ritual, and are given their most intense and overt expression in the rituals of the male initiatory cult. Outside of these ritual contexts, the relations which men and groups have with one another are relatively egalitarian, and extremely competitive. But what they are struggling constantly for are hereditary positions of high status in ritual, and the goals of all political competition are these 'ascribed' ritual prerogatives. For men hereditary stratification is a powerful religious ideology. Yet it is only episodically, in the actual staging of large-scale rituals, that they are able to bring this stratification into existence and live it in collective experience. A major initiation ritual requires years of complex planning and preparation. During those years, innumerable negotiations and intrigues take place as men, and the groups they represent, begin competing for the most important roles in the ritual. When the ritual takes place it is, in effect, the brief crystallisation of the power relations which have provisionally been established through these protracted struggles. The current balance within a constantly shifting field of power relations is transfigured, momentarily, into a ritually-validated hierarchy of status. A major ritual is a difficult and, in terms of time, energy and social conflict, *costly* achievement by political groups and the men leading them. It is the accomplishment of a short-lived moment of consensual and legitimate hierarchy among themselves.

This brings me to the significance of Avatip debating. When two groups compete in a debate for the ownership of a personal name, they are in fact competing, in the allusive and metaphorical language of oratory, for a secret prerogative in male initiatory ritual. Although debates are entirely public

4

events, only initiated men, supposedly, ever understand the real issues at stake. So far as women and noninitiates are concerned, debates are disputes purely over personal names. Quarrels over names, although noninitiates do not 'officially' know it, are actually the back-stage politics of the rituals of the male initiatory cult.

The debates are, in fact, an integral part of the preparations for an Avatip ritual. When plans are laid for an important initiation, a prolonged and often complexly interconnected series of disputes break out, creating or reopening major political rifts in the community. These disputes are, in other words, geared in to the successive phases of the initiatory system and, together with the initiatory system itself, follow a cycle lasting about a generation. These cyclical patterns of conflict are the subject of the book's later chapters.

I focus on two subclans which, in very different ways, are pivotal in the network of political relations in the community. One is a small, politically weak but ritually very senior subclan whose cosmological powers are being, and have been for several generations, gradually appropriated by more successful rivals. The second is the largest and politically most powerful subclan at Avatip; although it is a junior group, its leaders have tried over the generations, with some success, to make it ritually the most important group in the community. This part of the book is, in a sense, the history of these two groups, and of the conflicts they have been involved in, or which have in one way or another revolved around them, and which had shaped the major political processes in the community in the post-contact period. What I particularly try to show is the way in which a descent group's fortunes in the ritual system are linked closely, both as cause and effect, to its reproductive fortunes. Underpinning the competition for names and ritual prerogatives, there is another kind of rivalry altogether: for demographic viability and for the reproductive powers of women.

Polity and cosmology in Oceania

Avatip ritual, myth and cosmology are constantly altered and revised as groups, and the leaders representing them, compete in debates and challenge one another's status. One of the aims of this book is to identify the patterns of change in ritual and cosmology which these processes of political competition produce.

At one level, the basic symbolism and organisation of Avatip ritual and cosmology seem to have remained stable over a very long period. Groups rise and fall in status, but most of their disputes result simply in redistributions of ritual privileges within the existing cosmology and do not alter the cosmology itself. Nor do these processes result in any overall transformation of the political system, because all that happens is that a succession of identically-constituted subclans displace each other in a fixed status hierarchy. But what I wish also to show is that these competitive processes have involved, for some political actors, a purposeful long-term aim of bringing about changes of a different order: modifications not just *within* the existing structure of political-cosmological relationships, but *of* it.

In writing this book, I have drawn much inspiration from the extended-case method, which I regard as a powerful technique for the analysis of long-term patterns of conflict (see Van Velsen 1967). But I use a time-scale somewhat longer than is usual in an extended-case study proper, because the processes I shall describe extend over a period of three, or in some cases more, generations. Sometimes, I shall write as though the political actors in Avatip society were descent groups. This is not an attempt to hypostatise these groups but an effect of the time-scale of the processes I wish to analyse. Many conflicts in the community are short-lived, but the ones in which I am especially interested, for reasons I shortly discuss, are transgenerational. In other words, they transcend the careers, and the lifetimes, of the political actors who actually carry them out. An Avatip leader, by being born into a particular subclan, is born also into a complex of long-standing ritual disputes. These define for him, as they did for his predecessors and perhaps shall for his successors, a set of major, long-term political goals and strategies which have been highly consistent over the generations. It was fortunate for my research that Avatip has had a large, stable and permanently settled population for several hundred years. There are extensive and detailed oral histories from which to reconstruct, fairly reliably, the political relations between groups over my chosen time-depth of somewhat under a century.

Although I have borrowed from the extended-case method a concern with recurrent cycles of conflict, I have not tried to borrow the theoretical perspective with which the method tended to be associated. This perspective, a sophisticated and late version of structural-functionalism, was an attempt to integrate the analysis of conflict into a view of society as founded ultimately upon moral consensus. The aim of the 'classic' extended-case studies (for instance, Turner 1957) was to examine the ways in which repetitive patterns of conflict function in the reproduction of social systems, and serve in the long term to maintain homeostasis and stability.

The conflicts I analyse are certainly cyclical, but I argue that they involve, and did so before European contact, a dissensus among men regarding the significance of ascribed inequality. Avatip men certainly consider hereditary inequalities to be fundamental in the organisation of ritual. But the intense inter-group disputes which precede every ritual are not only struggles for status but also pre-emptive attempts these groups are making to prevent each other from gaining excessively or permanently dominant positions in the ritual status hierarchy. It is quite clear from their consistent political strategies, that the leaders of at least one of the larger and more powerful subclans have for a long time actually been seeking this pre-eminent status, and that others are trying to prevent them from gaining it. The leaders of this subclan have been trying to bring about a basic change in the structure of the cosmology: the transformation of a system of cooperative reciprocities in which every group plays a role according to its specific cosmological functions, into a quite different pattern in which one powerful descent group, their own, dominates the community and controls all the key ritual powers.

Forms of ritual organisation analogous to both of these patterns exist in other Oceanic societies. The first resembles the ritual systems of the Aboriginal societies of central Australia such as the Aranda (Spencer and Gillen 1904), based on a collaborative interdependence of politically equal clans each with its own distinctive totemic powers. But the Oceanic societies in which the second pattern is found are the chiefly polities, in which the major ritual powers are a prerogative of those of high rank or chiefly status. A widespread feature of Oceanic cosmologies, in other words, is an association of particular cosmological functions with particular descent groups; but a rearrangement of the ritual responsibilities, of the way in which these ritual powers are distributed among groups, can imply wholly different forms of political organisation. Each of these cosmological patterns contains the possibility of the other because, in principle, one can be transformed into the other by degrees, and without any change at all in the substantive contents of cosmology, simply by a gradual alteration in their social distribution. The 'same' cosmology can remain, the same ritual symbols enduring timeless and unchanged over history, but their political *meaning* can be progressively transformed by a reordering of the key social roles and relationships among the actors in ritual. Depending on the degree to which ritual powers are controlled by a minority or dispersed equally among all descent groups, they can 'signify' either rank at one extreme or complete political equality of groups at the other.

My argument is that the reason why certain Avatip subclans are seeking to achieve a pre-eminent status in ritual and cosmology, is that they are seeking to use that dominance to legitimise claims to ascribed political authority. In the disputes over cosmology which have been taking place this century in the higher grades of the men's cult, some of the most senior custodians, and innovators, of Avatip ritual and cosmology have been trying to establish embryonic forms of rank and chieftainship. I am not suggesting that the political system could be transformed *simply* by transforming the structure of the cosmology: in order to change cosmology in this way, a subclan must in the first place achieve a real *de facto* political dominance over other groups. What the ritual system offers, to a group sufficiently effective in defeating all rivals, is a means of institutionalising that *de facto* power. That is, the cosmology contains within itself the conceptual possibility of a new form of political organisation, and it is that conceived possibility that some political actors are seeking to make real. What has made conflict between groups so incessant and intense for several generations is that the ultimate issue at stake in these disputes has been, implicitly, the actual political system of the community as it is represented in ritual.

Up until some years ago, it was common to distinguish two broad geographical patterns of leadership and political organisation in South Pacific societies: the chiefly polities of Polynesia, based on rank and ascribed leadership, and the egalitarian systems of Melanesia, in which leadership is gained by personal achievement (see Sahlins 1963). A number of authors have since then argued that this oversimplifies an often complex interplay, in these societies, between principles of ascription and achievement, as well as the complex diversity of political systems in the region as a whole (Allen 1981, 1984; Chowning 1979; Douglas 1979; Godelier 1986). In the same geographical region as Avatip, for instance, there is a very wide spectrum of forms of leadership. At one extreme there are small-scale, seminomadic groups with minimally developed political institutions, such as the Sanio-Hiowe (Townsend 1978) and Bahinemo (Dye 1984; Newton 1971: 18–32) of the Upper Sepik. At another extreme, forms of rank and ascribed political office are found among the speakers of Austronesian languages in the Schouten Islands (Hogbin 1970, 1978; Lutkehaus 1984a, 1984b; Wedgwood 1934) and, in more attenuated versions, in some of the mainland societies with which they have trade connections (Josephides 1982, 1984; Lipset 1984; Meeker et al. 1986; Meiser 1955). In the middle Sepik foothills, to the north of Avatip, the Abelam and other intensive yam-cultivators have 'Big Man' polities of a classically Melanesian type (Forge 1970; Kaberry 1971); while elements of ascription and incipient social stratification have been reported among some of the Iatmul fisherfolk of the lower Sepik River (Metraux 1978: 50).

But in contrast to this variety of political forms, certain basic similarities in Sepik ritual organisation stand out. Each local polity usually consists of a number of kin groups differentiated from each other by hereditary ritual accoutrements. These appurtenances commonly include, as they do at Avatip, totems, spirit-beings, personal names, initiatory sacra, myths, song-cycles and spells. A large and important part of these regalia usually relates to the community's male initiatory cult, each segment having its own cult-spirits, sacred objects, ritual functions, and initiatory lore.

In effect, the same basic structure of ritual serves to support a variety of political arrangements in Sepik societies: small-scale chiefdoms, egalitarian systems, and others in which, as at Avatip, ideologies of male egalitarianism and of hereditary privilege coexist in an uneasy and unresolved tension. These political systems are different actualisations of the possibilities of power offered by a widespread Oceanic configuration of ritual and cosmology.

Ritual and history

An often noted characteristic of ritual symbolism is its ambiguity: the fact that the same symbolic content can serve to represent quite different patterns of social relationships. It is in this ambiguity of ritual that its political utility lies, because the same symbolism can be put to quite different, and even contradictory, political ends (Leach 1954). An important recent analysis making this point is Bloch's (1986) study of the circumcision ritual of the Merina of Madagascar. Bloch shows that the symbolism of this ritual has remained remarkably unchanged over several centuries, despite enormous political transformations in the society. More or less elaborated, truncated or expanded at different periods, the ritual has nevertheless been carried across the centuries with its core symbolism unaltered; what has varied over history are the political functions or uses to which it has been put at different periods by different interest-groups. The history and function of the ritual on the one hand, and its symbolic content on the other, remained two largely autonomous dimensions that coexisted but did not strongly interact.

The function of a ritual, Bloch argues, is open to political manipulation and is therefore highly variable over history; its symbolism, on the other hand, is relatively impervious to time. The crucial point which Bloch thereby establishes is that ritual symbolism is not directly determined by political and economic circumstances, because the same system of symbols can be made to serve wholly different political-economic regimes. In that respect, religious representations have their own historical autonomy. But this autonomy seems, to Bloch, a kind of inertia: rituals are refractory to changing social conditions because they represent the world as unchanging, and do so in a way that is only semi-propositional, half way between a statement and an act, and so cannot easily be challenged. But it does not follow that ritual itself is necessarily static. All that follows is that, whatever changes occur in a ritual, it will always retain its semi-propositional character and the images of the world it portrays will always be ones of changelessness and stability.

The sources of the stability of ritual symbolism must therefore be sought elsewhere, in its uses rather than in its intrinsic characteristics. Among the Merina, the successive political groups that associated themselves with the circumcision ritual arose in processes of state formation, periods of nationalistic resistance to colonial rule, and so forth. That is to say, these groups came into being through political transformations quite extraneous to the ritual order itself. The ritual was simply a resource they used for their own ends as they came and went over history. What they sought from associating themselves with the ritual, and playing key roles in it, was the prestige or 'unchallengeable' legitimacy this could confer. The ritual remained highly stable over centuries of political upheaval, because it was to the advantage of these successive groups to conserve it, not alter it, and to put its aura of timeless authority in the service of their particular goals. The symbolism endured, contra Bloch, to the extent that its political function did *not* change, but remained that of legitimising traditional authority. All that changed were the political orders that used the ritual for this end.

Comparing Avatip and the Merina, I would suggest a general point about those ritual systems which are used to legitimise traditional authority: that what is manipulated for political ends, and therefore highly variable over history, is not indeed the symbolic content of ritual, but the social identities of the key actors in it, the social distribution of the rights of control or 'ownership' in the rituals. These are the components of ritual that articulate most closely with historical processes, because they depend wholly on, and more or less immediately reflect, the changing realities of power relationships. Fundamental political changes can happen, yet they leave the ritual system essentially unchanged, except that certain roles in the system are played by different categories of actors.

Avatip and the Merina differ in that the formation of new political orders among the Merina was simply *reflected* in these reapportionings of ritual roles; at Avatip new political orders form *through* such processes. Working within the existing content of Avatip ritual and cosmology, from which all power draws its legitimacy, new political orders *can* only form themselves through reallocations of the key rights and roles in ritual. I am not arguing that reallocations of this sort are in themselves a sufficient condition to transform the political system, but that they are a *necessary* one.

Where the two societies most basically differ, in short, is in their conception of the relationship between the ritual order and the shifting realities of power. When new political orders arose among the Merina, they only sought legitimacy from the ritual, not their reality. Their control of the circumcision ritual was not a necessary condition for their existence. As Bloch argues, the reality of all the successive regimes was based upon domination and violence, and their *existence* was fully guaranteed by wider political and economic processes quite beyond the ritual order.

But Avatip is a society in which political groups do not simply draw legitimacy, but also their identities, from the ritual order. They define themselves as intrinsically ritual entities. More accurately, it is the political system itself as a global totality that is defined in this way. The control of all the different rituals by particular descent groups, the organic interdependence of all their different ritual functions, are the conceived basis of their reality as a unitary political whole and the means by which they construct themselves in the first place *as* a system of political relations.

In such a society, real political changes can in principle originate as innovations in ritual, myth and cosmology, because forms of authority that do not yet exist can nevertheless be constructed *conceptually* as permutations of the existing organisation of ritual. This freedom of ideation is in fact historically highly determined; but the basic historical constraints are those imposed by the existing patterns of ritual and cosmology, on which the legitimacy of all power is based. That is, actors can imagine new forms of political relationships only by unfolding or developing the inner possibilities of these inherited structures of ritual in something like the activity that Lévi-

Introduction

Strauss (1966: 16–36) called '*bricolage*', a kind of play with existing patterns of symbolism.

In a ritually-constituted polity, in other words, the ritual system shapes the directions in which political change can occur (cf. Sahlins 1985). Every system of ritual symbolism is ambiguous, in the sense that it can 'mean' a variety of structural arrangements, but different ritual systems can offer quite different constraints and possibilities for this sort of political manipulation, and therefore open up different pathways for history. A cosmology of the Avatip sort, for instance, puts certain conceptual limits on the type of political system it can legitimise: the basic units of the political system must be kin groups, and their politico-ritual relations must lie somewhere along a spectrum from ascribed inequality to equality. What the cosmology does not determine is where along that spectrum the political system will lie at any particular point in time. That is determined wholly by the shifting distribution of power, and forms the universe of indeterminacies within which history can happen.

In every society, political actors in competing with one another must draw on a whole range of material and symbolic resources to further their interests. But what can vary between societies, sometimes radically, are the cultural languages or idioms in which these struggles are carried out. In some societies, they take the cultural form of conflicts over privileges in ritual because, out of the total range of forms of action in the society, ritual has been selected as the language in which all political relationships are cast explicitly. The crucial indicators reflecting shifts in the balance of power between different actors or interest-groups are changes in the organisation of ritual. In other societies they may be changes in the distribution of economic resources, or rights in women, or military force. All of these processes of course occur in some form or other in every society; what differ are the cultural registers in which political actors express these universal processes to themselves explicitly. My aim is to show that in a society whose culturally 'valorised' arena of political competition is its ritual system, this system exerts its own determinations upon historical change.

1

The Manambu

Physical environment and subsistence

The Manambu are a people of the East Sepik Province of Papua New Guinea, and live along the section of the Sepik River that flows between the Hunstein Mountains and the Washkuk Hills (see Map 1). Here and there along these forty-or-so kilometres of the Sepik, the hill-slopes abut directly onto the river; but elsewhere they recede and the Sepik, varying in width between three and seven hundred metres, flows in a broad meander bed and is subject to frequent shifts in its course. Where the river curves, the inner banks usually consist of mudbanks, while the outer ones rise vertically to some five metres above low water level. Both are lined with tall, dense stands of wild sugarcane (*Saccharum robustum*) and Phragmites reed. During the wet season, the river may rise five or six metres, flooding large areas of the surrounding plain.

The immediate meander plain of the river consists of complexes of parallel and intersecting natural levees, with pandanus and swamp-grasses as the predominant vegetation. The higher levees may also be lightly forested. Here there are also ox-bow lagoons – detached meander loops of the river – covered with floating grasses, water-lilies and other aquatic vegetation. Behind the levees lie large areas of back-swamp, much of which is permanently flooded to form shallow all-season lakes. Further inland, the terrain changes to swampy forest with sago-palm in the understory; parts of this may be flooded for a short time each year.

During the dry season, which the Manambu call *nyakamali* and which lasts from about May until September, the river is low and usually exposes wide foreshores in front of the Manambu villages. The current is slow, and the water warm and turbid as the river drains off seepage from the stagnant back-swamps and lagoons. Heat-haze rises every morning, growing increasingly dense until late afternoon. The prevailing winds are the south-east trades, called *walimangk* by the Manambu.

In the wet season (*kwaiyungkw*), between October and April, the river rises to within a few inches of the Manambu villages and sometimes floods them. The river is wide, fast-flowing and swollen, and can get choppy in windy weather; the water is cold and relatively clear. The direction of flow in its

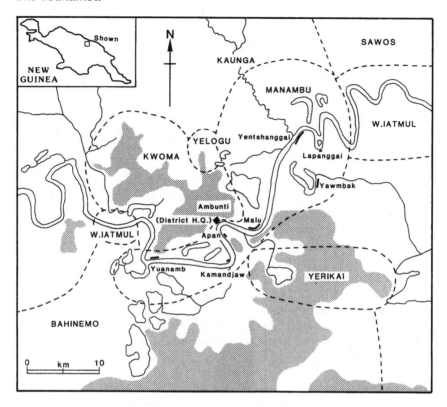

Map 1 The Manambu area.

smaller tributaries is reversed as the river feeds water back into the swamps. The Sepik brings down a constant supply of floating tree-trunks in the wet season, the better specimens of which the villagers take for house-posts and dug-out canoes. Mosquitoes swarm continuously but are at their worst at dusk. The Manambu know this time of day as *kupwukəpi*, 'the falling groundwards of the mosquitoes': they say the insects stay in the upper air during the day, and descend to the ground for feeding at twilight. The prevailing wind of the wet season is the north-west monsoon (*yambunma-nuwei*), and there are frequent, violent thunderstorms over the river.

The Manambu support themselves largely by fishing and the exploitation of the sago-palm, with hunting and swidden agriculture having a secondary place in their economy. Nowadays they also market coffee and crocodile skins for cash, while some individuals earn wages or salaries in towns.

The environment is rich, particularly in aquatic resources, and allows the Manambu to meet their subsistence needs easily by means of what was technically in the past a largely hunting-gathering economy. But neither the

13

environment nor their mode of exploiting it foster over-production. The only foodstuff regularly produced beyond immediate subsistence needs is fish, the surplus of which is traded with bush-villages in exchange for sago-starch. Yams are a ritually important prestige food, but because of the high and unpredictable water-table the cultivation of yams is limited and each household produces little more than enough for its own consumption. Few domestic pigs are kept, since there is little surplus food to support them, and wild pigs – and other large game such as cassowary – are in any case plentiful and easily hunted or trapped.

In many parts of Melanesia, traditional politics revolves around the competitive production and ceremonial exchange of food (see for example Oliver 1955; Sahlins 1963; Serpenti 1965; Young 1971). Among the Manambu there are no institutions of competitive feasting or food-exchange of this type. An important factor contributing to this, of course, is that the environment of seasonally flooded swamps does not encourage a mode of livelihood geared to the production of agricultural surpluses, and the economy is not one which would enable the Manambu regularly to build up large surpluses of the sorts of high-prestige foodstuffs, such as yams and pigs, characteristically used in Melanesian competitive exchanges. On the other hand, there are other Lowland societies in very similar ecological settings in which politics revolves around competitive exchanges of surplus food and wealth: the swamp-dwelling Frederik-Henrik Islanders of West New Guinea (Serpenti 1965), for instance, who cultivate crops on artificial garden-islands; and the Murik (Meeker et al. 1986), near the mouth of the Sepik River, who obtain much of the wherewithal for feasts by means of an extensive specialisation in trade. It would probably be feasible for the Manambu to produce surpluses only if they took very special adaptive measures such as these; that they have not done so is owing to several factors which interrelate and reinforce each other, and some of these have to do with Manambu politics and religion. I shall return to these in a later chapter, because they bear crucially on the theme of this book.

In their exploitation of the environment, the Manambu are deliberate conservationists and regard squandering any food resource as an offence against the totemic spirits of food species. The rotting yams of the Goodenough Islanders of the Massim (Young 1971: 162–4), for example, kept as symbols of their owners' status and prosperity, would appal the Manambu: the yam spirits, they say, would kill anyone who squandered his food in that way. A Manambu individual has to be hard-working and productive if he or she is to be respected and fulfil obligations to kin. But the Manambu do not place a value on competitive production, on production to excess, and lack any institutional framework for using food and wealth as resources in contests for status.

Each Manambu village is situated near one or more large lagoons, on which it depends for most of its supply of fish. Fishing is done by the women, using nets, and it is their main economic task. Manambu women, like their Iatmul and Chambri counterparts downriver (see Gewertz 1983; Hauser-Schäublin 1977) trade their surplus fish for sago-flour at markets (*takw*) held regularly with the womenfolk of neighbouring bush-villages. But the Manambu are less dependent on this trade than the Iatmul and Chambri appear to be, since the Manambu villages are partly self-sufficient in sago and much of their supply is home-produced. The production of sago-flour is carried out by husband-and-wife teams: the husband fells the palm, breaks open the cortex and pounds the exposed pith, while the wife leaches the pounded pith to collect the starch. An average household (five adults and five children) processes a palm about once a month.

Manambu households make yam gardens on the levees along the Sepik River. Because yams need a well-drained environment, these gardens are planted early in the dry season and harvested usually in December at the start of the wet. In each community the cultivation schedule is directed by a small number of hereditary ritual specialists: until these specialists have performed the necessary magic, the gardens cannot be planted, nor can they be harvested until these men inaugurate an elaborate first-fruits ceremony involving the entire village. Every four or five years, each village holds an especially complex version of this ceremony, which inducts novices into the second of three male initiatory grades.

Clearing garden sites and fencing them are tasks generally done by men. Planting the yams involves specialised tasks for both sexes and also children, while it is mainly women who weed the gardens and maintain them while they mature. In these respects the Manambu contrast with a number of other Sepik peoples of the foothills and mountains to the north, such as the Abelam (Forge 1966; Lea 1964) and Ilahita Arapesh (Tuzin 1972, 1976, 1980). In those societies, the cultivation of yams, at least the 'long yams' used in competitive exchange and men's ritual (*Dioscorea alata* grown under special conditions so as to produce very large tubers) is an exclusively male occupation surrounded by many sexual taboos. The Manambu do not grow long yams, because the annual rise of the river allows only a brief growing season. They do not hold competitive exchanges of yams, and there is only one part of the yam cultivation process from which women are ritually excluded: the harvest of the first-fruits of the yams, which can only be carried out by initiated men. It is perhaps because yam production is not an arena for status contests between men that it is not a focus of elaborate female pollution beliefs (see Harrison 1982).

Sugarcane, banana and leafy greens are also grown in the yam gardens. The gardens last for two years at most and are then left for a long period of bush fallow. Although swiddening ranks behind fishing and sago-production in economic importance, my impression is that it contributes more to subsistence than it does among the Iatmul, the downriver neighbours of the Manambu.

The Manambu

Presumably, this is because the Manambu have access to higher and less frequently inundated terrain. The relative importance of yam cultivation, and the male cult ritual associated with it, form the major feature distinguishing the Manambu from the Iatmul (Bateson 1932, 1958; Hauser-Schäublin 1977; Stanek 1983; Wassman 1982), to whom they are otherwise closely related socioculturally.

The Manambu communities

The Manambu speak a language of the Ndu family, a non-Austronesian language family which dominates the middle Sepik region and the most widely spoken members of which are Abelam and Iatmul (see Laycock 1965). Of the other Ndu-speaking peoples, the Manambu appear to be most closely related in language and culture to the Western Iatmul. The importance of yam cultivation in Manambu ritual and subsistence suggests also influences from the foothill-dwelling peoples to their north, such as the Abelam (Forge 1966, 1970, 1971, 1972a, 1972b, 1972c; Losche 1984; Kaberry 1941, 1942, 1971) and Kwoma (Bowden 1977, 1983a, 1983b, 1984; Whiting 1941, 1944; Whiting and Reed 1938–9).

The first recorded contact of the Manambu with Europeans was with the members of the German Sepik River Expedition of 1912–13 (Behrmann 1922), who made their main camp near the Manambu village of Malu. But regular administration of the area only began with the establishment of Ambunti Patrol Post, near the geographical centre of Manambu territory, by the Australian authorities in 1924 (Townsend 1968). Toward the end of the Second World War the area was occupied by the Japanese, and during this period the Manambu carried out their last headhunting raids and ambushes in a brief resurgence of traditional warfare.

Before European contact the Manambu lived in three politically independent villages: Avatip, Malu and Yuanamb. Yuanamb is known on official records, incorrectly so far as the Manambu are concerned, as Yambon. This is an abbreviation of Yambwundjendu, which is not the name of the village but of its site at the time of European contact. Since contact, Avatip has split into three separate settlements, called Yentshanggai, Yawmbak and Lapanggai. Yuanamb and Malu have both relocated to the north bank of the river, the latter producing a new offshoot, Apan, a few kilometres upriver and a small hamlet called Kamandjaw a little further upstream again (see Map 1). But each of the three communities retains a strong sense of separate identity, remaining largely endogamous and having an organisationally independent ritual system. The populations of the three communities in 1978 are given in Table 1.

Avatip is by far the largest of the communities, accounting for more than half of the total Manambu population. It is also the oldest Manambu

Table 1. *Populations of Manambu settlements in
1978 (includes absentees)*

Avatip	Yentshanggai	884
	Yawmbak	339
	Lapanggai	59
Total		1282
Malu (including Apan and Kamandjaw)[a]		561
Yuanamb[a]		362
Total Manambu population		2205

[a]*Source:* Government Census November 1978.

community, Malu and Yuanamb having been founded as its offshoots some
seven generations ago according to genealogical tradition. Avatip was militar-
ily the most powerful river-village known to the Manambu, and has a kind of
metropolitan status among them. Because of this and their relatively small
population, the Manambu have always had something of a sense of 'tribal'
unity, a state of affairs rare in traditional Melanesia. Warfare, for instance,
was prohibited between Avatip and its two offshoots, on the grounds of their
common language and traditions. Occasional feuds did occur, however,
between Malu and Yuanamb; these communities seem to have had stronger
political ties with Avatip than with each other. It presumably would have been
against the interests of Malu and Yuanamb to be on hostile terms with such a
sizeable neighbour; while from the point of view of Avatip, peaceful relations
with its two daughter villages would have kept it secure to the west and enabled
it to concentrate its warmaking northwards into the Amoku River and to
defend itself against the aggressively expansionist Western Iatmul.

There are minor differences between Avatip on the one hand, and Malu and
Yuanamb on the other, in language, ritual, social structure and economy.
Avatip claims to preserve the 'definitive' Manambu traditions and Malu and
Yuanamb tend, out of diplomacy, to defer to these assertions. For instance,
Avatip cultivates yams more intensively than the other two communities and
has, associated with this, a more elaborate yam cult. While the Manambu
believe these are ancient traditions that Avatip alone has preserved, the
available evidence suggests that they are in fact innovations dating from the
nineteenth century (see Harrison 1982). At any rate, Avatip ritual leaders have
a rather greater prestige than their Malu or Yuanamb counterparts, and are
regularly invited by those two communities to help preside over their male
initiation rituals. But the sphere in which Avatip has the greatest authority is
the cosmological complex of totemism, myth and ancestral names, and the

17

system of debating associated with this. The two smaller Manambu communities regard Avatip people as having almost a collective obsession with debating the ownership of totemic ancestors and their hereditary names, and their reputation for disputatiousness is quite justified. Disputes over names occur far more frequently at Avatip than at Malu or Yuanamb, presumably as a result of its larger size and consequently higher incidence of conflict. Avatip traditionally provides the authoritative experts in debating and totemic mythology among the Manambu, and those experts are sought after by Malu and Yuanamb men as teachers of myth and supporters in their own debates.

The totemic cosmology of the Manambu is integral to their clan system, which the Manambu believe is identical in all three communities and is in fact very nearly so. The communities are, in the terminology of Hogbin and Wedgwood (1953), 'osculant' multicarpellary parishes. Clanship provides the basis for trading and visiting throughout Manambu territory, as well as for the transmission of totemic and ritual lore, which is hereditary clan property, from Avatip to Malu and Yuanamb. The cultural pre-eminence which Avatip has among the Manambu is, in other words, maintained by means of – and presumably also helps to maintain – the pan-Manambu totemic clan system.

Relations with neighbouring social systems

The Manambu assume, in fact, that all human beings share their clan system. Many other peoples in the area appear to have similar beliefs that their particular totemic divisions are an inherent property of human society, transcending all linguistic and tribal boundaries (see for instance, for the Kwoma, Bowden 1977: 48, 50). This notion had an important function in this region of the Sepik since, as Gewertz (1983) has documented in her analysis of the history of the Chambri people, many of the cultural groups in this area were not self-supporting but depended for their existence on continuous trade with one another. Gewertz draws a number of conclusions in her study of the Chambri which are crucial for an understanding of this part of Melanesia, and there are two particularly important ones which I try to develop in this book. One is her view that the societies of the middle Sepik can only be analysed adequately as a regional political-economic system in which, intentionally or otherwise, they shaped each other's histories and social institutions. The other is that the fundamental economic resource in the region was not land, but trading relationships. A point I develop in this section is that, for the Manambu and their neighbours, it was the reciprocal assumption of a common totemic structure that provided the basis for all trade and communication with each other.

Off the river to the north, the neighbours of the Manambu are three land-based peoples: the Kwoma, Kaunga and Sawos. All along the middle Sepik, a symbiotic relationship exists between river-folk and bush-folk, and their two distinct but complementary ways of life. According to the Manambu stereo-type, the river-peoples such as themselves are essentially fishermen, with the lakes and waterways as their habitat, while the bush-peoples are forest-dwelling horticulturalists and producers of sago. The Manambu regard the bush as inhospitable and dangerous and they avoid travel on land. They are poor woodsmen and in the bush they were easy targets for ambush by the Numbundu, or 'dry land men' as they call the bush-folk. They believe that the Numbundu avidly practice exuvial sorcery (*wa'ai*) – a type of sorcery alien to the Manambu and greatly feared by them – and when in the bush the Manambu always dispose very carefully of their personal leavings. The Manambu consider everything to do with the forest and its inhabitants as crude and inferior, an attitude common among the river-folk (see for instance Gewertz 1978).

Each Manambu village has a traditional relationship with one or more Numbundu villages, with which it holds markets for the exchange of fish for sago. The Manambu villages were in the past constantly at war with neighbouring bush villages, and in traditional times all the Manambu villages were situated on the south bank of the river because of the danger of attack from these populations to the north. There are also two Numbundu peoples – the Yerikai and Bahinemo – to the south of the river, but they were too few in numbers to pose a significant threat.

The largest group neighbouring the Manambu are the Western Iatmul, a river-people like themselves with a similar ecological adaptation. The Western Iatmul outnumber the Manambu and their more westerly villages have been trying for many generations to expand upriver into their territory. The Manambu regard the Western Iatmul as their main enemies. This is particu-larly the case at Avatip which, as the closest of the Manambu villages to the Western Iatmul, fought constantly with these Iatmul neighbours. These hostilities usually took the form of ambushes or skirmishes between canoes, but there were sometimes full-scale battles between fleets.

At some stage in the pre-contact period a faction within the Western Iatmul village of Japandai – at the time the furthest upriver of the Iatmul villages – were allowed by the people of Yuanamb to settle with them, in this way leap-frogging Avatip and Malu (Bragge 1984; Staalsen 1965). Coexisting peaceably at first, the two groups later quarrelled and, in 1923, Yuanamb massacred these guests with the help of men from Malu and Avatip and some Kwoma allies (Bowden 1983b: 15). The survivors afterwards established the village of Brugnowi upriver from Yuanamb. This is now the most westerly Iatmul village, and is separated from the rest by Manambu territory.

It seems then that both the Manambu and the Western Iatmul were expanding, or trying to expand, upriver – but at different rates, the Iatmul moving faster than the Manambu and beginning, at around the time of European contact, to overtake them. It is conceivable that had European contact never taken place, the Manambu would have become an enclave within the Iatmul, perhaps eventually being absorbed by them.

The attitude of the Manambu toward the Iatmul is in fact a highly ambivalent one. The Manambu still suspect the Iatmul of wanting to take their land, and greatly fear their sorcery. On the other hand the Manambu and Western Iatmul villages traded with each other extensively in traditional times. The Manambu also seem to have imported throughout their history very many elements of Iatmul culture, particularly ritual, magic, totemism and myth. To the Manambu, the cultural forms of the Iatmul are surrounded by an aura of especially dangerous power, and are therefore valuable to acquire.

The Iatmul seem to have had a similarly dominating cultural influence on all the groups they traded with. They exported many elements of their culture to the Sawos and Chambri (Gewertz 1983: 80), for instance, as well as to the Manambu, while the Chambri and Manambu were in turn exporters of culture to their respective sago-suppliers to the south (Gewertz 1983: 109; Newton 1971: 18). The politically and ceremonially dominant position of Avatip in relation to the other two Manambu villages seems to have been an effect of proximity to the Western Iatmul, and the privileged access to Iatmul culture which this gave to Avatip. From an historical perspective, the circulation of ritual forms in the regional trading system seems to have been a key formative influence on Manambu society (see Harrison 1987), because the most valued scarce resources among the Manambu, and the items of strategic prestige value in the political systems of their villages, were rights in ritual property, much of which the Manambu acquired from the Iatmul. Manambu ritual and cosmology seem, in fact, to be not only a kind of patchwork of the ritual and cosmological traditions of neighbouring societies, but a largely *bought* patchwork, acquired piecemeal through trade.

The trading of ceremonial goods (songs, dances, rituals, magical spells, art styles and so forth) as commodities, the treatment of cultural or symbolic forms as transactable goods or wealth, has been noted in many areas of traditional Melanesia (see for instance Allen 1981; Kahn 1986: 96; Keesing 1982a: 54–5; Lawrence 1984: 145–6; Scoditti 1983: 260–3; Weiner 1977: 152–3). But it has been reported particularly often in the Sepik, ever since Mead (1938) first described the Mountain Arapesh as an 'importing culture'. Lipset, for instance, (1984:16) refers to an intertribal trade in ritual insignia carried out by the Murik in exchange for pigs. Bowden (1983: 67) mentions the Kwoma making gifts of cult sacra to their enemies to compensate them for deaths in war and seal truces. Forge (1984: 9) refers to the practice, among the Abelam, of selling or leasing whole ritual complexes; and, of particular relevance to this study, there are Bateson's (1958) references to the incessant quarrelling between Iatmul clans over the ownership of ancestral names and totems. This attitude could perhaps be summed up as a tendency to treat cultural items – particularly elements of ritual culture – as more than just meaningful or expressive forms, but as political and economic resources, as values to be bought, sold, exchanged, stolen, hoarded and so forth.

On first sight, it may be difficult to see how cosmological and ritual knowledge can be treated as a commodity, in the same sense that pots or axe-blades clearly can. If one sells a pot, one loses possession of it, but if one sells a myth one loses nothing because one still knows the myth and indeed can sell it again to others. This is a misunderstanding of the political and economic significance of knowledge in societies such as those of the Sepik. As Barth (1975) has shown for the Baktaman of the East Sepik, the value of ritual knowledge in such societies is inversely proportional to the number of individuals who share it. What one loses in selling a myth or a spell is not, of course, knowledge of it but one's monopoly or control of the knowledge, and that is indeed a real loss in societies in which knowledge is important political capital.

The ritual forms circulating among the middle Sepik societies were not only trafficked as commodities but conform closely to Appadurai's very useful definition of luxury goods:

I propose that we regard luxury goods not so much in contrast to necessities (a contrast filled with problems), but as goods whose principal use is *rhetorical* and *social*, goods that are simply *incarnated signs*. The necessity to which *they* respond is fundamentally political.   (Appadurai 1986: 38)

These ceremonial trade goods can usefully be viewed as forming a distinct exchange sphere of the regional trading system, a universe of luxury or prestige values separate from prosaic, subsistence goods. Divisions of this sort are of course common in nonmonetised economies (Kopytoff 1986), and in the middle Sepik commoditised ceremonial forms seem to have been the functional equivalents of the bird-plumes, shell valuables, pigs and other high-status goods that formed the prestige-sphere of the New Guinea Highland economies (Feil 1987; Salisbury 1962; A.J. Strathern 1971). In the remainder of this section I should like to outline the salient differences between the subsistence and ceremonial spheres of intertribal trade, at least so far as the Manambu participated in this system.

At Avatip, and in the other two Manambu communities as well, all trading rights are owned by subclans, each subclan having its own hereditary trade partners with whom it shares putative totemic 'clanship'. These relationships are an important and – though less so nowadays than in the past – economically valuable part of a subclan's patrimony.

There is a marked tendency for subclans to have their trading relationships in different cultural-linguistic areas. Some subclans have their main ties with the Iatmul, others with the Kwoma, and so forth. The trade carried out in this way is, or was, to some extent specialised. With the Iatmul, for instance, Avatip in the past traded canoe-logs, yams, coconuts, areca nuts and Campnosperm oil (used in body decoration) in return for shell valuables.

Sometimes, Avatip also obtained from the Iatmul the pottery and mosquito-proof sleeping baskets produced by the Aibom and Chambri peoples, for whom the Iatmul acted as middlemen; sometimes Avatip obtained these directly from their producers. With the Kwoma, Avatip traded fish, coconuts, pottery and shell valuables, mainly in return for sago. This trade with the Kwoma still continues, and Avatip also still buys its pottery, nowadays mainly for cash, from the Aibom potters or from Iatmul middlemen, but otherwise much of the traditional trading system has disappeared. Avatip no longer depends for shell valuables, as it did almost exclusively in the past, on the Iatmul. Nowadays, motorised canoes enable Avatip men to travel long distances to buy shells for cash from peoples, such as the Murik people near the river's mouth, with whom they had no direct contact in traditional times. Some of the traditional trade items are no longer manufactured: the sleeping baskets, for instance, made formerly by the Chambri, have now been replaced entirely by store-bought mosquito nets (see Gewertz 1983).

In the past, a subclan's allies – individuals connected to the group by affinity and uterine kinship – automatically shared its trading rights and had access to its trading relationships, and still do so to the extent that these relationships still function. A subclan tends to spread its alliances widely, and therefore the specialised trade rights held by these groups did not lead to economic inequalities developing between them. All individuals were entitled to use, besides their own subclans' trading relationships, also those of subclans to which they stood as allies: that is, the subclans of their spouses, mothers, and spouses' mothers. As a result each subclan usually had access, through its individual members, to the trading partnerships of all the other subclans in the same village.

All ordinary goods acquired in trade – sago, pots, shell valuables, and so forth – were the property of the individuals who obtained them and were theirs to consume or dispose of as they wished. But this did not apply to ritual entitlements obtained in trade, because the Manambu regarded these as the immemorial property of subclans and, ultimately, of the pan-human totemic categories of which local subclans were conceived as the representatives. A man whose maternal subclan had trade links with the Iatmul could, for instance, quite legitimately buy a spell from his maternal subclan's Iatmul trading partners. But he could only buy the spell on behalf of his mother's subclan; he would be expected, in other words, at some stage to impart the magic to his matrikin, and it would thereafter be treated as part of the patrimony of his maternal subclan. Each subclan had, in short, monopolistic rights in all ritual goods obtained from its trading partners, and these goods could only be transmitted legitimately between local descent groups conceived as belonging to the same totemic category.

Although it is true that some types of everyday trade – notably fish-for-sago barter – were considered the special province of women (Gewertz 1983;

Hauser-Schäublin 1977), subsistence trade could in principle be carried out by anyone. Trade in ceremonial rights, on the other hand, was subject to strict ritual restrictions and could be carried out only by initiated men. The male cults of the middle Sepik societies were comparable enough for a man's ritual status to be recognised by his trading partners. Men bought these goods principally with shell valuables. A minor Iatmul spell could be bought for a single shell, while more complex and important techniques of magic might require a fee equivalent to a Manambu bridewealth payment. This commerce has continued well into modern times, often using cash and, as I discuss in a later chapter, the Manambu seem in the past to have acquired in this trade whole initiatory ritual complexes from the Iatmul.

The Manambu were situated at something of an important node in the regional trading system, since they traded with eight different cultural-linguistic groups: the Bahinemo, Chambri, Iatmul, Kaunga, Kwoma, Sawos, Yerikai-Garamambu, and Yesan-Mayo (see Map 1.) Because each subclan tended to have its principal trade connections with one of these neighbours, and because these trade-links were also avenues for the diffusion of magic, ritual, and other forms of ceremonial property, the ceremonial attributes of subclans tend to reflect the cultural identities of their trading partners. This is the crucial legitimising 'charter' of a subclan's trading rights. That is, it is by identifiably sharing common ritual and ceremonial attributes with its trading partners that a subclan and its trading-partners are recognised as belonging to the same totemic 'clan' or clan-like totemic category. This is why the adoption of new elements of ritual, totemism and so forth, never seems to have been conceived as involving change in the structure of the totemic-ceremonial system. To Avatip people all ritual powers and attributes are held only 'contingently' by particular descent groups, villages or tribal groups, and are ultimately the immemorial property of totemic categories conceived as transcending all social and cultural boundaries.

To put this in a slightly different way, men make an implicit, but radical, ontological distinction between the two spheres of exchange. Subsistence commodities are inherently temporal and perishable, products of human labour and the phenomenal world. But ceremonial forms are values conceived as 'outside' of time and history, attributes of the totemic world-divisions, creations not of men but of the totemic ancestors, and part of a transcendent, timeless world to which those ancestors belong.

Lastly, subsistence and prestige goods are destined for different forms of 'consumption'. By this, I am not referring to the physical differences between, say, a yam and a spell that make one edible and the other not. Consumption, as Gell (1986: 112) has argued, does not consist in the metabolic or otherwise physical transformation of goods, but in their incorporation into a system of social relations which the goods thereby serve to reproduce. My point is that subsistence and ceremonial goods are incorporated into the social system of

The Manambu

the village in different ways, or rather in different organisational spheres. The significance of subsistence goods is that they are used to reproduce essentially egalitarian domestic and kinship relations, while ritual goods serve the reproduction of hierarchical political relations based on the control of ritual and cosmological knowledge by senior men.

2

Avatip

The community of Avatip

The comparatively large population of Avatip is a result of its location, which is unusually favoured for a middle Sepik riverain community, opposite the confluence of a sizeable tributary – the Amoku River – with the Sepik (see Map 1). The land along the Amoku is the only well-drained alluvial plain in the Manambu area. Haantjens et al. (1972) have rated its agricultural capacity as high, while giving a rating of nil to almost all other Manambu territory. Avatip acquired this valuable land in the nineteenth century, by making war against its original occupants, the Kaunga. The villagers of Avatip have ever since then made yam gardens in the secondary forest on the Amoku, in addition to gardens on the Sepik levees, and in this way produce two crops a year on a staggered schedule of cultivation. In the Amoku 'bush' gardens, the villagers grow mainly the yam species *Dioscorea esculenta*, while they devote the levee gardens to the cultivation of the species *D. alata*. The villagers attach great ritual importance to the cultivation of *alata*, as do many other peoples of the middle Sepik, and they celebrate the harvest of the levee gardens in an important annual ritual (see Harrison 1982).

The Amoku also provides Avatip with extensive hunting grounds and areas of sago palm, as well as forest for building materials. As a result, Avatip has a more diversified economy than most of the other settlements along the Sepik. Besides its comparatively intensive cultivation of yams, the community is self-sufficient in building materials and very largely so in sago. Many of the other river peoples, by contrast, are fairly specialised fisherfolk who must trade with their inland neighbours for these resources. During the 1960s the villagers began to grow coffee along the Amoku, and nowadays the sale of this cash-crop provides almost every household with a regular if modest income.

When European rule was imposed in the 1920s Avatip was a single village, which I shall call Old Avatip, with a population of about 800 people. In 1918 the villagers ambushed a German labour recruiter and his party as they tried to land. In reprisal, the Australian Naval and Military Expeditionary Force, which was then administering New Guinea, made a punitive expedition against the village (Rowley 1958: 202–3; Townsend 1968: 100). According to the villagers, Old Avatip was shelled from the river and, although these details do not appear in the official records, burned by a landing-party, and some half a dozen people were shot dead while being pursued by police through the swamps behind the village. The villagers abandoned Old Avatip for many months, living in small groups in isolated bush-camps for fear of further attack. Some eventually returned and rebuilt the village. Others established what is now the village of Yawmbak, on the eastern shore of the Walǝmaw lagoon, where they felt secure from further raids. It was during this period that the first Avatip men were taken to the coast as indentured labourers, to return two years later with a knowledge of Pidgin and some acquaintance with the new colonial order. One of them was appointed *luluai*, the Government official for the village, and two others his assistants, or *tultul*.

At the time, the course of the Sepik River was shifting northwards, moving away from Old Avatip and starting to leave it landlocked and, to the villagers, therefore uninhabitable. In the mid–1930s, the people of Old Avatip began to abandon it, some moving north to the new bank of the Sepik, where the village of Yentshanggai started to grow, and others east to establish the hamlet of Lapanggai. The last people to leave Old Avatip did so in the 1960s, the village being by then quite landlocked. Its site is now entirely overgrown, except for what used to be its main path, which now forms part of the footpath connecting the three new settlements with each other. For a while, Lapanggai was quite a large settlement, competing in size with Yentshanggai. But it became evident that it too would one day become landlocked, and over the years many of its residents moved to Yentshanggai. In 1979 the Sepik finally broke through the loop on which Lapanggai is situated (see Map 2), and that loop will eventually become a detached ox-bow lagoon, leaving Lapanggai cut off from the main river. That is an unattractive prospect to its remaining residents in these days of motorised river-transport, and they all plan to resettle at Yentshanggai.

Toward the end of the Second World War, a small force of Japanese soldiers based themselves at Yentshanggai, and the village was occasionally bombed and strafed, though without casualties. At the time, some of the villagers were in contact with an Australian guerilla unit operating in the foothills to the north, who persuaded them to kill the Japanese. The village men carried out a carefully planned ambush, taking the soldiers off their guard and killing them all except for their officer, whom they handed over to the Australians. This attack had all the magical and ritual preparations which traditionally preceded a headhunting raid, and was the last time these procedures were used. Many of the older men wear, during ceremonies, the special regalia of homicide for their part in it, and the villagers look back on it as their final act of traditional warfare.

Avatip underwent intensive evangelisation in the 1950s, mainly by the

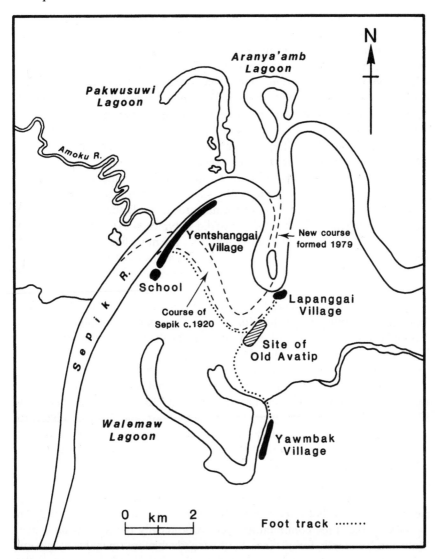

Map 2 Avatip and its vicinity.

Catholic Mission. A church was built at Yentshanggai and catechists visited regularly to give lessons. Yielding to pressure from the mission, the men abandoned their traditional initiation rituals for some years. But disillusionment with the missions eventually set in. Older men now speak bitterly of the period, claiming that the catechists deliberately withheld from them the skills –

now highly valued – of literacy and numeracy, and taught them only, as they now put it, mere bible-stories. Their dissatisfaction came to a head when one of the two tutelary spirits of Avatip possessed a man as he sat in his ceremonial house, and demanded that the abandoned rituals be reinstated and the church pulled down. This was done, and nowadays only a handful of adults at Yentshanggai profess to be Christians. The missionaries at Ambunti regard the Yentshanggai people as intractable, and focus their evangelical activities elsewhere. Yawmbak, rather differently, has had resident for a number of years a native evangelist of the Seventh Day Adventist Church, whose services are popular among the Yawmbak teenagers.

Because of the large population of Avatip, the Government established a primary school at Yentshanggai in 1961, and since then many young Avatip people have gained a high level of formal education. Before the school was founded, young men who left the village did so typically as wage-labourers on short contracts of a few years. Nowadays, they are more likely to be taking up well-paid careers as teachers, policemen, clerks and so forth. In general these young salary-earning absentees maintain close ties with their kin. They come home on leave and are an important source of money and goods.

Avatip was subjected to heavy labour recruitment until the end of the 1950s. But it has not experienced the same levels of permanent outmigration, and depopulation, that some of the other river-villages have suffered from (Curtain 1978; 1980: 324, 332). The villagers, both residents and absentees, strongly disapprove of anyone migrating to towns without a definite prospect of employment, and becoming a burden on town-dwelling kin. The pattern among outmigrants up till now has been to return to the village permanently on retirement or after a few years of contract labour, and this seems likely to continue because the community offers economic opportunities in the form of its Amoku River territory. Just before I left Avatip, the villagers had begun planting a new cash-crop, chili, on the Amoku, and one man had established there a small cattle-project.

With its large and relatively affluent resident population, Avatip seemed to me paradoxically both the most aggressively pagan and 'traditional' in outlook of the three communities, yet economically the most progressive. Malu and Yuanamb, for instance, have been much more amenable to mission influence than Avatip, and also experienced a short-lived cargo cult in the 1950s, quickly suppressed by the authorities. Avatip, on the other hand, has never been involved in an organised cult of this sort. Comparatively self-supporting in traditional times, and now able to earn cash and acquire European goods from its own resources, the community has kept a strong sense of independence and is hostile toward attempts by outsiders to interfere in its affairs. Among government and mission personnel its people have a reputation for refractoriness and have done so since the earliest days of European administration on the Sepik (see Townsend 1968: 100, 136).

Settlement and residence

The three villages comprising the community of Avatip are thin ribbons of settlement built along natural levees of the Sepik: Yentshanggai and Lapanggai on the river itself, and Yawmbak inland on a detached meander loop. Behind the levees the villages are situated on, the land drops away into uninhabitable swamp.

Each village is divided by rows of coconut palms into the wards (*yerəngk*) of patrilineal subclans. Every ward is identical in plan. At the back of it, nearest the swamps, stand the subclan's domestic houses (*wi*). In front of these are two or three small club-houses, called *sa'ai*, for the subclan's uninitiated men and boys. In front of these again, overlooking the waterfront, stands the subclan's *kara'amb*, or ceremonial house. This large building is a centre for the rituals of the men's cult, and the club-house of the subclan's initiated men. Along the ward's foreshore are the log-jetties (*yimbun*) of the subclan's households, where they moor their canoes. The ward, the junior club-houses, and the ceremonial house, bear the names of totemic ancestors of the subclan and, to the subclan's members, they *are* the material forms of those eponymous beings.

Along the more densely settled sections of the village run two parallel paths, one near the ceremonial houses and the other by the domestic houses. The first path is for the sole use of initiated men, while the second may be used by everybody and is the main thoroughfare of the village. Women and male noninitiates cross the initiated men's path all the time, whenever they go to the foreshore; but when they do so they have to avoid the ceremonial houses and must not walk along the path. These rules are less stringently enforced than they were in the past, and uninitiated males are usually allowed to use this path and enter most of the ceremonial houses, except during rituals.

Men regard the domestic houses, and the rear of the village in general, as the preserve of women and children. They tend not to spend much time in their own houses, except for sleeping there, wishing to avoid the ennervating 'heat' that emanates, they say, from women, domestic cooking, and small children. Men spend their leisure-time in their club-houses relaxing in an all-male atmosphere, removed from the constant traffic of women and their babies along the main path.

In other words, the ground-plan of the village codifies distinctions of ritual status: the swamp-side of the village is associated with women and children, the middle with uninitiated males, and the waterfront with full initiates. Viewed along its length, on the other hand, the village is simply a succession of identically laid-out wards; there is no central plaza or focal area of the village as a whole, and this reflects the highly uncentralised and segmental structure of the society. The layout of the village in this way diagrams the two basic, and similarly cross-cutting, dimensions of Avatip social structure: the division of

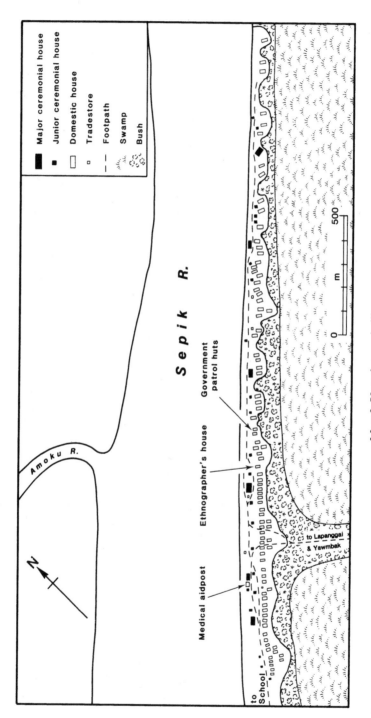

Map 3 Yentshanggai village.

the society into politically equal descent groups, and the ritual hierarchy of initiatory grades.

Residence after marriage is normatively patrivirilocal (a woman leaves her natal ward on marriage and takes up residence with her husband in his) and is almost totally so in actual practice. A man may live temporarily with his affines if a quarrel with his agnates causes his household ghosts to afflict him. But long-term uxorilocal residence would be thought extremely anomalous, and only one couple were living in this way during my stay at Avatip. People would say of this marriage, derisively: 'That woman is the husband; she took the man as her wife and fetched him away' (*a ta'akwa lanand; kəran kəraynda*). The villagers tend to speak of marriages as physical movements of women between wards; from the domestic area of their natal wards, to the domestic areas of their husbands' wards. A man's life-cycle, on the other hand, involves a slow progression within his ward from the domestic area to the riverfront. It is men who give the subclan its residential identity and continuity, simply taking on an increasingly senior ritual status as they mature. Women, on the other hand, are dispersed 'laterally' at marriage; the permanent ritual inferiors of men, they create the transverse ties which link the wards together.

The domestic houses face the river, their front doors overlooking the women's and children's thoroughfare. A household consists of a set of actual or classificatory brothers and their wives, children and elderly dependants. The genealogically senior brother, and his wife or wives and children, are domiciled at the front of the house (*tanggawi*). His younger brothers and their dependants are quartered behind him along the main axis of the house in order of seniority, with the junior brother and his family at the rear (*mbanggawi*). A subclan usually consists of two lineages, and in the past all the men of a lineage were quartered in this way in a single house. Nowadays, domestic houses are smaller and households are about half their traditional size, usually consisting of two or three adult males and their dependants.

All along the length of the house, the central floor-space is the preserve of its adult men, and the sides of the house are the women's and children's area. Each wife has a cooking-hearth by one of the side-walls, opposite the living-space of her husband, and the area around her hearth is her and her children's living-space. Whenever a woman menstruates, this central/lateral division of household space is heightened and emphasised. She must avoid the central 'male' living-area completely, and therefore may not use the front door of the house. She has to leave and enter through a hatch located for this purpose in the side-wall by her hearth. The euphemism used to refer to a woman's menstruation is, 'she sits at the side of the house' (*malawiam rəna*).

The household's ghosts (*wundəmb*) are quartered in the same way as its living occupants. The ghosts of dead fathers live, in their order of seniority, in the line of central posts supporting the roof-ridge. Their wives live by the hearths they used in life, inhabiting the row of short posts that run along each side-wall supporting the eaves. So long as their descendants remember them with occasional offerings of food, and keep on good terms with one another, the ghosts look after their welfare: protecting them from sorcerers and malicious spirits, and inflicting fatal illness on would-be thieves or other intruders. Because it is imbued with these tutelaries' presence, a house is conceived as very much a living thing: if a man has to go at night to the storage-area under his house, he takes the precaution of assuring the house that it is he, not some malefactor, in case its ghostly custodians unwittingly harm him.

The ordering of space within the household reflects, in miniature, the principles of spacial organisation of the village as a whole. Just as men form the residential core of their ward, so the central axis of the house is their living-space; while their wives, as outsiders, occupy the sides. Secondly, inside the house, and within the village as a whole, the direction of the waterfront signifies an order of increasingly senior male status. The seniority encoded in the layout of the village is ritual seniority; in the house, it is genealogical seniority. The two are closely linked, in fact, as I shall show later.

Avatip subclans claim a high degree of political autonomy, and their relations with one another tend to be intensely rivalrous. Every subclan has a strongly proprietorial attitude to its ward, as it does toward all its patrimonial property: names, myths, magic, ceremonial privileges and all the rest. When they visit other wards people are guests and their hosts expect them to behave circumspectly; even a wife takes several years to feel entirely on home ground in her husband's ward. Children are warned not to play outside their wards; and even the dogs seem to know the boundaries and guard them against each other. It is rather as though the village was conceived not as a unitary whole, so much as a series of contiguous little republics. This is, in fact, essentially the way the society is represented in Avatip myth and cosmology. The atmosphere of the ward is domestic, secure, and a little dull: to Avatip people, it is their interactions with other subclans that offer the real rewards – and risks – of sociality.

Subclans and marriage alliance

Each descent group at Avatip has a set of hereditary magical and ritual powers, which is called the group's *ndja'am*. The *ndja'am* is personified as a named female spirit, and the role of this spirit is to punish incest and breaches of exogamy among the group's members. In their conception of the prohibition of incest, what the villagers stress is not the prohibition of sexual relations itself, but the injunction on men to make their sisters and daughters available to others. Distantly related kin may quite safely have incestuous sexual relations, if – and only if – a legitimate potential husband of the woman copulates with her immediately afterwards. For this reason, when a man has an illicit rendezvous with a distant clan 'sister', he will usually bring an appropriate accomplice along to do the lovers this favour. The 'bestowal' of the woman on this legitimate mate completely neutralises the incest and prevents any punishment by the *ndja'am*. It is not the act of incest as such which the group's *ndja'am* sanctions, so much as the implied refusal to yield up female consanguines to other men. A group's *ndja'am* does not signify simply that its members are forbidden to mate or marry; but, more positively, that they are an active source of partners for outsiders.

A group's fund of ritual powers, personified as an incest-punishing spirit, symbolises what to Avatip people is a fundamental aspect of every descent group's identity: that is, that these groups are linked permanently by marriage and by nurturing one another by means of their ritual and magical powers. Each group's *ndja'am*, together with its *vei* or apical ancestor, are the twin symbols of its enduring identity. *Vei* literally means 'spear' and its connotations are masculine, phallic and agnatic. A *ndja'am* on the other hand is represented as a womb. Together, the *vei* and *ndja'am* signify the 'male' and 'female' aspects of a group's social identity: the *vei* an axial, male principle – the patrilineal continuity of the group by which its hereditary powers pass from one generation to the next; and the *ndja'am* a distal, female principle – the lateral ties of reciprocity which link a group with others and whose paradigm are the uterine relationships formed by the marriages of its female members.

These concepts of group identity are reflected in the villagers' beliefs about the biology of kinship. They say that bone (*ap*) is formed from the father's semen and transmitted by agnation. The term *ap* is in fact highly polysemous and signifies, alone or as a prefix, a complex of ideas having to do with patriliny, centrality, strength, age and durability. For instance, the villagers derive the name Avatip from the phrase *apa təp*, 'the strong/old/large/central village', referring to the status of the village as the 'metropolitan' centre from which the other Manambu villages were founded. Blood is inherited by matrifiliation and derives from the mother's womb-blood. An individual is regarded as sharing blood in some loosely defined way with all his or her matrikin, so that blood is transmitted between social groups by marriage, while bone is inherited only within them. The conceived constitution of the body in a sense reflects the structure of society, in that it reiterates the same opposition between a 'central' patrilineal aspect and a 'distal', uterine one. At the risk of carrying this imagery further than the villagers do themselves, one could in fact describe agnation as the 'skeleton' of Avatip society, and uterine alliance as its flesh and blood.

Subclans are the basic ritual and political units of the society, and are the groups which arrange marriages and between which debts and credits in women are reckoned. A subclan stands as a unit in an important relationship with the husbands of its female members, with the sons and daughters these women bear, and with these daughters' husbands. I call these individuals the subclan's allies. A subclan's allies contribute to all bridewealth and marriage-related payments which the subclan makes. They support it in brawls, debates and all political affairs. They help the subclan with maintaining its ceremonial house and with carrying out all its ritual activities. There are no circumstances whatever in which a subclan acts alone. It always does so in concert with its allies and with their support.

The closest of all the subclan's allies are the children of its women. They are called sisters' children (*nggambəro*) by all the men of the subclan, and children (*nyanungkw*) by all the women, who are of their mothers' generation or of any subsequent generation. They are known collectively as the subclan's *nggambəro-nyanungkw*. I shall call them sisters' children.

Sisters' children are conceived as having a uterine relationship with the whole of their maternal subclan. When they rally to its support in some context or other, they do it because they 'once lay in the womb' (*ya'al rəndiyan*) of that subclan; they say 'our mother's blood is pulling us' (*amei nyiki langgwundan-diyan*). This uterine tie strongly forbids marriage and sexual relations.

People may marry the sisters' children of other subclans of their clan or wider exogamous group. There is demographically almost a moiety system at Avatip, as I describe in the next chapter, and such marriages are therefore in fact the statistical norm. A mature woman who has been widowed or divorced is free to choose her next husband, or indeed to remain unmarried, but young women marrying for the first time usually have their marriages arranged by their parents. Senior men and women have a considerable say in the marriages of their sisters' daughters as well and can have them marry into subclans collateral with their own. Subclans of the same exogamous group maintain indirect alliance relations with one another by exchanging their sisters' daughters in this way, even though they are not marriageable directly.

A subclan's policy is generally to spread all its alliances as widely as possible. Its senior members try to ensure that the group always has at least one of its women married into every other marriageable subclan; and at least one sister's daughter married into every subclan collateral with itself. The reason for this is security: people want allies in all the other subclans in the community, to inform them if any of those groups are hatching plots against their own.

The villagers do not practise sister-exchange marriage, considering it almost incestuous, but they feel strongly that a balanced flow of women between groups should be maintained in the long term. For every female agnate or sister's daughter bestowed, another should eventually be given in return. Occasionally, an imbalance develops between two groups. If the offending subclan does not redress this, the senior men of the aggrieved group will make a curse preventing the women of their subclan, or their sisters' daughters as the case may be, from marrying into it until it makes good its debts.

A subclan has obligations to all its allies, but its most important ones are to its sisters' children. A man has a nurturant, solicitous, quasi-maternal relationship with all the sisters' children of his subclan, often referring to

34

himself as their 'mother' (*amei*). But his closest ties are with his own sister's children. He sends them food gifts throughout their lives, and contributes to the bridewealth payments of his sister's sons. He provides sacrificial pigs or fowl when his sister's children are ill. He helps them with housebuilding, with making their canoes and gardens, and with their other everyday tasks, and plays a special role in all their rites of passage. All of a man's agnatic descendants stand, terminologically, as 'mothers' and 'mother's brothers' of his sister's children; and when he becomes old they inherit his role of 'giving mother's milk' or 'giving the mother's breast' (*amei muň kwina*) to them. The Manambu term *muň* means both breast and breast-milk. A woman has similar responsibilities to her sister's children, the more physically demanding of which are carried out on her behalf by her husband. And women have special responsibilities to the sisters' children of their husbands, as well as to their own. For instance, women practise a special system of food-exchange among themselves, called *awarəwa kəkəvat* ('raw food back-and-forth'), which is partly a means of levelling out short-term fluctuations in each domestic unit's food supply. If a woman has a surplus of fish or sago-flour on a particular day, she gives it away to various female kin, who repay her in kind when they themselves have a surplus. Every evening, women and girls bustle back and forth along the main path through the village, carrying baskets of raw food to their sisters' children, or to other kin or friends.

A subclan has no alliance relationships with its sisters' children's children. It establishes a uterine alliance through the marriage of one of its women; and when the offspring of this marriage die, the alliance comes to an end. When a sister's child dies, his or her mother's agnates receives a large mortuary payment of shell wealth and cash, called *kəkətəp*, which repays them for their gifts and services to the dead person. The recipients redistribute the wealth within their subclan, repaying those of their subclan-agnates who gave them shares of previous mortuary payments. To the members of a subclan, one of the most basic expressions of their unity as a group is that they 'eat sisters' children together' (*nakaləmb kəkwanandiyan nggambəro-nyanungkw*); in other words, they are co-recipients of their sisters' children's mortuary payments. The 'eating' of the sister's child in the mortuary payment closes the alliance. The payment is made by the dead person's subclan and its allies, together with the subclan and allies of the dead person's spouse.

The other main type of alliance-related transaction made at Avatip is the payment of bridewealth (*ta'akwayu*), which inaugurates an alliance. It is always a smaller payment than *kəkətəp* and less social importance is attached to it. Avatip recalls the 'brideservice' societies identified by Collier and Rosaldo (1981), in that it is not so much wealth that men seek from the marriages of their sisters and daughters; what they want are sons- and brothers-in-law owing them a lifelong debt and allegiance. A bridewealth payment goes to the woman's close agnates who redistribute it, as with mortuary payments, to those members of their subclan who have previously given them shares of their own bridewealth receipts.

A young man marrying for the first time does not have the resources to fund his own bridewealth payment, and the payment is made by his subclan and its allies, together with his mother's subclan and its allies. For this reason, he can only contract a marriage of which these kin approve. If he marries again, he is expected to fund the payment from his own resources but also has a correspondingly greater freedom to choose his own spouse. Bridewealth payments still continue to be made up largely of traditional shell valuables, and cash has not so far entered the system in a large way. People say the reason is that certain types of traditional valuables are required in the payment in order to ensure the bride's fertility; but I suspect the real reason is that older men and women, who may have less access to cash than their junior kinsmen, wish to keep cash out of the bridewealth nexus because they seek to keep control of these young men's choice of spouses.

A subclan remains a social unit in the system of alliance payments only so long as no marriages take place between its sisters' children and its own members. Any such marriage would bring the rules of the system into conflict with each other and make the subclan donor and recipient of the same payment. This is precisely what happens when a subclan fissions: one branch begins marrying the sisters' children of the other, treating them, in other words, not as sisters' children but as unrelated marriageables (*mamandu*). This automatically makes the two segments separate units in the system of alliance payments, because each becomes a recipient of payments to which the other is a contributor.

In short, what holds a subclan together as a social unit is not patrilineal descent, but the group's collective relationship to a set of unmarriageable sisters' children. It is the matrifilial ties which flow from it which make a subclan a solidary group and distinguish it from the other subclans of its clan or larger agnatic group. What effectively differentiates collateral subclans from one another is not their separate patrilineal identities, so much as the fact that they are separate units for creating and reckoning uterine relationships. Any incestuous relations between the subclan's members and the group's sisters' children are thought to be punished by the subclan's *ndja'am*, the named spirit personifying its hereditary magical and ritual powers, and the spirit represents, implicitly, the subclan's unity and identity as an alliance group.

In contrast to groups in many of the New Guinea Highland societies, Avatip subclans recruit their members strictly by agnatic descent. They do not recruit affines, uterine kin or other non-agnates or incorporate them into their genealogical structure. The 'flexibility' of agnation in the Highland societies has been a long-standing problem in Melanesian studies (see Barnes 1962), and some of the more recent Highland studies (for instance Feil 1984; Sillitoe

1979) come close to suggesting that the apparent 'clans' in some of these societies are illusory and that all that exist are individuals and the networks they create. Although Avatip descent groups seem in this respect quite different from those of the Highlands, the underlying mechanisms are very similar.

The strictly agnatic structure of Avatip descent groups is not the result of an emphasis on patrilineal values as such. It is an effect of the structure of alliance relationships. If a subclan were to incorporate sisters' children, it would make itself a donor to their mortuary payments, instead of a recipient. It would deprive itself, in other words, of its main source of shell wealth, and cease to be viable in the system of alliance payments. Secondly, a man has an almost identical relationship with his maternal subclan as he has with his own agnates. He may use the land of both groups, learn both groups' magical specialties, have his bridewealth financed jointly by both, and may marry into neither of them. Conversely, both groups can call upon his support in political affairs, his contributions to their alliance payments, and his labour in major tasks such as housebuilding. There would be no particular advantage in incorporating sisters' children, either to the subclan or to the sisters' children themselves, because it would not alter their relationships in any significant way. It would simply prevent the subclan from carrying out alliance transactions effectively.

What keeps Avatip subclans purely patrilineal in composition, and constantly generates strictly agnatic lines of descent within them, are therefore the uterine alliance relations they create through the marriages of their female members. Subclans would remain rigidly agnatic groups *de facto*, whether or not the society espoused patrilineal values. As a norm or value, agnation plays the essentially ideological role, so far as I can see, of disguising the basic contradiction inherent in the tie of uterine alliance. Ostensibly, the gifts and services bestowed on sisters' children are motivated wholly by 'maternal' generosity and altruism; in actuality, they are self-interested and given in expectation of the reward of wealth in the mortuary payment. Indeed, the size of a mortuary payment depends very much on the degree of 'generosity' the matrikin are deemed to have shown the dead person over the course of his or her life. The 'norm' of agnatic descent disguises what is in fact an affinal relationship, based on the economic interests inherent in the structure of marriage alliance, as a relationship, to use the Fortesian term, of complementary filiation: that is, as a tie of personal sentiment between consanguines. The entire ritual and totemic system of Avatip is, from one perspective, an elaborate ideological 'mystification' of uterine alliance. It is the ideology of maternal sentiment projected onto the plane of cosmology and religion (see Harrison 1984).

People who share the same maternal subclan have close social ties and stand to one another, terminologically, as siblings. They say they 'came from a single womb' (*ya'al nakamwi rəndi*); they 'once lay in the womb' of subclan such-and-such. I shall call them uterine siblings (cf. Kelly 1977). Marriage and sexual relations between uterine siblings are prohibited, and would be punished by their maternal subclan's *ndja'am* if they occurred.

A category of uterine siblings carries out all the alliance functions which a subclan does. Its members 'nurture' their sisters' children with goods and services, make bridewealth and mortuary payments on one another's behalf, and share the receipts of these payments with each other. Every bridewealth or mortuary payment made at Avatip is, organisationally, actually two transactions taking place simultaneously and involves two distinct types of social unit: subclans, and categories of uterine siblings.

Because of the policy of spreading alliances widely, a category of uterine siblings consists of men and women of many different subclans, and these categories entirely cross-cut descent group structure. It is partly for this reason that alliance payments are not an overt focus of competition for status and prestige between kin groups. One does not find for example, as one does among the neighbouring Chambri (Gewertz 1977a), patron-client relations between descent groups in which large groups give small ones help in meeting their affinal exchange obligations in return for their political allegiance. An Avatip subclan can remain autonomous and viable in these exchanges even if it is virtually extinct, because its members can continue making the exchanges perfectly adequately through their membership of uterine sibling categories. For this reason, a small subclan will try to intermarry with very large ones so as to equip its members with many uterine siblings.

Although subclans are only one of two types of social unit carrying out alliance payments, they are the defining units in these transactions. A uterine sibling category is not itself a subclan, but it is defined in reference to one: its members' common maternal subclan. There are two distinct, cross-cutting types of alliance unit, but both have as the focus and symbol of their identity specific *ndja'am*-spirits: in the case of a subclan, its own *ndja'am*, and the *ndja'am* of their common maternal subclan in the case of a category of uterine siblings.

Sisters' children usually have a strong interest in ensuring the continuing unity of their maternal subclan. The fission of this subclan would split them into two uterine sibling categories, and, if these were small, it could jeopardise their ability to make and receive alliance payments effectively. It is difficult, in fact, for a subclan to fission without the assent of its sisters' children; unless its sisters' children are numerous enough to consider themselves capable of forming two viable uterine sibling categories, they will simply continue to operate as a single one. They can hinder the fission by refusing to marry with one another, or with any member of their maternal subclan, and by continuing to treat it a single unit in all alliance payments they make to it.

The system of bridewealth and mortuary payments does not give rise to Big Men who figure prominently in some other Melanesian polities – the self-made leaders who rise to prominence through skilful manipulation of wealth-exchanges. Women take part in bridewealth and mortuary transactions on an absolutely equal footing with men; even children may ask their parents for a shell valuable or two and invest them in the system with the same personal independence as an adult. Although these are transactions between political groups they are essentially domestic in character; when political groups transact *politically* they do not use material wealth but an entirely different medium as the later chapters of this book will, I hope, explain.

Competition between groups at Avatip is not for prestige in wealth exchanges, but for a number of closely interconnected values, the most basic of which is reproductive viability. This is a competition solely between descent groups; uterine sibling categories cannot by definition compete in this way because they are not agnatic groups and cannot increase their size by accumulating wives. In short, they are not and can never be political entities; nor are subclans, for that matter, so far as the wealth-exchanging functions they share with uterine sibling categories are concerned. The key material resource in the society is not wealth but reproduction, and the competition for it is between agnates. Subclans of the same exogamous group are, implicitly, permanent rivals for wives and compete for them by offering their marriageables valuable alliance relationships. In the next chapter, I shall describe the forms of 'value' with which these groups endow themselves for their potential affines.

Part of the reason why the system of bridewealth and mortuary payments does not give rise to Big *Men* as such is that the minimal structural actors in the exchanges are not men, but married couples. Individuals only begin participating fully in the system of affinal and matrilateral payments on marriage. When people marry, they take on a heavy load of obligations: not only towards their parents-in-law, but also to their spouses' sisters' children, and they also begin to assume responsibility for their, and for their spouses', fathers' sisters' children as well. Every transaction a married couple makes is to kin on either the wife's or the husband's side, but the gift is made in the name of the couple as a unit. In order to establish a newly-married couple as an exchange unit, their respective kin give the bride and groom each a small fund, called *ndjuwi*, consisting of a dozen or so valuables to start the couple off on their career in the exchange system. Whenever the husband has to make some gift or other – to contribute to the mortuary payment or bridewealth of some relative – he draws the necessary valuables from his wife's fund. And when she has to make some payment on behalf of her kin, she draws from his fund. Whenever either of them receives wealth in return, they pool it in a common fund. So, by these self-negating exchanges of wealth, the husband and wife become a single exchange unit after a few years of marriage, operating from a joint store of wealth. If a man is a polygynist, he maintains quite separate funds with each of his wives, though co-wives do often lend and borrow among themselves.

At a conceptual or ideological level, the units which give and receive all alliance payments are the subclans and uterine sibling categories. But in practice, the exchanges are not made by these entities acting as blocs, but are carried out through complex contractual networks between these husband-wife dyads. Firstly, the members of a subclan, or uterine sibling category, do not all necessarily contribute to, or receive shares of, each other's transactions. They only do so with those co-members with whom they have personal credits or debts, or with whom they wish to create such credits and debts. Energetic people may have large networks of agnates and matrilateral siblings with whom they exchange receipts of, and contributions to, bridewealth and mortuary payments. The more dilatory are only able to maintain small networks, especially couples who are lax in their duties toward their sisters' children and are therefore rewarded with only small mortuary payments on their sisters' childrens' deaths. People tend to keep considerable pressure on their agnates and matrilateral siblings to be dutiful to their sisters' children, so as to maximise incomings from mortuary payments. People habitually negligent to their sisters' children risk being dropped from the networks of many of their agnates and matrilateral siblings.

Secondly, people have very large numbers of classificatory mothers and mothers' brothers who can potentially 'nurture' them with gifts and services. These matrikin not only comprise all the members of the mother's subclan, of the mother's generation and all subsequent ones, but also all of those individuals' matrilateral siblings as well. People dissatisfied with their matrikin can simply cut them out of their mortuary payments, and find new maternal kin to succour them and receive their mortuary payments when they die. Women in particular have considerable power to appoint 'mother's brothers' for their children. A woman dissatisfied with her own brothers' efforts towards her children can simply establish relations with new 'brothers'. Men sometimes say they 'fear their sisters' (*ndjəkwa'arək yangganandiyan*) because these women have this powerful sanction of disinheriting them from their sisters' children's mortuary payments. In other words, the status of 'mother's brother' or classificatory 'mother' is partly an achieved and contractual one: it must be continually validated by 'giving mother's milk'. Again, conscientious couples tend therefore to have larger networks of sisters' children than lax couples do, and are rewarded with larger mortuary payments when their sisters' children die.

Conclusion

In contrast to some Melanesian exchange systems (see M. Strathern 1972), these exchanges do not create a division between men as transactors, acting in a political domain, and women as producers acting within a domestic one. Instead, like wives among the Tombema Enga of the Highlands (Feil 1978, 1984), women are full participants in the exchange system. Husbands and wives are wholly equivalent and interdependent halves of one dyad in the transactions, and what they are acting cooperatively to reproduce are the total set of affinal and kinship relations of this dyad.

But, in contrast to the Tombema Enga, these exchanges do not constitute the political arena of Avatip society, and I have described this nexus as being governed by a domestic ethos. But the system is not equivalent to a domestic *sphere*, because there are no feasible structural limits on the number of these exchange relations a couple can form. The 'domestic' at Avatip is not so much a domain of action, enclosed within a political one, but a form or modality of action existing as an alternative to a political modality and in implicit antithesis to it. The political mode of action is ritual, and specifically the men's cult with its hierarchy of ritual grades and initiations. It is men who are the actors in this system, and women are excluded from it.

In discussing the exclusion of women from the male political sphere among the Highlanders of Mount Hagen, Marilyn Strathern (1984) argues that women are not thereby infantilised, dependent or less than full persons. Within the domestic sphere, both men and women are full persons because domesticity is not, to the extent that it is in Western industrial society, materially and structurally dependent on the world outside the domestic circle. The locus of the political at Avatip is a men's cult, rather than a system of ceremonial gift-exchange as it is among the Hageners, but Strathern's point nevertheless applies. The reproduction of kinship and affinal relations in the exchange system is the fundamental preoccupation of everyday life, and a person's participation in this system is the public measure of his or her full humanness. The men's cult, so far as I can see, could disappear or be abolished, yet the whole system of everyday transactions between kin and affines would remain entirely viable and continue unchanged. These two dimensions of Avatip social life, the domestic and the political, are indeed interdependent, but this is not a functional interdependence but a semantic or meaningful one. It is a contrast between secular equality and ritual hierarchy (see Harrison 1985a, 1985b) as two opposed ideal conceptions of the structure of social relationships.

3

Magic and the totemic cosmology

Introduction

Reciprocity has long been recognised as an important theme of Melanesian social life, and especially of traditional Melanesian politics (Forge 1972a; Gregory 1982; Rubel and Rosman 1978; Schwimmer 1973). It is by making gifts to one another that groups, and ambitious men, form alliances and compete for reputation and power. These prestations often include ritual services (Rubel and Rosman 1978), but the main medium of the exchanges in most Melanesian societies is material wealth: pigs and shell valuables in many of the New Guinea Highland societies (Feil 1987; Lederman 1986; Sillitoe 1979; A.J. Strathern 1971), and yams or other prestige foodstuffs among many of the Lowland peoples (Malinowski 1935; Serpenti 1965; Tuzin 1976; Young 1971). In this chapter I discuss Avatip cosmology as a system of ritual reciprocities between groups, and suggest some parallels between it and the material reciprocities characteristic of Melanesian Big Man polities. My argument is that Avatip ritual and cosmology function as a gift economy, transposed from the sphere of material production into the idiom of magic and ritual.

Just as in other Melanesian societies, it is important in everyday life at Avatip for men and women to be productive, particularly so as to fulfil their obligations to their uterine kin and affines. They are respected for this in their ordinary domestic lives, and it is the means by which men and women create and reproduce their personal kinship and affinal relationships. It is precisely through these sorts of exchange relations, described in the previous chapter, that in many other Melanesian societies Big Men operate and develop networks of credit and political patronage (A.J. Strathern 1971). But, as I shall try to show, political actors at Avatip cannot earn political credit in this way. It is the hereditary ritual powers of descent groups that are the politically important resources, because these powers are conceived as creating the basic conditions for men and women to produce to fulfil their affinal obligations.

The totemic descent groups

The population of Avatip is divided into three intermarrying clan-groups. The

42

two largest are called Nggəla'angkw and Wuluwi-Nyawi. They each contain a pair of clans and account for about 44 per cent and 49 per cent of the population respectively. The third group, Nambul-Sambəlap, is a single clan representing some 7 per cent of the community. Wuluwi-Nyawi and Nggəla'angkw each contain seven subclans. Nambul-Sambəlap has two.

In demographic terms, there is therefore very nearly an exogamous moiety system at Avatip. The villagers themselves, in fact, speak of the three groups as though they had the idea of moieties in mind, and try to assimilate them conceptually to a dualism. Orators refer to Nambul-Sambəlap in their speeches as 'standing in the middle' (*nyəndəm tənand*), and by the epithet 'the hole/gap in the middle' (*nyəndəm tap*). This second expression was explained to me in the following way:

It is just like your house here at Avatip. It has two rooms, one at the front and one at the back. Nggəla'angkw and Wuluwi-Nyawi are like those two rooms. Nambul-Sambəlap is like the doorway between them. It can be entered from both sides.

The term 'entered' was meant to convey, as it does in English, a double *entendre*: Nambul-Sambəlap is 'entered from both sides' in the sense that its women are married by the men of both Wuluwi-Nyawi and Nggəla'angkw. My informant was representing the two larger groups, implicitly, as halves of an exogamous dual division, as though they alone exchanged women and Nambul-Sambəlap was merely a stock of women existing 'in between' them. He was trying to describe the three exogamous groups as a dualism, by identifying one of them with the relation – the 'hole' or 'gap' – between the other two. He 'feminised' Nambul-Sambəlap because, to the villagers, it is women who by their marriages form the link between Wuluwi-Nyawi and Nggəla'angkw.

The villagers derive the name Nggəla'angkw from the term *nggəlanggwu* ('black water'), a reference to the dark, clear water distinctive to lakes and ox-bow lagoons, with which this clan-pair is closely identified. The name is also connected with the notion that the totems of this group are 'dark' or 'black things' (*nggəlanggəla ndja'av*): dark-plumaged birds, plants with dark leaves and flowers, and so forth. Wuluwi-Nyawi, on the other hand, is said to have red (*nyikinyiki*) totems, and Nambul-Sambəlap white ones (*wamakawam*). Some Wuluwi-Nyawi men, however, harbour a more 'dualistic' view of this totemic colour-scheme: they claim both red and white as their totemic colours, and deny that Nambul-Sambəlap totems have any particular characteristic colour.

As is common among Melanesians, the skin-colour of Avatip people varies from very dark to a light, coppery brown. The villagers say they inherit the totemic colour of their descent group, Nggəla'angkw people being generally black-skinned (*nggəlasəp*) and Wuluwi-Nyawi people having coppery-red complexions (*nyikisəp*). It hardly needs saying that observation does not bear out this belief. But exceptions do not compromise it, since most can be accounted for as cases in which people have inherited the totemic skin-colour of their mothers' descent group. This is one dualism from which Nambul-Sambəlap is quite effaced: this clan has no hereditary skin-colour and most of the villagers, if pressed, suppose that its members inherit their mothers' colour only.

The most important attributes distinguishing the three groups are their specialised hereditary functions in magic and ritual. Nggəla'angkw is the autochthonous group at Avatip, according to myth, and owns the surrounding lagoons which are the principal economic resources of the community. It holds the ritual power to control the fertility of these fishing grounds and of the economically most important types of fish, all of which are its totems. It owns two of the four initiatory rituals in the men's cult, both of which promote the abundance of fish.

The two other male initiation rituals are owned by Wuluwi-Nyawi. This clan-pair owns all the magic and ritual to do with the growing of yams, which are one of its major totems, and all the main stages in the yearly yam-gardening cycle have to be inaugurated by its hereditary magicians. Its most important gardening ritual is the annual first-fruits ceremony of the yam harvest. Every few years, the community holds an especially elaborate version of the harvest ritual, and this amplified version is one of the two male initiation rituals owned by this clan-pair. In association with its hereditary powers over yams, Wuluwi-Nyawi owns a weather-magic complex called Nyava'at. In the old days, its magicians used to perform this magic annually in a public ceremony, to bring the dry season and give good weather for clearing and firing the new yam gardens.

Nggəla'angkw and Wuluwi-Nyawi are, in short, the 'owners' (*asa'ai*, literally, 'fathers') of fish and yams respectively. Nambul-Sambəlap owns the Sepik River and has sorcery to make it flood. But it does not own a male cult ritual controlling the fertility of a major food. One of the lineages of this group is affiliated to the ritual complex owned by Nggəla'angkw, another to the Wuluwi-Nyawi ritual complex, and its other three lineages to neither.

It is the organisation of ritual and totemism that assimilates the triad of groups most explicitly to a dualism, and encourages the villagers to think in terms of a moiety system. Nambul-Sambəlap is maritally a marginal group, because of its tiny size, and ritually an 'empty' group. The basic division of ritual powers in the society is between Nggəla'angkw and Wuluwi-Nyawi, and the emphasis of ritual and totemism is upon the relationship between these two clan-pairs. When men speak of this relationship in ritual, they say that each clan-pair is 'mother' and 'child' to the other: whenever one of the two groups carries out its magical functions, it does so to sustain and nurture the other. It is 'giving mother's milk'. This conception, of two groups in an immemorial and self-reciprocal uterine relationship, is the basic organising theme of Avatip ritual, totemism and mythology.

Beside the basic division of ritual functions in the community between the two major clan-pairs, with their hereditary powers over yams and fish, most subclans have their own, individual magical proficiencies as well. Some own love-magic. The men of some subclans are hereditary shamans, and own the shamanic curing and sorcery techniques the villagers call *yanu*. Other subclans have hereditary powers over particular foods: coconuts, taro, bananas, or the mayflies that now and then swarm on the river and are gathered by the villagers as a delicacy. There are many other hereditary powers of this sort, which are the *ndja'am* of specific subclans. Some of them, such as the hereditary ritual offices called *simbuk* which I discuss later in this book, are especially prestigious and important.

There is, in other words, a subsidiary division of ceremonial functions at the level of the subclan, and this too is spoken of in the idiom of uterine kinship. Whenever a subclan exercises its special powers, the villagers say it is 'giving mother's milk' to all its sisters' children. What they mean is that it is rendering these services to every other subclan in the community: because its sisters' children either belong to, or are married into, all those groups. That is to say, the villagers conceive of this exchange of magical services between subclans as paralleling the movement of women between them in marriage.

Cosmology

The villagers say that in the beginning, the world was a featureless, flooded plain, existing in complete darkness. Near the present site of Avatip was a village, where the totemic ancestors of Nggəla'angkw had their home. The totemic ancestors of Wuluwi-Nyawi lived in a settlement far to the east, and those of Nambul-Sambəlap in a similar settlement to the west. From these villages a number of other mythologically less important ones were founded, associated with specific subclans. All these ancestral villages are known as *sakitəp* ('myth-villages') and, according to mythology, it was in these that almost all things that exist first came into being. Nowadays, some of these villages are identified in a loose way with distant place-names such as Sydney, London, Papua and America.

A time came when all the totemic beings emerged from their settlements and created the world. Some fashioned the mountains, lakes and rivers. Others issued forth in the form of the winds, animals, plants and birds. Some founded Avatip, metamorphosing into its wards, its ceremonial houses, initiatory flutes, slit-drums, and all its male initiatory sacra. The ancestors of Nggəla'angkw created, among other things, the land and lagoons around Avatip. The sun, moon and the Pleiades (whose annual appearance signals yam harvest time) rose out of the ancestral village of Wuluwi-Nyawi, where they have ever since continued to rise. From the village of Nambul-Sambəlap, ancestors went out and made the Sepik River, which has ever after had its source in that village.

Magic and the Totemic cosmology

The villagers call living human beings *kwamakanduta'akw*: people with revealed, or visible, faces. The totemic ancestral spirits, they say, are men and women too; but their faces (*mak*) are hidden because these beings do not show themselves to living people in their true forms. They are only visible as animal and plant species, as rivers, mountains, ritual sacra, and so on: that is, only in their outward, transfigured forms:

You realise that this tree isn't really a tree. It is actually a man, but you and I can't see him because we are only living people. Our eyes aren't clear. We are not able to see things as they really are.

The villagers speak of there being two 'paths' (*ya'amb*) in the world; one path of living human beings, and another for the totemic ancestors and the ghosts of the dead. What they mean, implicitly, is that there are two separate orders of existence: the everyday world of sense experience, in which living human beings exist, and a second, concealed world, in which all things exist in their real forms, which are human forms. The image of the two 'paths' is perhaps drawn – though it did not occur to me in the field – from the village layout, with its separate paths for initiates and noninitiates. Living human beings are excluded from the invisible world of spirits, in the same way that women and noninitiates are excluded from the male domain of initiatory ritual. The idea that an invisible but more 'real' world lies behind the visible one, is compelling for the villagers because it is grounded in their everyday social experience and appears to them to reflect it. There are two parallel spheres of life in Avatip society: a secular, exoteric one shared by men, women and children alike in everyday life; and a second, ritual sphere, hedged around with secrecy, in which only initiated men can participate (see Harrison 1985b). Sometimes, a ghost or totemic spirit makes itself visible to a solitary hunter in the forest, or to a woman fishing alone on a lake. When this happens to someone, it is an omen that he or she is soon to die. To 'see things as they really are' is an experience the villagers fear, because they assume it signifies one's death – just as a noninitiate who trespassed into the ritual sphere of men would be killed by the spirits of the male cult.

Every descent group at Avatip, from the clan-pair to the lineage, traces its origin, and the origin of all its totems, to one of the mythical villages. When a man and his wife die, their ghosts go to his group's origin-village to live there with his totemic ancestors, and the mythical villages are sometimes referred to as *wundəmbatəp*, 'the villages of the ghosts of the dead'. I mentioned earlier that the villagers also say that ghosts dwell in the houses of the living as domestic tutelaries. This dual theory of the afterlife – that ghosts inhabit the mythical villages and, simultaneously, the houses of the living – seems to involve no inconsistency for the villagers. It is rather a corollary of their basic assumption that their community and the total world order share the same structure. The mythical villages are, in effect, their own residential wards projected into cosmology.

The mythical villages, Avatip people say, still exist, though they are only visible to the dead and to those about to die; and the totemic ancestors continue, in some undefined way, to live in them and to be embodied in the visible world at the same time. When a magician says spells to make yams abundant in the gardens, or to increase fish, or crocodiles in the hunting season, he 'calls them forth' (*wandjalina*) from their origin-villages, which are their permanent, inexhaustible sources. The mythical first emergence of things into the world is, implicitly for Avatip people, not so much a completed event in the past, as an act that must be repeated or sustained constantly by human agents in magic and ritual.

For their spells to be effective, increase-magicians must abstain periodically, and in some cases permanently, from eating the foods they control. Once a yam magician has said his spells over a newly-planted garden, he cannot eat yams again until the crop has grown and been harvested. Some subclans have the *ndja'am*, or ritual proficiency, of increasing crocodiles before the large-scale hunts held in the dry season. The men who practise this magic must never eat crocodiles themselves; as one of them explained:

When the men hunt crocodiles, it is I who tell the crocodiles to come out into the open and not be afraid of the men's spears. Because I know their [secret] names, they call me father and obey me. It is because they call me their father that I cannot eat them. If I ate them, they would say: why is he eating us? He cannot be our real father. Then they would no longer obey me. I make those things abundant, but it is other men who must eat them.

His magic powers are effective, in other words, only as long as he uses them for the welfare and benefit of others, and not for his own. Before their emergence into the world, so Avatip myths say, the totemic ancestors of the different descent groups often killed and ate each other. They concealed the existence of their totemic foods from each other as well, keeping them for their own secret consumption. Such acts, to Avatip people, are extreme images of the denial of sociality, and in fact the totemic ancestors are constantly referred to in myth and debating by epithets which stress their powerful, but wilful and non-social nature: *apǝl* (wild, uncontrolled), *ka'awndu* (the fierce one), *sǝpanǝmbi takwun* (bespelled with lethal war-magic). The mythical villages represent Avatip in a primordial state of disassembly, before proper sociality was established between its component groups.

In myth, each origin-village contained only those species and other elements of the natural environment owned by one specific descent group. In other words, besides being a partial, truncated society, each mythical village was a fragment of the yet-to-be physical environment as well. Avatip myth is the charter for the division of cosmological powers among social groups; and, rather like an 'exploded' diagram of a piece of machinery, it emphasises the design by representing it as having been taken apart.

When the totemic ancestors emerged from their villages and took up their present places in the material world, they brought society into being in the same process. Social groups renounced their independence by making their totemic food species and other resources available to each other; and in doing so they entered into social relations. A senior man of Nggəla'angkw put this to me in the following way:

If our ancestors had said it must be so, we Nggəla'angkw would now build our houses only with *mbanggər* and *marək* [two totemic trees of his clan-pair] and Wuluwi-Nyawi would build theirs only with *tawuk* and *miyemb* [totemic trees of Wuluwi-Nyawi]. We Nggəla'angkw would only drink the black water of the lagoons, while Wuluwi-Nyawi would drink only rain-water [a Wuluwi-Nyawi totem]. And so it would be; with house timbers, with drinking-water, with food, land, with everything. But our ancestors did not do that. They shared all these things with each other, and we must share them too.

People take pride in their totemic ancestors' creative acts, and like to boast of their importance. The men of Wuluwi-Nyawi, for instance, claim credit for the existence of daylight because their ancestors created the sun, and they often remind other groups, even in casual conversation, of the debt they owe:

It is because we Wuluwi-Nyawi made it so that night now alternates with day. If we had not done so, there would be no daylight, just darkness all the time.

There is a strong notion of consubstantiality between people and their totems, an idea that in allowing one another the use of their totemic resources they nourish each other with their own flesh. People often say, for instance, that when they eat yams they are eating human flesh and blood. Each group therefore expects the others to treat its totems, and particularly its edible ones, with respect and gratitude. To allow a yam or fish to rot uneaten, or to kill an animal gratuitously without making use of it for food or some other responsible purpose, is an offence against its totemic owners called *sa'al*. This expression means to vandalise someone's property, or to treat someone's possessions in such a way as to insult or threaten him. If such an act came to their notice, the totemic owners of the food would cause it to become scarce, making magic to 'send it back' (*kawlana*) to its origin-village or to 'block the path' (*ya'amb təpəna*) along which it comes into the phenomenal world. As one magician explained:

Suppose a man fells his breadfruit trees to take their fruits. The fathers [i.e. totemic owners] of the breadfruit tree would become angry with him for destroying his trees, saying to themselves, those are our very bones he has cut. Or suppose the man harvests the immature fruits, throwing them carelessly on the ground and leaving the ripe ones on the tree. The fathers would see this and be angry, saying to themselves, why has he damaged the tree? It is not just a tree, it is a man. It has a name, and a father, a mother and a mother's brother, and the fruits are his children. Why has he harvested the younger siblings before the elder siblings? Then the fathers will call the [secret] name of the tree, and tell it to stop bearing.

48

Magic and the Totemic cosmology

To the villagers, all food resources, wild and domesticated, are held by the community in a kind of usufruct from their totemic owners; they are gifts or loans that can be taken away if they are squandered. Land is treated in this way as well. There is no shortage of land at Avatip, and each subclan allows the others freely to hunt and fish on its territories, to gather wild plant foods and materials, and to cultivate gardens. It does not let them plant or husband sago palms, coconut and areca palms, and nowadays also coffee trees, because these are hereditable fixtures of land that imply an enduring relationship with it. But it allows sisters' children to use and harvest these resources all their lives. The ownership of land, in other words, entails only very limited rights of exclusive use. To own land is, primarily, to have the magical and ritual responsibility for its fertility. To the villagers all land and bodies of water are fertile because they contain the rotted bodies and body-fluids of totemic ancestors. Many parcels of land are criss-cross complexes of old levees left by shifts in the course of the river; people say these have a human outline, and still bear the shapes of the ancestors who 'fell down' (vakərəndi) upon them in mythical times. It is the responsibility of these ancestors' human descendants to make sure their substance is conserved. If a lagoon is being over-fished, or the game are being driven from a tract of land by too intensive hunting, its owners will put it under a ritual interdiction. They invoke the ancestral spirits of the locality, bidding them to visit sickness or accident on anyone who tries to use it. Although land ownership gives few exclusive use-rights, it can confer real economic power. The owners of an important fishing-lagoon, or a prize area of gardening land, can use the threat of interdicting it to compel other groups – owners of less valuable land resources – to keep their territories always open for general use. The rights of the clan-pair Nggəla'angkw to prohibit use of the community's vital fishing grounds is the most powerful of all sanctions of this sort. Wuluwi-Nyawi, in turn, have quite a powerful sanction of their own: as they often like to remind the people of Nggəla'angkw, nobody in the community could eat yams without their annually granted ritual permission.

In this whole scheme of reciprocities the two ritually most important resources are yams and fish. An act of sa'al against these foods is a serious ritual offence. The offender would have to appease their ancestral spirits, and their human totemic owners, with an offering of areca-nut, a chicken, or even a pig if the offence was a particularly serious one. Otherwise he would fall sick and die: in a grim reversal of the normal roles of man and food, the food he had misused would 'eat him' (kəkəndanand).

There are many special restrictions to do with the exploitation of yams and fish, and it is a sa'al to break any of them. The most important one concerning yams is the prohibition of harvesting the levee gardens, or even disturbing their surface unnecessarily, between the time of their planting and the performance of the harvest ritual some six months later. There is a similar taboo with regard to fishing. Several times a year, big shoals of fish appear in the lagoons for a day or two, and virtually the whole able-bodied population go out onto the lagoons to spear them. On these occasions, it is forbidden to disturb the water's surface unnecessarily. If people need to bail out their canoes, they must pull in to the shore to do so and cannot do it on the open water. Any breach of this rule, even the accidental capsize of a canoe, would offend the totemic spirits of the fish, and of the lagoon itself, and make the fish disappear.

All these sorts of ritual restrictions have quite real ecosystemic consequences of which the villagers are highly conscious, and help to prevent the over-use or over-exploitation of natural resources. In this respect, one may speak of the community and its environment as, in Rappaport's (1968) vivid phrase, a ritually regulated ecosystem. But these implications for the ecology are not, as in Rappaport's functionalist argument, *unintended* consequences that must necessarily remain unperceived by the actors themselves in order to be effective. Rather, religion and the villagers' common-sense practical knowledge of their ecosystem work in tandem and reinforce each other.

Nggəla'angkw and Wuluwi-Nyawi are represented in ritual as using all their powers for each other's 'maternal' nurture. But this reciprocity has also, latently, a sinister underside as well. Both groups own highly feared forms of sorcery capable, so the villagers believe, of destroying their community entirely. Nggəla'angkw owns two such weapons of magical mass destruction: one for infesting the community with plagues of venomous insects and snakes, the other for destroying everyone's livelihoods by silting-up the fishing lagoons. Wuluwi-Nyawi, likewise, owns two, both of which relate to its totemic associations with the sky. One is magic for calling up storms and destroying the community with thunderbolts, which the villagers believe hurl down fist-sized stones. The second is magic to cause the total collapse of the sky, which Wuluwi-Nyawi ancestors are said to have shored up in its present position on posts, having separated it from the earth in mythical times.

There is a balance between the two clan-pairs, not just in their life-giving powers, but in their destructive ones as well. As one of my magician friends put it:

We Nggəla'angkw control the things of the earth, while Wuluwi-Nyawi control the things of the sky. Wuluwi-Nyawi could destroy the village from the air. But we could destroy it from the ground.

The villagers say that these destructive powers have been fully unleashed only once, when their ancestral home, the village of Asiti, was destroyed by the thunder-magic in an internecine feud. The destruction of Asiti is not totemic myth (*sakima'andj*) but legend (*wasekima'andj*). It is considered to have been an ordinary historical event, involving human beings. It is one of the most important Avatip legends, and is a kind of object lesson in the consequences of a major breakdown of social ties between groups:

According to this story, a man was tricked into killing his wife by cutting off her breasts and making soup with them. According to another version, he was driven mad by sorcery and cut his wife's throat. His brothers-in-law decided to avenge the killing of their sister, and speared to death the man's two children, their own sister's children, while they were fishing in a canoe. The husband in turn took his revenge by trying to kill the whole population of Asiti with the storm-magic. He waited for a day when all the villagers were out fishing on Kamiar, the main fishing-lagoon of Asiti. He placed a bespelled stick against a coconut-palm, called on the thunder-spirits by their secret names, and snapped the stick with his foot. A storm-cloud immediately gathered over Kamiar, and the thunder-spirits came hurtling down on the villagers in the form of thunder-stones. Everyone was killed except for a few who managed to capsize their canoes and take shelter under the hulls. The survivors abandoned Asiti, moved upriver, and founded Old Avatip. One man and one woman from each lineage survived, and they are the progenitors of all the present-day lineages.

The important point about this tale is that it describes the destruction of Asiti as having been caused by a breakdown of affinal and uterine ties. Its lesson is that if affines and matrikin feud, groups will use their magical powers to destroy the whole of society. Like totemic mythology, it describes a negation or inversion of sociality as a way of stressing the fundamental ties conceived as holding the community together: ties of intermarriage, and the use by groups of their hereditary powers for each other's welfare and sustenance.

Each group's origin-village represents, implicitly, the total fund of positive and negative values which its ancestors are conceived as having first brought into the world, and which are now under the social, responsible custodianship of the group's senior men. Almost all the resources considered necessary for people's existence and well-being are perceived as emanating from one social group or another; even, as I mentioned, such a commonplace utility as daylight. In such a conceptualisation, it is impossible for individual or collective needs to be met without continually reproducing relations of credit and debt between social groups. All ritual powers, including the destructive ones that groups hold constantly in abeyance for each other's benefit, confer on their owners the status that Mauss (1966: 72) called *magister*, the dominance and superiority of the giver, making the beneficiaries dependent and obliged. These groups' claims to grandiose magical powers express the narrow segmentary allegiances that divide the community against itself. But they also express an opposite and equally strong drive by these groups to keep to a maximum the number of ways in which they are *accountable* to each other (see Harrison 1988a).

Avatip totemism is reminiscent of the classic totemic systems of the Aranda and other central Australian peoples (Spencer and Gillen 1904), in which groups are responsible for the ritual 'production' of their totemic species for one another's consumption. Lévi-Strauss (1966) has argued that these imaginary economies, and the hereditary occupational specialisations in caste systems, are transformations of the same underlying structures. Exogamous totemic clans 'produce' women for one another, and imagine themselves as magically manufacturing their totemic food species for one another's consumption. Endogamous castes imagine themselves as 'species', incapable of intermarriage, yet are interrelated by a real exchange of goods and services. Whatever the merits of Lévi-Strauss' ingenious argument, an implication of it which I wish to develop in this book is that cosmology in one society can be structurally cognate with economy in another. Specifically, I shall argue that the structures that manifest themselves at Avatip in the form of a ritual system and cosmology are those on which prestige-economies and gift exchange systems are based in some other Melanesian societies.

A basic feature distinguishing gift exchange from the exchange of commodities is that gifts symbolise social relationships or, to put it slightly differently, stand for persons or for aspects of persons (Gregory 1982; Mauss 1966; M. Strathern 1983, 1987, 1988). I have noted the close identifications made in ritual between men and their totemic food species and other resources. In offering one another these resources they represent themselves as giving away a part of their own substance, an aspect of their own identities. Although the values that Avatip groups transact in ritual are immaterial, they represent in exactly the same way as do material goods – the pigs, pearlshells and other wealth in other Melanesian gift economies – the social identities of their donors.

Personal names and totemic classifications

The most important part of a subclan's patrimony are the names of its totemic ancestors. These names are considered the source of all the magic powers of the subclan and are its jealously guarded property. They are the personal names borne generation after generation by its members, and in this section I describe the place of names in the system of totemic classifications.

Lévi-Strauss (1973) has argued that it is artificial to try to isolate totemism as an institutional complex. Totemism is simply one of the many manifestations of the human propensity to impose categorical order upon experience, and the 'problem' of totemism is part of the wider problem of understanding systems of classification. According to Lévi-Strauss, the use of animal and plant emblems by social groups is a way of representing these groups as forming a unified-yet-differentiated whole in parallel with an identically-structured 'nature'.

The nature/culture dichotomy which Lévi-Strauss presupposes is difficult to apply to Avatip totemism.[1] The problem is that a great range of quite different sorts of entities are used as totems of Avatip groups. A subclan's totems do not only include 'naturally' distinct categories such as animal and plant species. They also include 'culturally' bounded tracts of land, ritual sacra, ceremonial houses and their architectural parts, and shamanic spirits and other superna-

---

1 See MacCormack and Strathern 1980 for other critiques of the structuralist assumption of the universality of the nature/culture dichotomy.

Magic and the Totemic cosmology

Table 2. *Some single-subclan totems and their derived personal names*

Subclan	Totem	Totemic name
Makəm	Rainbow (*walimawndi*)	Walimawndindu ('Rainbow-man')
Yimal	Campnosperm tree (*sunggwar*)	Sunggwarwakən ('Campnosperm-shamanic spirit')
Nyakaw	Moon (*mbapw*)	Mbapata'akw ('Moon-woman')

tural beings. Different positions of the sun are 'owned' as totems by subclans. The heat-haze which surrounds the village each afternoon in the dry season is divided, by quite arbitrary cultural *fiat*, into named sectors, each one belonging to a specific subclan. To the villagers, all those disparate entities are, as totems of groups, equivalent in kind because they are all the metamorphosed forms of totemic ancestors. But they do not constitute a category of existence equivalent to 'nature'. Many of the distinctions made in Avatip totemism, and which are vitally important to the villagers, are not perceptual distinctions at all but exist purely in myth. There is no difference, for instance, between a personified canoe, or shield, or fish-trap, or egret, appearing in one subclan's myths, and others figuring in the myths of another subclan, except that they are named differently. In fact, the only characteristic that all Avatip totems have in common, the one feature which makes all these disparate entities or pseudo-entities serve as emblems of groups, are the personal names they are accorded.

A second problem with Lévi-Strauss' approach is that the social groupings which the totems define are not entirely discrete or mutually exclusive. They tend instead to overlap and rather untidily cross-cut each other. A subclan may have some totemic species which are exclusively its own and others which it shares with a number of other subclans. In short, a subclan may have a unique complement of totems. But many of these will be shared by other groups, although none of those subclans perhaps has an exactly identical set. It is a subclan's hereditary names deriving from its set of totems, and only the names, which completely individuate the group and make it distinct from others.

Let me illustrate these remarks with some examples. Table 2 gives a small selection of totems owned exclusively by single subclans. It illustrates the way in which many personal names derive etymologically from the terms for totems.

In the case of totems such as these, which are exclusive to specific subclans, the 'classification' of groups by means of personal names simply duplicates the way in which the groups are 'classified' by their totems. But a totem shared by

Table 3. *Totemic names of the sun*

Group	Totemic name	Position of the sun
Nyakaw	Tundimi/Nyakawndu	sunrise
Wanaki	Samnap	
Nanggwundaw	Tuwai	↓
Nawik	Mbaliamb	
Wanɔkaw	Wimbus	midday
Maliyaw	Yuanap	
Ambasarak	Tupukuman	↓
Sarambusarak	Kwarumbaliamb	sunset

several subclans is 'refracted' into several personal names; it is then the different names which distinguish the subclans, while their common totem associates them. For instance, an important totem of the clan-pair Wuluwi-Nyawi is the sun. This totem is also shared by the Nambul-Sambɔlap lineage Wanaki, as part of a totemic tie which that lineage has with Nyakaw, the senior subclan of Wuluwi-Nyawi. Table 3 gives the personal names of the sun, and the corresponding positions of the sun, owned by Wanaki and the Wuluwi-Nyawi subclans.

Here, these groups are differentiated not only by personal names, but also by the perceptually distinct 'sun-positions' to which the names refer. But there are many totems whose 'name-refractions' have no objective referents at all. For instance, there is a special ceremonial association, relating to the yam harvest ritual, between the subclan Ambasarak and certain other descent groups (see Chapter 8) and, as part of that association, Ambasarak shares some totems with those descent groups. The most important of the totems, and the corresponding totemic names, are given in Table 4.

The different totemic names each of these groups has for the cassowary or yams do not refer to different 'kinds' of cassowaries or yams. They do not have different perceptual referents at all, but simply refer to different individuals in myth.

The totems these descent groups share serve at least to distinguish them as a ritual association from other ceremonial groupings in the community. But there are many totems which do not have the effect of differentiating social groups at all. For instance, every subclan at Avatip has the dog, pig and eagle as a totem; all that distinguishes subclans are the ancestral names they have for these creatures. Every subclan has ancestral canoes, spears, suspension hooks, and many other items of material culture, which exist only in its myths and are distinguished from those of other subclans purely by their totemic names.

To summarise, the role of totems in 'classifying' groups is a variable one. A totem may be an indigenous animal or plant taxon; or quasi-natural entity such as a heat-haze sector; or a category of material culture such as 'axe' or

Table 4. *Totemic ties between the member groups of the Yanggǝlimbaw yam harvest ritual association*

	Ambasarak subclan	Sarambusarak subclan	Ndjǝmalwan lineage	Makapangkw lineage
Cassowary	Mǝndanggǝn	Mǝndapa'akw/ Ndapa'akw	Kundapa'akw	Apwinǝmbǝr
Male Eclectus parrot	Kwarulukǝn	Waiyakǝndu	Wapilaw	Apakwaru
Yams	Kawmbar	Mbapañ	Selikeiñ	Parmeli
Red-leafed Cordyline	Sarakandu	Sarambundu	—	Ndjukwulndu

'spear-thrower'. It may be an emblem of one subclan, or of several, or of every subclan in the society. The only constant, uniform and thoroughgoing differentiae of groups are their hereditary totemic names.

Avatip totemism is not, to use Lévi-Strauss' (1966: 115) terms, an homology between a 'natural series' (animal and plant species) and a 'cultural' one (social groups). It is more accurately described as an homology between a series of groups and a series of name-sets, and does not involve a nature/culture dichotomy. The villagers do not consider personal names to be 'natural' phenomena. But it would also misrepresent their ideas to say they think of names as products of 'culture'. They think there is a fixed, finite number of personal names in the world, which have existed since the world's creation. The names were neither created by human beings nor can they be changed or added to. Together with natural species, the landscape, the ritual system, and the social groups whose immemorial property the names are, they were brought into existence by the totemic ancestors and are simply objective properties of the total world order.

I mentioned earlier the villagers' idea of two 'paths', or basic orders of being: the world of outward, phenomenal appearances in which ordinary men and women live, and the hidden but more 'real' order peopled by spirits and ghosts. It is those two categories, not nature and culture, which are given a common structure in Avatip totemism and organised into a conceptually related whole. The 'message' of Avatip totemism is that the world of everyday life exists in counterpart to another, the world of the totemic ancestors described in myth, and that these are the basic parallel categories of the world order. That is, Avatip totemism does not arrange social groups in a merely semantic or classificatory relationship with animals, plants and so forth: it gives each group an hereditary efficacy over a particular sector of the environment, and puts these groups in contact with the conceived sources of power in the world. In the next section, I examine the conceived nature of these magical powers.

Personal names, myth and magic

To the villagers, the most important expression of the relationship between the two orders of existence is that the totemic ancestral spirits, and living men and women, are each other's namesakes. All the men and women of a subclan consider themselves namesakes of their mythical forebears and carry their names with great pride whether or not they actually know their mythological significance. Many of the names have an esoteric significance, known only to the senior men of the subclan and their close allies, and are the highly secret 'real' names of the group's totemic ancestors. Other names are purely exoteric, and are considered mere pseudonyms by which to refer to the totemic ancestors and their mythical exploits in public. In other words, many of the members of the subclan, without knowing they do so, carry their ancestors' esoteric names, and these names are therefore in fact spoken constantly in everyday life. It is not the names themselves that are secret, but their mythological referents, the relationship between these names and the figures in the subclan's myths. That is known only to the senior men of the subclan and to their close allies.

Only when they start learning secret myths, do men come to know that the ultimately 'real' names of the totemic ancestors are just the names of ordinary human beings. When they learn that these secret names are simply those of their own kin and neighbours, many men are incredulous at first. Some accuse their instructors of deceiving them. But, as their teachers emphasise to them, it is no lie but a basic ritual truth: the secret names of mountains, rivers, plants and animals and all other things in the world are the names of ordinary men and women, *because those things are themselves in reality men and women*. Many men speak of the first time they learned secret names as having had a deep and powerful impact on them. It was such tangible evidence of the unity between the familiar world of living people and the world of myth.

The origin-myths of different subclans tend to be quite similar, and this is particularly the case with subclans of the same clan, whose myths are often virtually identical, only differing from each other by the names of the actors figuring in them. Almost every object appearing in a myth is personified as a totemic ancestor and given personal names, and the names are in many cases all that define the myth with complete certainty as 'owned' by a particular subclan.

As a result, the function of myth as a charter for the subclan's ritual prerogatives is borne very largely by the ancestral names contained in it. Only if it keeps the names of its totemic ancestors associated with itself exclusively, by having its own members always bear the names, can a subclan stay in undisputed possession of its ritual powers. A subclan must constantly affirm its mythological rights by keeping, or trying to keep, a collective homonymy in existence between the actors in its myths and its own living members.

Magic and the Totemic cosmology

The secret names of its totemic ancestors are the basis of all of the subclan's magical and ritual powers. It is by these names, and only by them, that men can address and communicate with their totemic ancestors, and so control the forces they personify. All spells consist essentially of lists of esoteric names. These secret names are known as *ap* (bone/strength). Sometimes they are called *mutam* (faces) or *maka'ap* (foreheads, a synecdoche for *mutam*). They can also be referred to simply as 'the men' (*ndu*) and 'the women' (*ta'akw*). The totemic ancestors' exoteric names, on the other hand, are called *ndjambi*.

A spell contains – and, to the villagers, must contain to be effective – the secret names of the ancestor it invokes, and of that figure's father, mother and mother's brother. The mother is called the *sakwuna amei*, 'the mother who bore (the ancestor)'; the mother's brother the *səsakwunandə awai*, 'the maternal uncle who bestowed (the mother)'; and the father the *wus kwinandə asa'ai*, 'the father who gave the urine' (a euphemism for semen). The magic has full efficacy only by the presence in the spell of the names of those four beings: two belonging to the subclan which owns the spell, and two belonging to a subclan with which it exchanges women. Just as a subclan cannot create human life by itself, but only by a marriage with another group, so it acquires magical powers only through a kind of onomastic exogamy, an exchange of magic names with its marriageables. Marriageable subclans draw part of their magical power from each other; all of a subclan's spells are frozen records of mythical alliance relationships, and are claims not only to magical powers but to an identity as a marriage alliance unit as well.

I should note that the spells construct the social identities of totemic ancestors on the same pattern as those of real people. The basic elements of a person's social identity at Avatip are, first of all, his name, and secondly his paternity and matrifiliation. An individual's paternity gives him his identity as a member of a particular descent group; his matrifiliation distinguishes him and his full siblings from the other members of his group; and his name distinguishes him from his siblings. To put this slightly differently, a spell is actually an artificially constructed person. It is a verbal formula that imaginatively creates (though the villagers would claim it really contains) the power of agency of an individual. Magical power, just like human agency, can only be brought into existence through a creative interaction between *two* groups.

Taken collectively, a subclan's spells specify the secret names of all its totemic ancestors, both male and female, and of each of those figures' mothers and mothers' brothers, and these ancestral affines and matrikin are of course recognised as totemic ancestors of particular subclans. Implicitly, marriageable subclans in this way ratify each other in their myths and magic as holding rights in women. To be recognised in this way a group must, obviously, own its own corpus of named totemic ancestors. A group must be an independent name-owning unit, and magic-owning unit, to be acknowledged by its marriageables as an independent unit in marriage alliance.

The important point here is that marriageable subclans share highly secret knowledge of each other's totemic ancestries. Their spells contain overlapping configurations of ancestors, and so confirm each other. In their secret myths and magic, marriageable subclans implicitly validate each other's ritual powers.

By and large, marriageables are not in competition for these prerogatives. A subclan's main rivals are its own agnates, and most conflicts over ceremonial rights take place within the clan and clan-pair. The principle that agnates compete and challenge each other's status, while marriageables are interdependent and support one another in these disputes, expresses itself in Avatip social organisation in many different forms, and is a theme I will often return to in later chapters.

In summary, the totemic ancestors of marriageable subclans, like the human members of these groups, stand in specifiable affinal and matrilateral relationships with one another. The details of its ancestors' marital and uterine ties are the most closely guarded hereditary secrets owned by the subclan, and are called *ndja'amama'andj*, or 'talk concerning the *ndja'am*'.

A subclan's spells are its charter for contracting present-day marriage alliances. Its members may marry only into the same subclans as did their totemic ancestors. Every real-life marriage should recapitulate a mythical one, otherwise it would invite affliction by the *ndja'am*-spirits. Men say that one of the most important reasons for making sure their magical lore is passed from one generation to the next, is so that people can know where they may marry.

For instance, in Avatip myth, the ancestress of the coconut palm is the mother who bore the ancestors who personify yams. Thus in Avatip totemism coconut palms and yams are related to one another as mother and child. Ceremonial houses are related as brothers and sisters, as brothers-in-law and so on and, in ritual contexts, people address and refer to their totems by kin terms. Wuluwi-Nyawi, for instance, has the sun and moon as totems and, to a man of this group, the moon, personified as the ancestress Mbapata'akw, is his sister and the sun is his father or, in an alternative usage, his paternal grandfather. To a man of Nggɔla'angkw, the moon is his mother and the sun his mother's brother. Thus the villagers integrate into their own kinship ties the phenomenal world of animals, plants, the landscape, ritual sacra and so forth. To them it is the visible form of a vast, invisible connubium that forms the timeless pattern after which living people must marry.

Let me bring this section to a close by suggesting how notions of magical efficacy are generated out of the dichotomy the villagers posit between the order of everyday life and the timeless order of myth and totemism. First of all, Avatip cosmology is a systematic animism, a thoroughgoing socialisation or humanisation of the conceived elements of the world. It projects notions of human identity and agency upon animals, plants, ritual objects and all the rest: they share kinship with human beings, have names, belong to subclans, marry and so forth. But secondly, there is in turn an introjection of that humanised world back into society in the form of imagined powers to influence those beings through their names and kinship statuses. That is, this is an introjection in which the magical powers become bound, through the names of their owners, into their owners' very identities as persons. Or to put it more clearly: a subclan's members do not so much 'own' magic powers at all; they *are* those powers embodied as living men and women.

The naming system

On average, a subclan owns between one and two thousand names. The names represent, implicitly, the idea of all its past, present and future members. The members themselves change as the generations go by. But the names they 'occupy' or 'are in' (*tǝna*) are, supposedly, the fixed names of the subclan's members forever. As personal names for human beings, in other words, the names are classes, each in principle is occupied by an infinite series of individuals in succession. They are like little corporations sole, though implying no continuity of social personality other than membership of the same descent group. They are just the empty forms of persons of specific subclans.[2]

No subclan at Avatip has enough members to bear all its names at once. My estimate, that a subclan of average size owns between one and two thousand personal names, gives a total, for the whole community, of some thirty-two thousand names, a figure compatible with Bateson's estimate that an erudite Iatmul man 'carries in his head between ten and twenty thousand names' (Bateson 1958: 222). The naming system has, as Lévi-Strauss puts it

a reserve of unoccupied positions sufficient to accommodate all the children born. The available positions beings always more numerous than the population, synchrony is protected against the vagaries of diachrony, at least in theory. (1966: 197)

Even the largest and most rapidly expanding subclans are in no danger of running short of names. For all practical purposes, the naming system has no attainable upper limits. But this tolerance of demographic flux does have a very real lower threshold. If a subclan is to remain the unchallenged owner of all its names, it must be capable of having most of them – particularly the mythologically more important ones – occupied at least once every two or three generations. If it is declining in size and cannot do this, reproductively more successful subclans will try to appropriate its vacant names.

A child is named when it is a few months old and its parents decide that it is

2 The ownership of personal names by groups is quite widely reported in lowland Melanesia. It is found, for example, in the Trobriand Islands (Malinowski 1954: 199–200; Weiner 1977: 126–7), among the Kove of New Britain (Chowning 1974: 179, 190), in the Madang area (Morauta 1973: 141), among the Keraki (Williams 1936: 117, 177), the Baruya (Godelier 1986: 19) of the southern fringe Highlands, and among the Tanna of Vanuatu (Lindstrom 1985). It seems especially widespread in the Sepik, being reported among the Iatmul (Bateson 1932: 401–413; Stanek 1983; Wassman 1982), Chambri (Errington and Gewertz 1987; Gewertz 1977b: 48–9), Kwoma (Bowden 1977: 54), Abelam (Kaberry 1971: 58), Bun (McDowell 1975: 212) and Ilahita Arapesh (Tuzin 1976).

likely to survive infancy. Despite the great political implications of naming children, no important ceremony accompanies it and it is an informal, almost casual event. The father may name the child himself, if he is adequately versed in his subclan's myths. Otherwise, he will ask one of the senior men of his subclan to do so. Sister's sons, again if they are knowledgeable, are expected to name children of their mother's subclans from time to time. The villagers have a notion that once a person is named, an intrinsic connection is created between the bearer and the name, in which the name comes to contain the person's Spirit or life-force (see Harrison 1985a). Some older and more conservative men were for this reason unwilling to give me their genealogies, for fear that by writing down their names, their life-force might be trapped in my note-books and taken away to Australia when I left. Partly for this reason, I have used pseudonyms for all Avatip individuals referred to in this book. The reaction of the Manambu to the first experience of having their names written down by officers of the Australian administration gives an interesting insight into their attitudes towards names. In 1925 the District Officer, Townsend, added a month to the sentences of five men from Yuanamb (he calls this village Jambon) who had escaped from the gaol at Ambunti. His account of the court proceedings is worth quoting in full (I thank Rob Crittenden for bringing this passage to my attention):

When questioned through our interpreter, the five men each admitted breaking from custody. Police evidence was then taken, the Gaol Register being produced and the names read from it. This was, in fact, the only part of the proceedings that really registered with the Jambons. The other evidence was merely going over well-known ground and was, as far as they were concerned, not worth repeating. But the evidence that showed that the Government had 'imprisoned' the men in a *book* was disturbing indeed.
    When the Court gave judgement of the extra sentence, this and the names of the men were again written in the book so that they were thus more firmly 'held' than ever. This feeling amongst these people that the writing of a name had some magic quality was so strong that no special care was needed to see that the prisoners did not escape again. Indeed, I think that throughout the remainder of their terms they would not have gone even if we had helped them on their way.   (Townsend 1968: 130)

All forms of sorcery are assumed to act upon the victims' life-force through their names. Even the 'foreign' technique of exuvial sorcery, the villagers believe, requires that the sorcerer possess both the leavings and the *name* of his victim.

An individual is given names from his or her subclan's name-corpus once only, on this one occasion in infancy, and can never again receive patrilineal names. These agnatically-transmitted names are called *apasə*, or 'bone names'. The number of such names given to the child is kept within quite strict limits, for reasons I explain shortly, and a child is rarely given more than five. One is the child's *taisə*, or 'first' name, the name by which the child will be principally known. The others are given as secondary names, or *sənggəliyak*. Those names tend not to be used often, because only close kin are usually familiar with each other's secondary names. Although children are named after totemic ancestors, they do not have to be of the same sex as their mythical namesakes. Most names have a suffix indicating gender and can be made masculine or feminine as needs be.

The naming system is of a type which seems common in the Sepik, in which names are owned and inherited patrilineally but are also regularly 'loaned' to sisters' children (see Bateson 1958; Harrison 1985c; Tuzin 1976). At Avatip, a subclan's names are bestowed on sisters' children in the following circumstances. When people are bereaved, whether they are children or adults, they are given by their matrikin a new name belonging to their maternal subclan. This name-change is carried out to ward off the ghosts of the kin whose deaths they are mourning. The recipients still keep their patrilineal names, because a person retains those for life. But if people have been given a bereavement name, it is good manners to address and refer to them by it, and avoid speaking their patrilineal names. When matrikin bestow a bereavement name, they take the recipient a small ceremonial gift of food, and the renaming is known idiomatically as *kəmbi kawarna*, 'carrying up the food basket' (i.e., into the mourner's house). The recipient of a bereavement name bears it until death, or until bereaved again and once again renamed. Most people go through many bereavement names during the course of their lives. Whenever someone relinquishes his or her current bereavement name, the name returns to the maternal subclan. It is the property of that subclan and the erstwhile bearer cannot give it to his or her own descendants. Bereavement names are called *kəpakwur sə*, or 'dirt-taking names', a reference to the custom of smearing oneself with dirt as a sign of mourning.

Men also give their subclans' personal names to their domestic pigs and dogs, and these animals bear the subclan's ancestral names in exactly the same way as do their human owners. Occasionally, names are even bestowed on domestic fowl and the European-introduced house cat. These are practices usually confined to declining subclans, and are regarded as something of an extremity to which their dwindling numbers have driven them.

When men are choosing a name to bestow, there are a number of important considerations they have in mind. These apply whether they are to bestow the name agnatically or as a bereavement name, and whether the recipient is human or an animal. The first and most important factor is the pressing need to keep as many as possible of the subclan's names in regular use. Any which remained idle for long would tempt other subclans to lay claim to them. Secondly, the men must make sure that the name they choose is not already in use. It is acceptable to give an infant a name being carried by an old person who is likely to die and vacate the name before the child is mature. But otherwise every person must be completely individuated by his or her names and no coevals may be namesakes. Lastly, no one branch of the subclan should use the same name or names many times in succession. If one segment has used a name continuously for several generations, it should give it up for the next few generations and let other branches of the subclan have it.

A subclan's collective rights in names are an important public expression of its unity as a group. Formally, all of the subclan's names and ancestors belong to particular lineages within it. But if the subclan is to stay united, its lineages must let each other use one another's names, so that the names circulate freely within the whole subclan over the generations. The main rules of the naming-system are precisely devices for preventing any of its segments from monopolising names. These are: the limit of five names or so per individual; the convention that an individual receives patrilineal names only once, in infancy; and lastly, the prohibition of creating namesakes.

If one branch of the subclan were to insist on using certain names repeatedly, or give its members excessive numbers of names, or duplicate names already in use elsewhere in the subclan, it would be viewed as trying to claim for itself a separate social and political identity. The circulation of names within the subclan over time is a sensitive barometer of the political relations between its segments. In a later chapter, I show that when competition breaks out within the subclan for control of personal names it is always a part of fission or of other structural changes.

Time and hierarchy

I have noted the marked distinction made in Avatip religion between a perceptual order of existence (the everyday world of sense experience) and a parallel invisible order of spirit beings represented as the source of all fertility and well-being. One of the basic features distinguishing this hidden order of existence from the phenomenal order is that it is conceived as atemporal. For example, an important, magically powerful object in the men's cult, such as a slit-drum belonging to a particular subclan, may be physically replaced many times over the generations as it wears out or decays. But men do not speak of there having therefore been several such drums. Because the same, named ancestral spirit always inhabits it, there was and is only one such drum and its identity continues through any number of physical incarnations. In a similar way, each subclan's cult-house is believed to embody an ancestral spirit of the subclan and always carries that being's name; however many times the cult-house is rebuilt men speak of it as being always the same house, because it is simply so many renewals of that ancestor's material form.

A related aspect of Avatip religion is that it associates descent groups with the control of whole classes of material resources. For instance, in Avatip totemism, the tree called *ma'angk* (used for house-building timber) is personi-fied as a totemic ancestor called Manggandimi, and all such trees are his outward, visible forms. The villagers may in some context or other speak of two, three or more *ma'angk* trees, but not of there being therefore two, three or more 'Manggandimis'. To them, each tree of that species in the world 'is' him and there is only one Manggandimi however many his manifestations. The premiss here is that under the aspect of Avatip religion any number of things classed as instances of the same totemic ancestor – flocks of birds of the same species, a quantity of yams, a succession of versions of the same ritual object – are an individual and have the quantity *one*.

What men seem to be trying to represent in ritual and cosmology is the idea that their own social groups are perpetual and control the sources of all material growth and plenty. They are trying to portray their groups to each other as entities that provide in ritual the means to one another's production but in themselves transcend time and exist outside of the productive process.

In some other Sepik societies, where environmental conditions facilitate the intensive cultivation of yams, the production and ceremonial exchange of yams are politically significant activities in which aspiring Big Men compete for influence and reputation (Kaberry 1971; Tuzin 1976). At Avatip, the politically significant value of yams is that they are manifestations of the ritual control that Wuluwi-Nyawi has over yam-fertility; and, to a lesser extent, manifestations of the ritually-sustained fertility of the land on which they are grown (which is to say, not necessarily the land of the grower's own subclan). According to Avatip religion, yams are not actually created by gardening but, like all other cultivated and wild foods, they come into the phenomenal world by being 'released' from the mythical villages by means of ritual. In the men's religious conceptions, all yams that could ever be grown exist already in the ritual powers of Wuluwi-Nyawi, and their growers are not their creators but their recipients. Implicitly, these kinds of religious representations seem to be attempts to subvert those strategies of competitive production and exchange – and the ideologies of male egalitarianism associated with them – which are the means to power and prestige in those Melanesian societies in which Big Men figure (Forge 1972a; Josephides 1985; Sahlins 1963; Sillitoe 1979).

I should say that Avatip men and women are perfectly aware that successful yam-growing is the result of yams having been grown on the right kind of land, tended properly while they were growing, and so forth. These sorts of technical skills are everyday knowledge common to all socialised adults, and part of what I have elsewhere (Harrison 1985b) called the cultural system of the domestic sphere. Men and woman know *how* yams are grown successfully. But Avatip religion, like Azande witchcraft beliefs (Evans-Pritchard 1937), poses and answers a different question: *why* the yams grew successfully, and to whom the social and political credit is owed. To Avatip men, the credit belongs to the custodians of the relevant secret, ritual knowledge. The prestige and authority of these men derives from their access to a hidden, atemporal reality, beyond the world of sense experience and inaccessible to practical, unrestricted knowledge (see Bloch 1977).

Magic and the Totemic cosmology

Bloch (1974; 1977; 1986) has argued that religious ideologies that deny time or history are supports for hierarchical social orders, because they legitimise an order imagined to be unalterable and therefore unable to be changed or challenged. Avatip religion, in much the same way, is an assertion of static hierarchy, in the sense that it makes the claim that political prestige in food production belongs to whatever descent group is the totemic owner of the relevant food and land and ritually responsible for its fertility, and denies that it can accrue to the physical producer. Competitive production would challenge the established basis of status among men and groups, because it would imply that political credit was not an hereditary right of the ritual owners of natural resources but something that anyone with ambition and energy could earn by exploiting those resources. It is largely for this reason that Avatip groups and their ritual leaders have such a strong custodial concern with protecting their land from too intensive use, and with discouraging any use or production of their totemic food species beyond subsistence needs. There are of course sound ecological reasons of which the villagers are well aware (especially the need to ensure adequately long fallow cycles) for this systematic inhibiting of surpluses. But the idea that any excessive production is the 'squandering' of some descent group's fertility, that it is a ritual offence against that group and punishable by affliction, is also, I suggest, a way of suppressing surplus production as a possible alternative form of political action.

Conclusion

The basic structures and cultural values on which the Melanesian Big Man polities are based indeed exist at Avatip: the high respect given to productive and generous individuals, and the importance of marriage ties as the basis of life-long transactions of goods and services between affines. But Avatip religion defines these everyday-life exchanges as part of an essentially private sphere of interpersonal kinship, and prevents them from acquiring a political dimension by creating above these mundane exchanges a kind of higher-order system of magical and ritual exchanges.

In these ritual transactions Avatip groups represent themselves as maintaining political relations, like groups in many other Melanesian societies, through the creation and exchange of material values. But Avatip differs from those societies in which Big Man politics prevails in that groups are portraying themselves as corporations for a kind of 'meta' production and transaction: the role they claim is to create and exchange for all time, in magic and ritual, the conditions of one another's members' *physical* production and transaction (Harrison 1988b; see also Young 1985). What simultaneously distinguishes and interrelates them are their specialised powers over the weather, the fertility of animals, plants, land, lagoons and so forth, so that it would not be possible conceptually for any one of the clans to exist by itself, as a kind of independent social monad. An Avatip totemic category existing in autarky (sky existing without the earth, a world of lightish-reddish things with no blackish-darkish things, and so forth) is not simply a practical impossibility to the villagers, but also a conceptual one. The social world of Avatip is divided in such a way that the idea that groups require each other comes close to being a kind of necessary truth, not only a contingent one. What is assumed to be prior to all actual social groups is a closed system of archetypal categories forming a kind of organic totality. Local descent groups 'are' those pre-existing categories brought into the world of social practice, and groups are assumed to draw their social existence and identities from that closed world of social classifications 'above' them, rather than from an immediate instrumental relationship to land and physical resources 'under' them.

Second, and closely related to this, the material values by which men measure status, and which they represent themselves as having the power to exchange in ritual, are entire categories of things (all yams, all fish and so on), and not quantities of things as in the Melanesian Big Man societies. Avatip cosmology can be viewed as a typical Melanesian prestige economy, but one in which 'wealth' has been defined as whole classes of values instead of tokens of those classes. Wealth, as a specifically political resource, is culturally defined in such a way as to immobilise the status relations established by exchange and prevent the development of any politically significant exchanges that are real temporal processes in which men must compete to produce or control more or less of some circulating, finite fund of goods. Each clan and its members are conceived to differ qualitatively from the others. All the groups have their own, distinct hereditary 'essences' and it is those differentiating essences or substances, embodied also in their totemic food species, land and other resources, that are the gifts which these groups transact. In other words, it is themselves they exchange, their own social identities objectified as classes of substances, as the basic categories of the world order. The reciprocity between groups has been lifted out of political process, which is its axis in the Big Man societies, and immobilised in ritual and cosmology to establish notionally permanent, hereditary status relations between groups reified as the basic, timeless categories to which everything in the world belongs.

4

Ceremonial rank

Introduction

I have argued that Avatip cosmology is an ideology inhibiting the use of material wealth in political competition, because it transposes the political significance of affinal exchange relationships out of the sphere of material production into the medium of magic and ritual. In this chapter I examine the consequences of this transposition for the structure of political relations between groups.

In an important paper, Morauta (1973) has identified what she calls a 'magical division of labour' – an hereditary division of ritual powers among social groups – as a common pattern in Lowland New Guinea social systems. Besides the societies which she cites as examples, some recent ethnographic studies indicate the existence of ritually specialised descent groups among some of the fringe Highland peoples (Godelier 1986), and there is evidence of this pattern in many Sepik societies in addition to the Manambu.[1] A particularly important conclusion Morauta makes, and one which I should like to develop in this chapter in relation to Avatip, is that these ritual specialisations are typically associated in Melanesian societies with ideologies of rank. In some of these social systems – the Trobriand Islands (Malinowski 1935; Powell 1960) for instance, and the Mekeo (Hau'ofa 1981) – the inequalities of status are relatively strongly institutionalised. In others, such as the village of Kalauna on Goodenough Island (Young 1971) they take a weaker form that Young (1971: 63) calls submerged rank. Morauta's argument applies well to Avatip, because Avatip descent groups are considered to have unequally important and prestigious ritual responsibilities, so that there are ascribed inequalities between groups in their cosmological and ritual status. In rather the same way that Young describes for the Goodenough Islanders, these inequalities are little in evidence in everyday life, where they remain a largely latent organisational form. But I shall not refer to them as submerged rank because they are emphasised and displayed quite manifestly in ritual life, especially in the rituals of the men's cult. I shall call them

1 The Iatmul (Bateson 1932: 446), the Chambri (Errington and Gewertz 1986; Gewertz 1977b: 48–9; Mead 1963: 247), the Sissano (Haiveta 1984), and some of the societies of the upper Sepik (Newton 1971: 34, 36, 51–3, 83, 89).

ceremonial rank, because they are a structure of relations specific to the ceremonial world of men.

These inequalities of status are cast in the idiom of totemism, and I begin this chapter by describing the features of the totemic and mythological ties between groups by which relations of ceremonial rank are validated. I then consider, in the light of these inequalities, the structuralist argument that totemic societies are specially committed to resisting change, history and social conflict. Finally, I discuss the implications of the ceremonial stratification of Avatip groups for some theories of the evolution of rank in Melanesia.

Totemism and descent

Totemic ancestors are known generically as *nggwa'al-asa'ai*: 'the fathers and fathers' fathers'. They are conceived to be, like people, members of the clans and subclans and the agnatic descendants of those groups' apical ancestors. But their genealogical ties with the apical ancestors and with each other (and in fact many other details concerning them) are highly secret. People do not claim descent from their totemic ancestors. They posit them as collateral, not as lineal, ancestors and these figures are not reference-points of segmentation. Conceptually, the founding ancestors of descent groups are quite distinct from these totemic beings. They have no 'totemic' characteristics; they do not take the form of species or other totemic phenomena, and mythology does not give them an important role in the creation of the world. Nor are they an especial focus of secrecy. Their genealogical connections with one another are public knowledge.

Although the relation between the members of a descent group and their totemic ancestors is treated as one of shared patrilineal descent, what in fact defines this relationship is simply that it is validated by myth, and that it entails the rights to use these ancestors' names and to perform the magic relating to them. Many totemic ancestors are associated with particular descent groups not by descent from those groups' apical ancestors, but on the basis of myths describing their transfer from other descent groups. I discuss the causes of this 'non-agnatic' recruitment of totemic ancestors later. Here, the important point is that matrifiliation, fosterage and co-residence are often used in myth as modes of 'recruiting' totemic ancestors to descent groups, and are considered to be as valid as agnation. Those modes of recruitment are not, as they are in the societies of the New Guinea Highlands (Barnes 1962), used in real life because descent groups recruit their human members strictly by agnation. It is the manipulability of myth and totemism that gives this society its political flexibility, not manipulable recruitment rules.

Totemism creates important political relationships between descent groups. In the simplest case, of a totemic relationship between two descent groups, the charter for the tie is a mythical partnership between a pair of their totemic ancestors. The two figures are usually described as having the form of the same species, as living in the same mythical village and performing their cosmogonic exploits together. Many other subsidiary ancestors usually appear in the myth. The two figures' weapons, tools and ornaments are personified as named ancestors, as are the canoes in which they travelled together, the houses they built and lived in, and in some cases certain of their own body-parts. Each of these ancestors, and their names, belong to one or other of the two descent groups, so that each group derives a specific set of personal names from the myth. The ownership of these linked name-sets is an important part of the charter for the relationship between the two groups. The two groups may share the secret details of the charter-myth, including the secret magic deriving from it, and are prohibited by their relationship from intermarriage. A relationship of this type, using exactly the same principles, can exist between three, four or more descent groups.

These totemic 'sibling' relationships between groups correspond quite closely to their agnatic relationships. But they are conceptually distinct from relationships based upon descent. They can exist between groups that are unrelated agnatically. And they do not employ the notion of descent in any way. They are based on the sharing, not of common descent, but of a common *ndja'am*.

Groups linked together in this way stand in senior/junior relations with one another. To take, again, the simplest case of a totemic tie between two groups, one group always has precedence over the other in the mythology which links them. Typically, their pair of ancestors are described in myth as having settled in the origin-village of the senior group, and as having taken the form of one of that group's totemic species. Most importantly, the ancestor of the senior group is described as having laid his hands first to all the cosmogonic tasks which the pair undertook together. He is referred to as the 'elder brother'. Often, he is the main creative figure in the myth, while the younger brother is described as his helper or follower. But sometimes, the precedence of the senior ancestor is quite nominal and, for reasons I discuss later, it is the ancestor of the junior group who actually plays the more important role in the myth. All that matters is that one ancestor is given some type of formal seniority over the other, and that this establishes a senior/junior relationship between the two descent groups.

This difference in seniority between the groups, although represented in an elder brother/younger brother idiom, does not imply common descent in any way. It simply refers to the form of a mythical partnership between certain of their totemic ancestors. It is not a relationship of seniority of descent, but of differential precedence in cosmology, totemism and cosmogonic myth.

Ceremonial rank

All subclans belonging to the same exogamous group are graded by their totemic relationships with one another in an order of ritual precedence and status which I call ceremonial rank (see Table 5). The ceremonial ranking of these subclans corresponds largely, but not entirely, to their order of seniority by agnatic descent. Where it conflicts with agnatic seniority, it overrides it. People of ceremonially junior subclans call the members of senior subclans by classificatory kin terms indicating seniority, such as elder sibling (*ma'am*) and father's elder brother (*nyasa'ap*). These acknowledge the differences in ceremonial rank between their subclans.

This ranking extends down to the level of the lineage, the minimal named unit of group structure. A subclan normally and, to the villagers, ideally, consists of two such lineages. These groups claim descent from the senior and junior sons, by different mothers, of the subclan's apical ancestor and are called *tanəmb*, or domestic hearths. They are usually seven or eight generations in depth. The senior of the two is called the *va'ak*, 'the sago storage pot', and the junior *ya'andj*, 'the lid of the sago storage pot'. What these figures of speech refer to is the joint role of the two lineages as a source of nurture for their collective sisters' children.

These inequalities in ceremonial rank do not exist between the three basic exogamous groups in the community. These groups themselves are not ranked, because they each form a separate mythological-totemic complex. Although Nambul-Sambəlap has relatively few ceremonial powers, it is not lower in ceremonial rank than the other two groups, because marriageables are not conceived to be commensurable in this way. Agnates, on the other hand, are commensurable; and all relations between agnates intrinsically involve inequality in ceremonial rank.

High ranking subclans tend to have the greatest number of magical and ritual prerogatives, and to own the most important and prestigious ones: the most powerful forms of sorcery, the economically vital magic relating to agriculture, fishing and the weather, and so forth. Within the subclan itself, the subclan's hereditary powers should ideally be held by the men of its senior lineage. But it is in male initiatory ritual that ceremonial rank is most emphasised, and most overtly displayed. None of the cult rituals owned by Wuluwi-Nyawi or Nggəla'angkw can take place without first being inaugurated by its owners' senior subclans. The ritually senior men of these subclans must give their consent before the ritual can be held, and they control the timing of all performances of cult ritual. Throughout the course of the rituals, the men of all the 'owner' subclans have many special responsibilities and entitlements; but these are rigidly graded in importance according to each subclan's order of ceremonial rank. A major organisational principle of every male initiation is the order of ceremonial precedence of the descent groups which collectively own the ritual.

All the rituals of the men's cult are a display of two complementary group relationships: mutually 'nurturant' equality between marriageables; and, between agnates, unequal power to provide marriageables with this nurture. The yam harvest ritual, or any of the other male rituals, is a prestation by its

Table 5. *Size, ceremonial rank and ceremonial powers of Avatip subclans in 1978*

Subclans in order of ceremonial rank	Size in 1978	Main trade links with	Holds simbukship	Holds key rights in initiatory ritual	Other ritual powers
Nggəla'angkw clan-pair: (unnamed senior clan)					
Makem	36	Chambri/Sawos		Scarification ritual Ndumwi ritual	Fertility of main fish species, crocodiles, some sago-palm, duck and cocunut species
Yimal	178	Iatmul		Scarification ritual Ndumwi ritual	Fertility of main fish species and of lagoons; sorcery to destroy the lagoons; love-magic
Nggambak	83	Iatmul/Kaunga	Yes	Scarification ritual Ndumwi ritual	
Valik	133	?	Yes		
Nggəla'angkw clan-pair: (unnamed junior clan)					
Wopunamb	22	Yerikai-Garamambu			
Kambuli	85	Yerikai-Garamambu	Yes		Fertility of crocodiles, and some sago and duck species; love-magic
Waranggamb	24	Yerikai-Garamambu			
Nambul-Sambalap clan					
Nambul	33	Yesan-Mayo			Fertility of areca-palm, breadfruit and edible mayflies;

					control of monsoons and Sepik floods; sorcery to cause mosquito-plagues
Sambalap	53	Yesan-Mayo			Fertility of edible mayflies; control of monsoons and Sepik floods; sorcery to cause mosquito-plagues; sorcery to cause earthquakes
Wuluwi-Nyawi clan-pair[a]					
Nyakaw	57	Iatmul	Maiyir ritual	Yes[b]	Magic to inaugurate the clearing of the river-gardens; planting-magic for the bush-gardens; Nyava'at weather-magic; lightning sorcery; love-magic; fertility of areca-palm, breadfruit, some turtle, crayfish and coconut species
Ambasarak	87	Kwoma	Maiyir ritual Yam harvest ritual	Yes	Planting-magic for the bush-gardens; fertility of taro, pitpit, some banana cultivars and leafy greens
Nanggwundaw	30	Chambri			Fertility of crocodiles, some duck, sago-palm and coconut

Table 5. *Size, ceremonial rank and ceremonial powers of Avatip subclans in 1978*

Subclans in order of ceremonial rank	Size in 1978	Main trade links with	Holds simbukship	Holds key rights in initiatory ritual	Other ritual powers
Maliyaw	246	Sawos	Yes	Maiyir ritual Yam harvest ritual	species; love-magic Nyava'at weather-magic Magic to inaugurate the clearing of the river-gardens; planting-magics for the bush-gardens; sorcery to cause earthquakes
Sarambusarak	136	Kwoma			Lightning-sorcery; fertility of some turtle, crayfish and edible frog species
Wanəkaw	59	Sawos			
Nawik	20	Chambri			

[a] The senior clan of Wuluwi-Nyawi is called Nyawi, and consists of the subclans Nyakaw, Ambasarak, Sarambusarak and Wanəkaw. The junior clan, Wuluwi, consists of Nanggwundaw, Nawik and Maliyaw. The order of ceremonial rank of the Wuluwi-Nyawi subclans bears little relationship to their order of seniority by descent and entirely cross-cuts the clans, for reasons I discuss in Chapter 8.

[b] This is not formally a simbukship, but has some of the functions of one in the yam harvest ritual. According to legend, it was a simbukship in the distant past, until the subclan Valik 'stole' the office (see Chapter 7).

entire 'owning' clan-pair to all its marriageables; but it is a prestation to which its subclans contribute unequally, according to their ceremonial rank.

These rituals validate, among other things, important economic rights held by senior subclans. The power to interdict the fishing-lagoons, and to lift these interdictions, is not held by all of Nggɔla'angkw but by its senior subclans. Similarly, the yam-gardening magic, and the right to grant the community permission to harvest their gardens, does not belong to all the Wuluwi-Nyawi subclans, only to the senior ones. What junior subclans have is the right to inherit these prerogatives should their seniors, through extinction or for any other reason, be unable to exercise them. These successorial rights are intended, firstly, to protect the ceremonial system against accidents of demography. Groups may become extinct, but each has its successor ready to assume its position in the system should this become vacant. Secondly, these rights are meant to preserve the rule of seniority, by ensuring that each position is always held by the most senior extant descent group qualified to fill it. The rank order of seniority in each of these clan-pairs, is a successorial queue, in which each subclan has rights of inheritance in all the ceremonial powers of the subclan next in seniority. Within the subclan, the junior lineage has these rights in the powers of its senior. These powers are not vested in any descent group absolutely, but only provisionally, for so long as the holders of the powers remain capable of exercising them. If they cannot, their prerogatives are taken over by their juniors.

Structure and history

A characteristic of 'totemic' cultures, and one which has made them of particular interest to anthropologists, is that they seem especially static and opposed ideologically to change. Lévi-Strauss describes such societies as 'cold', in contrast to more advanced, historically 'hot' ones:

the former seeking, by the institutions they give themselves, to annul the possible effects of historical factors on their equilibrium and continuity in a quasi-automatic fashion; the latter resolutely internalising the historical process and making it the moving power of their development.   (Lévi-Strauss 1966: 233–4; see also Lévi-Strauss 1978: 29–30; Charbonnier 1969: 32–42)

These two sorts of societies represent alternative choices made in the face of 'a sort of fundamental antipathy between history and systems of classification' (Lévi-Strauss 1966: 232). While hot societies commit themselves to history, cold societies commit themselves to structure, but in doing so face a 'permanent conflict between the structural nature of the classification and the statistical nature of its demographic basis' (Lévi-Strauss 1966: 232). They must therefore act continually to preserve structure against the demographic and other random vicissitudes of diachrony.

In ritual and cosmology, Avatip men represent their society as very much a 'cold' one in Lévi-Strauss' sense. As I shall shortly show, they still continue nowadays to try to maintain this conception of their society despite two generations of encapsulation within a new political and economic order, by incorporating elements of Western culture and state political authority into their totemism and cosmology. The rights of succession I have just described are intended to cope with a problem which Lévi-Strauss sees as the inherent dilemma of societies of this sort: the problem of preserving their classifications against historical change or, to put it more generally, the problem of the antipathy between history and structure (Lévi-Strauss 1966: 232).

But the problem with applying Lévi-Strauss' notion of a cold society to Avatip is that these processes of succession are associated with recurrent patterns of conflict which are the central dynamic of Avatip political life. And, as I shall argue later in this chapter, these conflicts seem in fact to have been an important cause of historical change in Avatip society before the advent of colonial power. Changes in cosmology do not simply 'occur', suppressed from consciousness by an ideology that denies change and conflict. They are publicly institutionalised in the debating system, and generated in ceremonial contests which are the central arena of Avatip political life. Indeed, it is precisely that conception, acted out in the initiatory cult, of the society as a timeless and transcendent reality, that *motivates* the incessant political conflict and the innovation in the symbolic order. These rivalries are encouraged and admired, precisely because of the high prestige attached to important 'hereditary' positions in the totemic system and, like many other Melanesian peoples, Avatip villagers are litigious and enjoy public competition over culturally valued goals. The constant demographic changes in the size and viability of the competing groups are integral to the disputes, as reproductively successful groups displace less successful ones from prestigious roles in ritual and cosmology.

The basic difficulty then, which I shall try to answer in this section, is that while the totemic cosmology is indeed assumed entirely to transcend time, groups continuously struggle for prestigious positions in the system, and constantly manipulate and dispute it in these rivalries. The answer to this conundrum hinges upon the distinction between groups and categories or, to phrase this in terms of Avatip ethnography, the distinction made at Avatip between the totemic clans as *conceptual entities* and the actual groups of people those clans contain.

The totemic clans, in the manner of those societies Lévi-Strauss calls totemic or 'cold', are assumed to be the utterly changeless structure common to society and the whole world order. I have said that the villagers assume that their clans and subclans are an inherent property of society everywhere, and that all human beings are divided into the same social categories as themselves. Animal and plant species, land, waterways and virtually all other conceived elements of the environment are also classified in the same way, and their descent groups are not, to them, simply social categories but the basic intrinsic categories of the world order. So far as the villagers are concerned, their own society could be obliterated, yet these categories would remain as basic properties of the world. Each of those totemic world-divisions is represented in society by two entities: firstly, by a patrimony of myths, totems, personal names, and cosmological powers and attributes (that is, by a particular *ndja'am*); and secondly, by a set of human beings having common agnatic pedigrees. To the villagers, neither of those two kinds of entities are the categories themselves. The first are magical and ritual powers that the categories make permanently available in society; and the second are simply the real-world collectivities of men and women that actually carry those powers through time. Men are aware that these groups can grow, decline, amalgamate, die out and so on, and that these contingencies pose a permanent problem: the problem of ensuring that every position in the totemic system always has a specific descent group installed in it. Hence the conventions to ensure this: groups related by common descent are each other's potential successors, and have rights to inherit one another's responsibilities in the system. If some position falls vacant – because the occupants have become either extinct or too few to carry out the associated ritual functions effectively – a junior group then has the right to take charge of its patrimony and all its functions in the totemic system.

To men, it is a vital necessity to prevent dying groups from carrying their cosmological powers into extinction with them. But the problem is that Avatip is a competitive society, and the processes by which declining groups are replaced by successors are by no means smooth or automatic. They invariably entail struggles, which are often intense and prolonged. A difficulty with Lévi-Strauss' notion of a 'cold' society is its supposition of an absence of conflict and of inequalities of power. At Avatip, the perceived need to protect the totemic system against change requires that viable groups displace groups which are less viable, and this is a major source of conflict. The reluctance of dying groups to yield up their cosmological powers is a major political obstacle their heirs must overcome. Heirs themselves are usually impatient for their legators' demise, and often try to take over the powers of groups still very much in existence. Avatip politics consists almost wholly in this competition between groups for prestigious positions in cosmology and ritual.

Men deny that the totemic categories have an historical character, but they do not try to suppress or deny history. What I mean is that they do not try to disguise the fact that descent groups are subject to change, and do not seem to have any special overall concern with preventing such change. They try to resolve the antinomy between the 'structural' classifications and the 'statistical' demographic flux, by making full use of the statistical fluctuations, not by denying them. To them, struggles between groups, conflicts drawing on the demographic differentials which arise between groups, are inevitable and necessary to guarantee viable representatives in society for all the categories of the totemic system.

This also explains the apparent contradiction at the heart of men's attitudes toward cosmology: on the one hand they envision it as timeless and unalterable, while on the other, as I shall try to show, they constantly manipulate and dispute it. The point, from their perspective, is that it is not cosmology they treat as negotiable but the way in which descent groups articulate with it. It is the relation between these groups and the categories of the totemic system that is the contentious issue, not the organisation of the totemic system itself. They are quite consistent to imagine their cosmology is immutable, though they well know it is their main arena of political conflict. For descent groups are, to them, simply contingent sets of persons that draw – for as long as they prove themselves capable of doing so against constant challenges by their rivals – an identity and prestige from cosmology. No group, however high its 'hereditary' ceremonial status, can take that status for granted, but its men must continually demonstrate that they have the political strength to keep it.

As categories, the totemic clans are purely conceptual entities. But the actual local descent groups instantiating those categories in real social life are *political* entities, continually reorganising themselves in relation to the totemic categories as they grow, decline, fission and so forth. These sorts of processes are openly recognised by the villagers. But these processes also act back upon the structure of the totemic classifications and – although the villagers themselves would deny it – work to alter the classifications over time.

The dispute between Maliyaw and Sarambusarak over their totemic relations with the state

I should like in this section to suggest some of the ways in which these processes of competition seem to have shaped the historical development of Avatip cosmology and the ideology of ceremonial rank. There are of course no means of tracing long-term historical trends in Avatip society before European contact. But there is a long-standing dispute between two large and influential subclans of Wuluwi-Nyawi, in the course of which these rival groups have made some modern innovations to the cosmology, and it contains some important clues about the way in which alterations to the cosmology, and to political ideology, may have been made in pre-colonial times.

For some years, the men of the subclan Maliyaw have made a large and quite complex claim to share common mythological origins with Europeans. The basic elements of their argument are as follows. Firstly, all Avatip subclans own honorific address-forms (*waiyepi*), by which their members may be addressed so as to express special courtesy and respect. The main address-form owned by Maliyaw is the title *wapi* ('bird'), which is also the term adopted many years ago by the Manambu for the European-introduced *laplap*, or loincloth. The leaders of Maliyaw claim on this basis that the laplap and, by extension, all 'European' clothes, must be totems of their subclan. Secondly, they claim that the coastal town of Wewak, the administrative and commercial centre of the East Sepik Province, is actually Ambianggai, the mythical origin-village of their subclan and the home of all their totemic ancestors and ancestral ghosts. They base this claim on the fact that Wewak lies in the same direction from Avatip as does Ambianggai according to myth. Finally, so the leaders of Maliyaw point out, their subclan is the largest in the 'red-skinned' clan-pair Wuluwi-Nyawi. Since Europeans are also red-skinned (in fact the Manambu call Europeans 'redskins'), they and the people of Maliyaw must have the same origins and be 'brothers' (I might mention that it is perhaps no accident that I was quickly 'adopted' by Maliyaw after my arrival at Avatip and given one of their hereditary names).

The subclan Sarambusarak, the second largest of the Wuluwi-Nyawi subclans and the major political rivals of Maliyaw within that clan-pair, have responded to these assertions of superior status by trying to prove that they too have important totemic connections with Europeans. The leaders of Sarambusarak point out that the crest of the Australian Government, which they used to see on school exercise books during the Australian administration, includes a 'cassowary' (actually, an emu), which is a major totem of Sarambusarak. On this, perhaps rather slender basis, these men now boast the Queen as one of their subclan's totems, and derisively dismiss their Maliyaw rivals' pretensions to superiority.

What these two subclans are actually making are totemic-mythological claims to positions on the Local Government Council. Avatip has two councillors, and they are responsible for settling minor disputes, and for organising community works such as the maintenance of footpaths and the primary school at Yentshanggai. One councillorship represents the village of Yentshanggai and is held by Maliyaw, and the other represents the village of Yawmbak and has for many years been held by one of the orators of Sarambusarak. In effect, the privileged access the two rival subclans have to those new sources of power requires mythical charters. They are interpreting the symbols of state power as their totems, and portraying the conceived elements of that external political order as their hereditary ceremonial property.

The neighbouring Chambri seem to have responded to the advent of European power in a very similar way. Errington and Gewertz (1985; 1986; 1987) have described the attempts made by the Chambri in recent times to harness that power for ritual purposes. In one particularly interesting case, a Chambri Big Man who had become an important figure in local government and, later, in the national parliament, returned to Chambri announcing himself its 'chief' on the basis of his privileged access to the new political order (Errington and Gewertz 1985).

Ceremonial rank

Like the Australian Aborigines described by Worsley (1955; 1967), the villagers nowadays in fact incorporate many perceived elements of European culture into their totemism. The subclan Kambuli, for instance, claim as a totem the tilapia fish, which was introduced very successfully into the Sepik by Europeans and is now an important item in the villagers' economy. The basis of this claim is that *makau*, the term for the fish in Melanesian Pidgin, resembles the personal name Makawei, which Kambuli owns. Some subclans at the village of Yuanamb nowadays lay claim to the ownership of certain European months, again on the basis of similarities between the names of the months and personal names owned by these descent groups: July, for instance, which resembles the personal name Ndjulai; August, because it resembles the name Awkasmeli; and March (*Mas* in Pidgin) because of its similarity to the Manambu term *ma'as* (areca palm), a totem of the subclan that claims ownership of this month.

There are two points I would like to draw out of this discussion, besides the obvious one that the totemic system at Avatip remains highly resilient. Firstly, totemism in this society is, and doubtless always has been, a focus of intense competition for status between groups and it is this competition which has 'pushed' the totemic organisation, over history, in the direction of greater and greater complexity and elaboration. Secondly, as Errington and Gewertz have shown for the Chambri, men seem always to have looked outside the society for their symbols of status and power. For the Chambri, the motive was a sense that their society was entropic, that the fund of ritual power it contained was finite and constantly diminishing. At Avatip, it was rather the aggressive competition between groups and ambitious men that created the constant and continuing drive to import foreign cultural elements, to draw into their competition what they perceived as prestigious cultural forms offered by their neighbours and other outsiders.

In the past, the most important source from which these forms were imported were the Iatmul. The Ndumwi ritual of third-stage male initiation, and the first-stage initiation ritual of scarification, both of which I discuss in the next chapter, were Iatmul imports, the scarification ritual apparently a comparatively recent one, since older Avatip men can remember Iatmul experts having been paid to help supervise performances of it in their youth. In very many ways the Manambu implicitly associate the Iatmul with the 'invisible' world of spirits. Shamanic spirits, for instance, speak through their human mediums in a special, arcane language, intelligible only to those with many years of experience of shamanic séances, which is actually a kind of Manambu-based jargon with exaggeratedly *outré* 'Iatmul' features. In fact all speech-registers used in contexts of ritual and myth-telling, all specifically 'religious' forms of speech, borrow heavily from Western Iatmul and, to Manambu ears, the Iatmul language is intensely evocative of the whole conceived world of myth and totemic cosmology. To the Manambu, the

Iatmul embody, far more so than any of their other neighbours, that other, hidden order of existence which is the perceived source of all power.

I mentioned earlier the large number of commodities the Manambu used to export to the Iatmul in trade. What is striking is how little in the way of material goods, apart from shell valuables, the Manambu appeared to have received in return. In some respects, the trade relations between the Manambu and Iatmul resembled the relations between Avatip junior and senior men, writ large. That is to say, Avatip men seemed to have been soliciting their Iatmul trading partners with material goods and services in return for ritual techniques and knowledge and for the 'power' these represented. It was the constant competition for status that drove men to seek these symbolic goods and made Avatip, for their Iatmul trading partners, a permanent market for their cultural products. The particular direction in which the cosmology and political institutions of Avatip evolved needs to be understood, in other words, in the context of the position of Avatip in the regional trading economy. Avatip was the neighbour of one of the major 'culture-exporting' – but, in relation to Avatip at least, commodity-*importing* – peoples in the middle Sepik. I have said that the community produces little material surplus apart from fish. Of this surplus, except for fish, a large part seems to have gone in trade to the Iatmul, in return for shell valuables and probably, over history, much of the edifice of Avatip ritual, totemism and cosmology.

This can help to explain why the organisation of Avatip ritual is based in the first place on a principle of hereditary status-ranking. The answer, I suggest, has again to do ultimately with the position of the Manambu in the regional trading system. I have explained that the ceremonial attributes of Avatip subclans tend to reflect the cultural identities of their trading partners. For instance, the senior owning subclans of the Ndumwi and scarification rituals are subclans with important trade relations with the Iatmul; the subclans with major rights in the yam harvest have their main trade links with the Kwoma and other northern groups from whom this ritual, or some earlier version of it, was almost certainly acquired (see Table 5). It is exactly this kind of charter for trading rights that the two Councillors' subclans are constructing for themselves nowadays. They are representing the government as their own, exclusive trading partner, and claiming special rights to acquire its ceremonial appurtenances.

The cultural goods offered by the various neighbours of the Manambu were not, at least to the Manambu, all equally prestigious. The cultural products of the Iatmul were in high demand and have certainly been so for many generations. At the other extreme, the Manambu regard what they know of the cultural forms of small, marginal, sago-supplying groups such as the Yerikai-Garamambu as without prestige value and in fact highly undesirable. The Manambu were, accordingly, exporters of culture to these trading partners rather than the reverse. In other words, those Manambu subclans with access to highly valued cultural traditions tended to channel them into the Manambu ritual system, adopting many elements of these traditions as their own ceremonial property and, in the process, acting as important sources of ritual innovation within Manambu society. As with the subclans Maliyaw and Sarambusarak nowadays, and their attempts to establish totemic credentials for their Councillorships, it was presumably in similar elaborations of myth and totemism that, in the past, new rituals or imported magic became added into the ceremonial system. On the other hand, subclans with culturally 'impoverished' trade-partners lacked this access to high-status ritual property; they tended to act, on the contrary, as the suppliers of such goods to the peoples culturally dependent on the Manambu.

The principle of ceremonial rank seems therefore to have derived ultimately from the perceived inequalities in cultural prestige between the societies with which Manambu descent groups trafficked in material and ritual goods. Subclans transacting with culture-exporters of high status such as the Iatmul gained more important positions in ritual than those linked with culture-importing peoples of low status, so that the ceremonial system of the Manambu became a kind of microcosm of the differentially-valued ritual traditions of the surrounding societies. It was because the Manambu perceived their neighbours as 'ranked' in ritual status, that the descent groups linked in hereditary trade relations with these neighbours were conceived as ritually ranked. Ultimately, the ideology of ceremonial rank reflected the position of the Manambu in a regional trading system between whose constituent social systems there were real and major differences in material scale and sociocultural complexity. It is quite possible, of course, that notions of hereditary privilege 'diffused' to the Manambu at some stage in their history. There are peoples such as the Murik, near the mouth of the Sepik River, who have forms of hereditary political office (Lipset 1984) and are perhaps close enough to the Manambu to have had an indirect cultural influence on them. But, obviously, 'diffusion' alone cannot explain why the Manambu should have adopted and institutionalised these notions rather than any others that also circulated in the region. My suggestion is that, 'diffused' or not, ceremonial rank was institutionalised because it corresponded to the way the society articulated with the regional political-economic system.

Conclusion

Allen (1984) has argued that one factor that may have served to stimulate or inhibit political evolution in Melanesian societies is the mode of descent these societies employ. The Melanesian patrilineal descent systems, he suggests, provide a highly flexible and adaptable ideology for the formation of political groups. But it is precisely these functional advantages of the 'agnatic model' that tend not to foster the evolution of political structures above the level of kinship and affinal relations. Matrifiliation, on the other hand, is not as manipulable by ritual and genealogical fiction as is patrifiliation; and matriliny therefore tends to have an inherent inflexibility as a mode of recruitment to political groups. But it is that inflexibility of matrilineal descent, the limitations it tends to have as a basis of large-scale political relations, which make it likelier to encourage the emergence of supra-kinship forms of political association.

Although Avatip is not a matrilineal society, its system of patrilineal descent is a very rigid mode of recruitment to groups. In other words, it has much the same limitations as Allen posits for matriliny. At Avatip, it is totemism which provides the political flexibility which the descent system itself lacks. The elaborate development of totemic relationships, as a form of political association to some extent 'above' the level of kinship, is perhaps, in much the same way that Allen has suggested for matriliny, a response to the structural limitations of agnation. It is totemism, for instance, and not descent, which provides the basis of trading relations and all social and political ties between villages and between the different cultural groups in the area. It was those putatively 'pan-human' totemic categories that provided the routes along which ceremonial forms, and all other sorts of material and symbolic commodities, were traded between the Manambu and their neighbours. Indeed, it is on the basis of those same totemic world-divisions that the subclans Maliyaw and Sarambusarak now claim cosmological entitlements to seats on the Local Government Council and to special totemic relationships with the state. Within the community, totemism and not descent provides the idiom in which relations of ceremonial rank are cast and is, or was, a potential basis of political stratification. The mode of recruitment by descent perhaps has influenced the development of ceremonial rank as a supra-kinship structure at Avatip, though the important factor would seem to have been the inflexibility rather than the actual mode of descent.

There are also a number of parallels between the situation of the Manambu, as I interpret it, and the circumstances described by Brunton (1975) in his persuasive explanation of the emergence of rank in the northern Trobriand Islands. Brunton argues that the elaborate development of rank and chieftainship in that part of Melanesia was the result of a set of ecological, demographic and other factors having combined to partially isolate that area from the Kula Ring, making it possible for a small minority of men to gain a monopolistic control of the circulation of Kula valuables. Generalising from this case to Melanesia as a whole, Brunton concludes that hereditary stratification is most likely to arise where men can limit the access of others to the main wealth items circulating in trade and exchange.

Irwin (1983) has criticised this argument on the basis of a spatial analysis of the Trobriand villages, suggesting that at least one factor involved in the development of rank was the central position of certain villages in the local network of economic and political relations. Perhaps similar factors were at work in the case of the Manambu as well since, as I explained earlier, the Manambu occupied something of an important node in the regional trading system, having access to the ritual traditions of eight immediately neighbouring peoples. But also, in very much the same way that Brunton suggests for the northern Trobrianders, the Manambu depended on their regional trading system for their items of strategic prestige value; and, as in the northern Trobriands, conditions among the Manambu were such as to create inequalities in access to these goods. The basic difference between the two cases is the substantive nature of the items of exchange: in the Trobriands these were Kula valuables, and among the Manambu they were items of (primarily Iatmul) ritual culture. While Brunton's general argument applies well to Avatip, I suggest he draws a misleading dichotomy when he concludes that the evolution of Melanesian rank and chieftainship is to be explained in terms of the economy rather than in terms of religion or culture (1975: 556). It is difficult to see why his otherwise persuasive argument should entail the necessity of treating economy and religion/culture as opposed explanatory categories in this way, and I have found it impossible in practice to apply them as alternative means of interpreting Manambu politics and history. The problem is that while the political evolution of the Manambu can indeed be understood only in terms of the regional economy, key items in this economy were religious and cultural forms.

In many Melanesian ceremonial exchange systems, such as those of the Papua New Guinea Highlands, important Big Men nowadays seek to include cash, cattle, motor-vehicles and other modern prestige goods in their prestations. The perceived forms of introduced 'wealth' that Avatip leaders seek to draw to themselves for political purposes seem instead, to a Western observer, to be elements of our symbolic or cultural order rather than our material commodities. But it is our own analytical and folk distinctions between economy and the symbolic order that these Melanesian peoples are implicitly calling into question in their responses to the advent of the European order. Avatip villagers, like Big Men in other Melanesian societies, indeed seek these new forms of material wealth, but the difference is that they define them as personal or private wealth and not as politically significant prestige goods. There are half a dozen or so young entrepreneurs at Avatip who run trade-stores in the community, cattle-projects, or other local business ventures, and some of them have significant cash incomes. My impression is that the community's ritual leaders have tended deliberately to keep these men in junior ritual grades long after they are due for promotion, so as to counteract the new forms of inequality they represent, and to keep their access to Western *material* wealth from challenging the *ritual* authority of their elders. The *political capital* that Europeans are perceived as offering – Councillorships, the totemic ownership of coastal towns, or Western clothes, or months, or of introduced species of fish, or the Queen or the coats of arms on school exercise books – are those emblems of state power that can be utilised as symbols of ascribed status. They are sought because they are the closest perceived equivalents to the symbolic insignia of ritual rank and status that Avatip sought in the past from the Iatmul and were their most valued and politically significant trade goods. The most important and prestigious of these ceremonial goods pertained to the men's cult and male initiation ritual, to which I should now like to turn.

5

Male initiation

Introduction

A feature of many Melanesian societies are male cults, in which men are promoted through a series of initiatory grades during the course of their lives, and at each stage are taught successively more secret, and more powerful, ritual knowledge (Allen 1967; Barth 1975; Herdt 1982; Tuzin 1980; Whitehead 1986). In this chapter I outline the male initiatory system at Avatip because the major political conflicts in the society, which I analyse in later chapters, are contests for pre-eminent positions in the organisation of the men's cult. It is this cult that provides Avatip men with their most powerful and compelling models of hierarchy, and it is above all the hereditary powers and privileges deriving from the cult which Avatip leaders are competing to control.

I begin by describing the stages of the initiatory cycle, starting with the ritual of first-stage initiation, and then discuss the privileges (these are primarily entitlements to different funerary rites) of the three ritual grades. I end with a discussion of the ritual elite, the men holding hereditary offices called *simbuk*, arguing that while these offices confer little authority in secular contexts, they are intensely significant symbols of the *idea* of ascribed inequality.

Ritual and social reality

The male cult, like most such cults in Melanesia and elsewhere, debars women and involves the deliberate hoaxing and deception of women and children. The cults have for these reasons sometimes been interpreted as expressing a polarisation or antagonism between men and women, or as being instruments of male domination (Allen 1967; Langness 1967; Keesing 1982b; Herdt 1981, 1982). There are difficulties with applying these interpretations to the cult at Avatip. The principal concerns of the initiation rituals are with the ranking of the sexes, and with the ranking of men themselves by seniority of descent. In the rituals, very real inequalities of power are enacted between men and women, and between senior and junior men. But, for a variety of reasons, these inequalities cannot be transposed wholesale into everyday life, and they therefore exist primarily in the context of ritual itself. Outside of actual performances of ritual, they can manifest themselves as inequalities of prestige or status, but rather weakly and equivocally as inequalities of power.

One way around difficulties of this sort is to view ritual as an idealised representation of social reality, to which people's empirical patterns of social life can never more than untidily approximate (see for instance Durkheim 1976: 420–4; Leach 1954). In this approach, the difference between everyday life and ritual is essentially the difference between the actual and the normative, between people's social existence and their ideal conceptions of it. The problems with this approach are, firstly, that it tends implicitly to define social life in non-ritual contexts as merely 'behaviour', as though it constructed no dimension of shared meaning of its own. It is not that the symbolic or communicative content of everyday life really is negligible, but simply that this content tends to be thoroughly 'embedded' in practical action. Secondly, ritual, for its part, is not simply a way of making statements or prescriptions about social action, but is itself a modality of action and therefore constructs its own, delimited, reality. Avatip ritual does not only 'represent' notions of inequality, but actually brings those inequalities, contextually, into existence. It is a *lived experience* of hierarchy and not just a model of it.

It is true that Avatip men may claim, in their rituals, to speak in the name of their society as a whole and on behalf of a common good. But it is men alone who control the ritual system, and these claims must therefore be treated as interested and ideological, as ethnographic data and not imported into theory as a premise of one's own analysis. Men's claims authoritatively to signify an ideal social world in ritual are self-validating, because the rituals signify nothing except the provisional worlds which the men themselves create in the rituals. To represent the discordances between these cult contexts and everyday life as discrepancies between 'norms' and 'behaviour' is simply to be drawn into a collusion with one's male informants and to convert their political interests into a theory of religion.

Another way of accounting for these discordances is to argue that ritual can get out of kilter with the realities of everyday life during social change. Geertz (1957), for instance, discussed the lack of fit between traditional funerary ritual and the realities of modern political life in Java, arguing that if social structure changes, ritual and the cultural order may lag behind. But the weakness of this early paper is the structural-functionalist assumption (later disavowed; see Geertz 1966) that ritual simply serves to reflect and support the structural *status quo* ideationally; if it does not do so, it is an abnormality or malfunction brought about by the disruptions of social change. My disagreement here is with the analytical division between religion and the cultural order on the one hand and, on the other, an order of social structure and political relations in which all change is assumed to originate. The assumption I make is that ritual is a mode of social action with its own meaning, principles of organisation and patterns of power relations. What gets disjointed or out of kilter during social change are therefore not culture and social structure but different structures of action. This sort of disarticulation is not an epipheno-menon of social change but *is* social change, seen at a particular moment in time.

In a later work, his study of the Balinese cock-fight (1972), Geertz argues that ritual should be approached as a kind of non-verbal text, an interpretative 'metasocial commentary' on everyday existence. The Balinese cock-fight, he shows, is actually a symbolic fight for prestige between men, a simulacrum of status-competition in a society in which rank is in actuality rigidly ascribed and can never truly be challenged. But in acting out this imaginatively constructed play-world in which status can be lost and won, the Balinese reveal to themselves the powerful tensions hidden behind the elaborately formal etiquette and ceremonial of everyday life. But a criticism rightly made of Geertz' approach is that it ignores the context of power relationships which rituals and other symbolic forms create and are created by, and therefore ignores their ideological significance (Asad 1983). In the case of Balinese cock-fighting, the central actors are the local elite; and, a striking exception in a society which Geertz (1972: 30) describes as an otherwise rather 'uni-sex' one, cock-fighting is an entirely male activity from which women are strictly excluded. The many inversions of normal Balinese behaviour which take place in this ritual are particularly stressed by Cohen (1985: 63–9), who describes it as 'a kind of speculative and harmless experiment in social change' (Cohen 1985: 68). What makes the ritual out of congruence with everyday life is that it constructs, not only a micro-world of egalitarian competition within a rigidly hierarchical order, but also an all-male world within a comparatively sexually undifferentiated one. It is a make-believe world, not of Balinese society, but of a minority within it, and presumably therefore primarily reflects the perspec-tive and preoccupations of that minority. But a more basic question concerns the sense in which the ritual can therefore be described as having a 'meta' relationship to the wider context of Balinese social life. In the ritual, men rise and fall in status, and a strict division between the sexes is imposed, neither of which seem to carry over into general social life. But in the context of the ritual, these patterns are enacted and made real. Objectively, the cock-fight is simply one of the many forms of social action in which the Balinese, or certain categories of them, engage and is neither a higher-order nor lower-order activity than any other. What 'lifts it from the realm of everyday practical affairs, and surrounds it with an aura of enlarged importance' (Geertz 1972: 26) are presumably the claims or views of its participants that it has such an enlarged significance. To regard the ritual as metaphor for everyday-life experience when it is itself a part of that experience, to treat it as an interpretative assessment of other contexts of Balinese social life when it is simply one of those contexts, is to view the ritual from the perspective of a particular set of indigenous political interests.

A rather different way of explaining dissonances between everyday social life and its representations in ritual is to interpret religion as a mystification of political and economic realities. Keesing (1982a), for example, draws on Marxist perspectives of this sort in his analysis of the religion of the Kwaio people of the Solomon Islands, referring to the 'veils of illusion' (1982: 217) which the religion draws over exploitative economic and power relations between Kwaio men and women, seniors and juniors. The most important basis of the power of senior Kwaio men is their control of sacred knowledge, and the religious ideology that represents women as dangerously polluting. Keesing shows that women themselves can turn this ideology back against men, and use the dangerous powers of pollution attributed to them as weapons to protect their own rights and interests. The difficulty here, it seems to me, is that the conflicts that men and women are fighting out in this way are not only between ideologies, but between modes of social action. To the extent that male ideologies of pollution among the Kwaio 'work', the sexual inequalities they create are real; to the extent that women successfully use these ideologies against men, women actually do protect their interests. That is to say, these religious beliefs are not a means only of conceiving or representing social reality, but of creating and living it. In a similar way, when men at Avatip act out ideas of hereditary inequality in ritual, those inequalities *exist*; when groups compete for ceremonial privileges as equals in the debating-arena, or husbands and wives act as equals in the gift-exchange system, those equalities also are real. I do not see how it is possible to privilege one context over the other, and to consider one to be the lived actuality of which the other is simply a distorted or illusory image. They are simply real forms of action in an antagonism with one another.

My approach to Avatip ritual is closest to those which view ritual and non-ritual action as dialectical counterparts, each drawing its meaning from the other by the contrast between them. I am thinking here, for instance, of Turner's (1967, 1969) notion of communitas, the period of anti-structure existing in the liminal, betwixt-and-between phase of rites of passage; and of those symbolic reversals of the everyday world that commonly occur in myth, ritual and symbolism (see Babcock 1978; Cohen 1985: 63–9; Gluckman 1955a; Leach 1961b). These inversions and violations of normal behaviour have tended to be interpreted from a functionalist point of view, as serving to accentuate everyday norms, or in one way or another to reaffirm them, and so in the long run to help maintain social stability. My view is that this presupposes the consensual legitimacy of norms, and that everyday social life and the contraventions of it which may take place in ritual are better interpreted as a kind of dialogue of argument and counter-argument. Which form of action is the norm and which the inversion, which is conventional and which abnormal, are inherently political issues. Patterns of action that exist as ritual inversions in one society can exist as conventional norms in another. All-male arenas of status-rivalry, for instance, appear in both Bali and in Melanesia, but in one case as ritual inversions of the official political *status quo*, and in the other as the very embodiment of it. All that defines such arenas as the political norm in Melanesia, and as the converse of it in Bali, is the overall distribution of power in these two societies.

My interpretation is that, underlying both secular life and ritual at Avatip, there are two conceptually distinct ideal systems of social classifications. In other words, everyday life and ritual are domains of action drawing on different schemes of values. As Dumont (1970) shows, hierarchy and equality imply each other and co-exist in every social system; what varies is their relative valorisation, the symbolic weight given to each. At Avatip, hereditary equality and inequality co-exist as the ideal principles of secular and ritual action respectively, as contraries entailing each other – to borrow Wagner's (1986) metaphor – like figure and ground.

I am not suggesting that Avatip society alternates, in ritual and everyday life, between two radically opposed social realities. The contrast I am drawing is between opposed ideologies or ways of conceptualising social reality. It is in the rituals of the men's cult that ideas of hierarchy are given their fullest and most complete expression, while an ethic of egalitarianism is manifested most fully in secular life. But, in both ritual and non-ritual contexts, people's actual patterns of action are negotiations of these two ethics and involve some degree of compromise between them. The ritual inequalities between men and women, seniors and juniors, can certainly obtrude into everyday social relations. And conversely, there are contexts in ritual in which, as I shortly show, women partly take on the ritual status of their husbands, so that the wives of ritually senior men actually have higher ritual status than junior initiated men and the status distinctions being drawn are between senior men-and-their-wives on the one hand, and junior men-and-their-wives on the other. These sorts of situations are outcomes, at the level of practice, of conflicts and compromises between the values associated with the men's cult and those associated with everyday conjugal and kinship relations. That is to say, the interaction between these two ethics is not static but an inherently dynamic and historical one.

Spirit and Understanding

An important theme of Avatip ritual, it will be recalled, is the promotion of the fertility of land, lagoons, crops and so forth, taking the form of a mutually 'nurturant' reciprocity between two moiety-like groups within a closed kinship universe. Outsiders are by definition thought of as playing no part in this reciprocity, and if they used any of the community's resources it would be a kind of theft of the products of the men's ritual labour. The men's cult, in short, is an assertion of the community's territorial rights against outsiders;

both Avatip and, so far as I can tell, neighbouring groups as well, conceive of a village's 'ownership' of its land as deriving from its ritual powers over the land's fertility.

This brings me to the second main theme of Avatip ritual: warmaking. The spirit beings conjured in ritual are believed to protect the community from its enemies and, in the past, to have ensured success in warfare and headhunting. The performance of ritual continues nowadays to be seen by men as necessary to keep themselves armed supernaturally and in permanent readiness for fighting. The essence of their idea of themselves as a ritual congregation is that they represent a politically and territorially distinct entity against outsiders, and combine in warfare and have a common focus for their aggression. As one can see, the themes of warmaking and natural fertility in Avatip ritual are closely connected, because they both arise out of the community's relationship with its territory.

Associated with both of these is a basic concern with preserving the community as a closed connubium. The attempts by the Western Iatmul in particular to encroach on Avatip territory were not only military. They also took the form, and continue to do so nowadays, of attempts at peaceful intermarriage with Avatip, aimed at gaining kinship rights in its resources. Avatip men assiduously resist such overtures, and the ritual system is preoccupied with the maintenance of symbolic boundaries (see Cohen 1985) around the community and an ideology of endogamy. Ritual and cosmology portray the community's descent groups as closed in upon themselves forever, reproducing and ritually 'nurturing' one another and maintaining their viability against hostile and dangerous outsiders. The descent groups are represented as the sole sources of one another's growth, in a complete interdependence in which the basic resources they exchange – of land, weather, and animal and plant fertility and so forth – are bound forever into their own identities, and could never become 'free' values that could be used in exchanges with outsiders.

The themes of fertility, warfare and marriage are also linked closely with one another in Avatip conceptions of the person and of personal ritual status. Every individual is thought to have from birth a *kaiyik* or, as I call it, a Spirit (see Harrison 1985a, 1985b), which is the animating energy or life-force of a living person. As men and women age, their Spirits become more potent, and by middle age a person has a capacity to curse and bless his or her juniors, and mild powers of witchcraft, which become stronger with age. With men, however, the powers of their Spirits are also augmented by their initiations into successive ritual grades. When a man is first initiated in the cult, his Spirit turns into a semi-autonomous personal spirit-guardian or potency called a *nggalaka'aw*, which is thought of as the source of his physical strength, energy, endurance and well-being, acting also as his protector in fights, keeping him from harm and striking fear and confusion into his enemies. A man's *nggəlaka'aw* is thus the key to the two qualities most admired in Avatip men, especially in the eyes of potential brides and fathers- and brothers-in-law: productivity, and warlike prowess. These qualities are supposed in general terms to develop with increasing ritual status, because the power of a man's Spirit is said to increase as he is promoted into higher ritual grades. Men's Spirits are supposed to take on especially heightened powers during the rituals themselves, becoming inimical to women and uninitiated males and automatically attacking them with sickness if they do not keep at a respectful distance from the performers.

A very basic concern of the ritual system is thus with the reproduction of persons, and specifically with the reproduction of male ritual status as embodied in the power of their Spirits. In this way, the cult maintains differences in status both between men on the one hand and women and non-initiates on the other, and also between adult men themselves according to their ritual grade. But to Avatip people, this hierarchy of ritual statuses is a relation between people's Spirits and not between entire persons. Spirit is only one of two conceived components of social identity, and relates principally to the sphere of ritual (see Harrison 1985a, 1985b).

In addition to a Spirit, all individuals are spoken of as having a *mawul*, or what I call an Understanding. Children are thought of as developing an Understanding, the essentially moral and sociable dimension of the personality, through the normal processes of socialisation in everyday-life contexts. To have an Understanding is to be rational, to possess all appropriate adult skills and knowledge, and to be aware of one's obligations and the rights of others. Above all it implies an empathic disposition and the capacity to identify sympathetically with other people. It manifests itself in the co-operation between spouses in their daily tasks and in the rearing of their children, in the everyday exchanges of goods and services in which kin and affines show their concern for one another, and in all the contexts of quotidian life that call for practical knowledge and a properly socialised disposition toward others.

The ritual system, in short, is concerned with the reproduction of one particular aspect of male personhood, and with a system of hierarchical social relations having a specialised relevance to religious contexts. I mentioned earlier that personal names are conceived to encapsulate their bearers' Spirits, and the dimension of identity which the male cult concerns is that dimension through which persons are connected to their totemic ancestors and to the timeless order of myth and cosmology.

The male initiatory system

All the conceived elements of the men's initiatory cult are personified as named totemic ancestors: the beings who first created the rituals in mythical times, the spirits the rituals invoke, and all the physical appurtenances of the rituals.

Male initiation

These include the men's ceremonial houses and their various parts – the posts, beams, spires, hearths and so forth; the slit-drums, secret initiatory flutes and wooden trumpets, and many other ritual sacra. Some ritual objects are stored permanently in the ceremonial houses. Others are remade each time a ritual is held and destroyed afterwards. But every one of them is conceived to embody an ancestral spirit who came from one of the origin-villages at the founding of Avatip. What men act out in ritual is an identification with these ancestral spirits or personified sacra whose names they carry; and, as will become clear, the rituals are in effect special contexts in which men temporarily *become* those beings.

In front of a subclan's ceremonial house stands a mound, or *tupwi*, which is an important focus of ritual. Many kinds of flowers and shrubs used in ritual are grown on it, some of them totems of the subclan. Inside the building there are three fireplaces (*yendjɔmb*), one for each of the three ritual grades in the men's cult. Men of the highest grade sit around the hearth at the front of the building, the *tanggayendjɔmb*. Second-grade initiates congregate at the second hearth, and first-stage initiates around the hearth at the rear of the building. A man may not approach the hearth of higher-grade men without their permission.

When any male initiation ritual takes place, the ceremonial house it is held in is enclosed in a tall cane fence, to hide the proceedings from the uninitiated. Women and noninitiates must stay away from the building and, above all, must never see any of the secret musical instruments which the men play in ritual. The main instruments are pairs of bamboo flutes. The uninitiated are told that the men summon spirits, called Ndakwul Wapi, to their rituals, and the music in the ceremonial house is the voices of these beings. Men describe the spirits as like men but with hollow tusks, through which they speak in their musical voices.

Before a set of novices can be inducted into any ritual, they must first pay their initiators a highly secret favour. They have to persuade at least one of their kinswomen, married or unmarried, to copulate with at least one of their initiators. It is the responsibility of the older men of the novices' grade, who are called the Ambasɔ, or 'head of the grade', to arrange this. They keep the identities of the women secret, even from their junior fellow-novices. Nor do the women know that they are being asked to do something with a ritual significance. Each woman is simply told that so-and-so wishes to have a rendezvous with her. Men and women often have casual liaisons, secretly arranged via kin, and women do not find such invitations in any way out of the ordinary. After the initiation is over, the newly-promoted grade must pay the same favour to their initiators again. Until this is done, they may not shave, and whenever they smoke or chew areca-nut they must first give some to their initiators.

An initiation ritual may last for a month or so, and during this period the

91

entire community is put under two principal restrictions. Firstly, nobody may marry. Secondly, nobody may make loud noises, such as chopping firewood or having domestic arguments. If these rules were broken, the initiators would send the novices to ransack the offender's house. This is called *wi wañgɔlna*, and involves taking all the food in the house, slaughtering the owner's dogs, pigs and domestic fowl, stripping his trees and palms of their fruit, and taking everything to the ceremonial house for the spirits, which is to say, the initiators, to eat. The culprit's gardens are left untouched, so as not to cause his household undue hardship. There are frequent minor infractions of the rule forbidding noise, and these receive small fines of food. At the initiation in 1978, a man slipped on his house-ladder injuring his testicles, and his agonised screams earned him a fine of several coconuts.

Because of schooling and employment, it is nowadays more difficult to assemble a large number of novices for an initiation, and as a result initiations are performed more frequently than in the past, but on a smaller scale with smaller numbers of initiates. In the past, the rituals of the men's cult were larger in scale, longer, but also more widely spaced. These changes in the scale and tempo of the initiatory cycle have had some important consequences, as I shall explain later.

Uninitiated males are called Nɔmbanyanungkw, a term essentially meaning 'children'. They are nowadays initiated into the first stage of the men's cult, singly or in small sets, on any occasion when the secret flutes are played, such as during repairs to a ceremonial house. They are shown the flutes, warned – often with a knife held to their throats – never to reveal their existence to women and children, and may then begin learning to play them themselves. In the past, Nɔmbanyanungkw were initiated into the cult in a large-scale ritual, owned by the clan-pair Nggɔla'angkw, in which they were scarified and secluded in the ceremonial house for several months while the cuts healed. The women were told that the novices were gored by the Ndakwul Wapi spirits, and that the scars the new initiates carried when they emerged were the marks of the spirits' tusks. These days, some young men have themselves scarified while they are away from the village, working as labourers on plantations. This is becoming less common now, but the villagers still regard these one- or two-year absences by young men as something of a 'modern' substitute for the old first-stage initiation ritual.

Second-stage initiation

Once he has learned the secret of the flutes, a novice can be initiated into the yam harvest ritual, at which point he becomes a member of the second ritual grade, the Mɔndja Sɔ. This ritual is owned by Wuluwi-Nyawi. It takes place in December, and the whole village looks forward to it eagerly because it lifts the interdiction on the levee gardens and allows their harvest to begin after an annual period of scarcity. A simple version of this ritual is held annually, but it is a special prerogative of Wuluwi-Nyawi men to perform this version by themselves and it does not normally involve initiations. The more elaborate, initiatory version is staged about once every four years, whenever there is a particularly good yam crop.

The most important prerogatives in the yam harvest ritual are held by three senior Wuluwi-Nyawi subclans: Nyakaw, Ambasarak and Maliyaw. In the ritual, all the Wuluwi-Nyawi descent groups divide into three ritual associations, each headed by one of those subclans. The ritual is performed simultaneously and to a large extent independently by these associations, at the three senior subclans' ceremonial houses.

According to myth, it was the totemic ancestors of the three 'core' subclans, as I shall call them, who first brought yams into existence. Each of these subclans had in its mythical origin-village a water-hole (*wa'anggw*), which kept itself magically filled with yams and provided the ancestral members of each association with an inexhaustible supply of the tubers on which they would secretly feast, keeping the existence of the holes and of yams themselves concealed from the ancestors of Nggəla'angkw and Nambul-Sambəlap. Eventually, the hole belonging to the subclan Ambasarak 'burst open' (*wila*), discharging yams into the world and making them available to all social groups. The price paid for that primordial act of generosity, Wuluwi-Nyawi people say, that ever since then they have had to produce yams by their own physical labour. On the basis of this myth, the three 'core' subclans are the joint owners of the magic relating to the cultivation of yams.

Both versions of the yam harvest ritual begin in the same way. The men of Wuluwi-Nyawi who are second-stage initiates go secretly one evening to their levee gardens and harvest their first-fruits. They smuggle the yams into the village and stay all night, with the yams, in the ceremonial houses of their core groups. During the night, they are bespelled with war-magic by ritual office-holders called *simbuk*, and the men take on a state of ritual potency dangerous to women and children. At dawn, the men take up position by their slit-drums, drum-beaters in hand, and wait for the first woman or child to emerge from a domestic house. As soon as a woman or child does so, the men start up a deafening chorus of drum-rhythms: this is the signal to the village that the ritual has begun, and all women and noninitiates must now stay inside their houses and keep silent. The village gives an eerie illusion of being deserted, except for the watching faces of children pressed to the gaps in the walls of their houses. The men emerge from the ceremonial houses and carry the first-fruit yams in procession along the village, presenting them to all the households of their sisters' children. The presentation to the sisters' children, the villagers say, is the annual re-enactment of the primordial release of yams into the world. It lifts the interdiction on the yam gardens, and once it is over the whole village sets off in their canoes to harvest them.

93

Male initiation

In its initiatory version, which was not performed during my stay at Avatip, the ritual is followed over the next few days by the construction, in the core groups' ceremonial houses, of three ritual effigies known as məndj (hence Məndja Sə, or 'məndj grade'). The effigies are large, personified representations of vine-covered yam-poles. Groups belonging to the same association are ranked in an order of seniority, with the core group being the most senior, and each of these groups is responsible for constructing a specific part of the association's effigy according to its position in the rank order. The senior groups make the upper part of the effigy, its 'head', while the rest of the effigy, down to its 'legs', is made by the other groups in order of increasing juniority. Once assembled, each association takes its effigy by raft to a spot on the river-bank opposite the village, where the three figures are erected one after another in the order of seniority of the three core groups. Of these three subclans, Nyakaw is the most senior according to myth and genealogy; Ambasarak is second and Maliyaw the most junior. Nyakaw, however, does not in fact hold the crucial privileges in the ritual; for reasons I explain in a later chapter, it is actually the two junior core groups who have the critical right to inaugurate the ritual and decide its timing. As a visual expression of their effectively more important status, the effigies of the junior core groups are very tall, ten or so metres high. Nyakaw, though erecting its effigy first, has to give it the diminutive and, to the villagers, slightly derisory height of about one and a half metres. It is during this phase of the ritual that novices are initiated into the Məndja Sə, and undergo beatings with stinging-nettles and other ordeals.

Third stage initiation

The third and highest ritual grade is called the Maiyira Sə or Ndjəpas. There are two alternative rituals giving entry to this grade, one belonging to Nggəla'angkw and the other to Wuluwi-Nyawi.

The one owned by Nggəla'angkw is called Ndumwi, and in it the Ndjəpas men summon up a huge female spirit of the same name, and escort her into the village on a raft. The key prerogatives in this ritual are held by Makəm and Yimal, the two most senior of the Nggəla'angkw subclans. The ritually senior men of these two subclans must give their assent before the ritual can take place, and have many other special rights during the ritual. These include the entitlement to build the gate through which the impersonators of Ndumwi enter and leave the initiatory enclosure, and many special prerogatives to do with impersonating the Ndumwi spirit. The ritual is usually held shortly after the initiatory version of the yam harvest ritual. The spirit is fetched to the village to 'fan' the ritual effigies of Wuluwi-Nyawi, which are her children, just as Avatip mothers fan their children to keep them cool.

To prepare for this ritual the men of the Ndjəpas grade make ready a large stock of sago, going each day for a week or so with their wives to the bush to process the palms. The sago is to last them and their families for the duration of the ritual, during which the men are taboo to their womenfolk and children, and unavailable for productive work. Some of the sago, so the women are told, is also for Ndumwi as well, for her to take away in her net-bag on her departure from the village.

The Ndjəpas men at this point seclude themselves for about a month in one of the Nggəla'angkw ceremonial houses. Each subclan's Ndjəpas are allocated a living-space with a hearth. The hearths of the Nggəla'angkw subclans are ranged along the swamp-side of the building, those of Wuluwi-Nyawi along the water-side, and those of Nambul-Sambəlap in the middle: as one of the Ndjəpas explained to me, just as in marriage Nambul-Sambəlap stands in the middle, so it does in Ndumwi also. This arrangement of the three groups also diagrams their mythological origins, Nggəla'angkw being autochthonous, Nambul-Sambəlap having originated at the source of the Sepik, and most of the Wuluwi-Nyawi subclans being immigrants from mythical villages in the foothills to the north. Within each row, the hearths are arranged in order of seniority, with those of senior subclans having the place of honour at the front of the building, and those of junior subclans toward the rear. By each of the Nggəla'angkw hearths, there is a slit-drum, and the men beat these drums almost continually, night and day for a month, to summon Ndumwi to the village. Just as a man has his own slit-drum signal, so does Ndumwi, and it is her personal call-signals (*ndja'amb*) that the men play. They are all fast, syncopated and very complex rhythms played on all the drums simultaneously in the two-handed style, and the volume of sound produced is enormous. Men say that their furious drumming can sometimes carry to other villages, and intimidates their enemies. Each signal is based on a different rhythmical theme, which must first be played by the men of Makəm and Yimal, who share the same hearth and slit-drum, and then repeated by each drum in order of seniority until it reaches the slit-drum of Waranggamb, the most junior Nggəla'angkw subclan. It then returns to the drum shared by Makəm and Yimal, and so goes on circulating from one drum to another until the men of Makəm and Yimal call a rest. It is exhausting work and as one man tires at his drum, another – a subclansman or a sister's son – takes over from him. During the day, the men take breaks and snatch sleep for an hour or two. But they allow themselves few breaks after dark: they say that if they spent the night asleep, not beating the drums, the ceremonial house would burst into flames and incinerate them.

Once or twice a day, the men take a break to play the flutes, letting the village know that the Ndakwul Wapi spirits have arrived and are with them. Another supernatural guest is Ndumwimalanmbandi, the brother of Ndumwi: she has heard the drums and sent her brother ahead of her, to confirm that the men are really calling for her. Ndumwimalanmbandi is a stone, hung from a suspension hook and beaten to make a faint ringing sound in time with the drum-rhythms.

The men rarely leave the initiatory enclosure but when they do so they must be avoided by everyone except the novices awaiting initiation, because they are in a ritually potent state. They carry their lime-gourds and serrated lime-spatulas, which are emblems of Ndjɔpas status; and they grate these wherever they go, making the sound the villagers onomatopoeically call *nggɔrɔkiya'ap*, to warn people to stay clear of them. They never leave the enclosure singly, but always in groups or at least in pairs, in case one of them is tempted to visit his family and thereby afflicts them with sickness.

Two or three times during this phase of the ritual the younger Ndjɔpas go to the bush to hunt pigs and cassowaries 'for Ndumwi to take away with her in her net bag'. The novices also hunt 'pigs for Ndumwi' and all this game is smoked inside the enclosure by the initiators and eaten by them. Because they are eating their usual daily diet, sent in to them by their wives, as well as the pigs 'for Ndumwi', they have noticeably put on weight by the end of the ritual. Ndumwi, as one man told me, is the ritual of fatness.

The novices make ready the personal accoutrements which, when initiated, they will be entitled to wear as members of the Ndjɔpas grade: a cassowary-plume headdress, a shell neck-ornament called a *kwalɔsapi*, a lime-gourd and serrated spatula, and a special shoulder-bag with a distinctive pattern in the weave. These are larger and finer versions of the ordinary net-bags worn by men, and are woven for the novices by their female kin. The novices send all these accoutrements into the initiatory enclosure, where the Ndjɔpas hang them on suspension hooks around the hearths of their respective subclans and bespell them with war-magic. They will present them to the novices at their initiation.

A few days before the initiation, three domestic pigs must be bought for Ndumwi: one by the initiators and two by the novices, one for each of the initiatory moieties to which the novices belong. A domestic pig is an expensive luxury at Avatip, costing the equivalent of K100–K150 in a combination of cash and shell valuables. At the time of my fieldwork, the Papua New Guinea Kina was equal to approximately £1 at current (1988) rates. All the novices and initiators carry the three payments in a big procession along the village and present them to the pigs' owners. A day or two before the arrival of Ndumwi, the pigs will be claimed and taken into the enclosure, where the initiators will butcher and smoke them as gifts for the spirit.

The day before Ndumwi is to come, the initiators go by canoe to a spot on the Sepik called Kwanawi, a few miles downriver from the village, where Ndumwi traditionally materialises. They cut enormous steps into the river-bank, for her to come down onto the raft they will bring for her. The Ndjɔpas also collect large amounts of stinging-nettles, with which Ndumwi is to beat the novices. When they return to the village, the novices repay them for this work with large bowls of yam soup. On this expedition, the initiators have also, secretly, gathered vines and other materials to make an apparatus impersonating Ndumwi in the initiatory enclosure. That night, the last before their initiation, the novices must leave their families and sleep in their ceremonial houses.

At dawn the next day, a large party of initiators leave the village for Kwanawi on a raft. The raft is a trimaran of three canoes lashed together under a platform. The two outside canoes are bound in place by the initiated men of Wuluwi-Nyawi and Nggəla'angkw respectively, and the middle one by the Nambul-Sambəlap men, the trimaran being in this way a kind of explicit nautical representation of the community's group structure. On the raft they have built a domestic hearth, such as every married woman has in her house, 'for Ndumwi to light her tobacco' as she rides the raft to the village. The departure of the raft is the signal for everyone, except the initiators and novices, to leave the village. They cannot witness the arrival of Ndumwi. All women, children and unauthorised men abandon the village, most of them going to the site of Old Avatip a couple of miles away. The novices as well are forbidden to see Ndumwi arrive; they gather in a ceremonial house a few hundred yards from the initiatory enclosure and out of sight of it.

Ndumwi is an enormously squat spirit, with huge strides. When the men on the raft reach Kwanawi, they plant a row of palm-fronds down the steps, to mark where the spirit's footsteps fell. The fronds are three or four metres apart; later, when the ritual is over, women and noninitiates who pass by the spot in their canoes will see these fronds and, so the men hope, be astonished at Ndumwi's awesome strides.

As the raft comes back to the village, supposedly with Ndumwi on it, some of the crew are playing flutes, and others short trumpets – the 'baying of the dogs' she is bringing with her. Her brother Ndumwimalanmbandi, the ringing stone, is on the raft as well. The paddles are struck against the sides of the raft in unison, in exaggerated imitation of the rhythmic knocking a woman makes when paddling a canoe. The raft comes to shore by the enclosure and its crew jump up and down on it together, to suggest Ndumwi marching across the raft and coming ashore. A Ndjəpas man emerges from the enclosure and greets her with a long list of her totemic names, and the men on the raft stream ashore and rush around the enclosure beating it with sticks. This is the sound of Ndumwi's aggressive entry into the ceremonial house.

The novices, who have meanwhile heard all these intimidating sound effects from a distance, are told that Ndumwi now awaits them in the initiatory enclosure, ready to thrash them. The novices of the senior ritual moiety are sent in first, passing down a corridor of Ndjəpas who beat them with nettles, and emerging at the end to take their places by the hearths of their subclans. Then the junior moiety are sent in and go through the same ordeal. All the novices are now presented with their third-grade attire. They are also decorated with *ndumwikupw* (Ndumwi's clay) a yellow clay which is an emblem of Ndjəpas status, and with palm-fronds in their arm-bands.

The initiators turn their attention now to constructing the Ndumwi apparatus. Ndumwi will dance inside the enclosure for the benefit of the women and children; she herself will not be visible, only the long palm-fronds she holds in each hand, nodding and swaying above the enclosure as she dances. The fronds are operated by one of the initiators, pulling on a vine which connects them. Two fronds are set up, about eight metres apart, indicating to the women and noninitiates the gigantic span of her outstretched arms. Once the Ndjəpas have tested this apparatus and made it secure, they beat the slit-drums to call the women and children back to the village.

The latter gather at a safe distance from the enclosure. There is a line of widely-spaced palm-fronds leading into the enclosure from the shore, to show the audience Ndumwi's footfalls. A loud bang comes from the enclosure as Ndumwi stands up to dance. All the Ndjəpas and novices are outside the enclosure now; except for one who, his absence unnoticed, works the apparatus inside. The two palm fronds rise up bobbing and swaying rhythmically above the enclosure, in time to a swishing sound made by the seed-rattles on the spirit's leg-bands. Every so often the fronds fall as the spirit sits down to rest before resuming her dance.

As evening falls, the women and uninitiated hurry to their houses. Ndumwi is about to walk through the village and go home, and there must be no light in any of the domestic houses and complete silence everywhere. When it is quite dark, there is an urgent shout from the enclosure, telling the women and children to get inside their mosquito-nets, and, a second later, a splintering sound as Ndumwi tears the gate off the enclosure and bursts out into the open. She starts marching along the village, taking away all her gifts of food in her net-bag. At the initiation in October 1978, she carried away in her bag six wild pigs, three domestic ones, several hundredweight of sago and a cassowary. She is escorted along the village by Ndumwimalanmbandi, by the Ndakwul Wapi spirits, by her dogs, and by all the initiators and novices. The men stamp their feet in time with each other, imitating her gargantuan footfalls, calling to her to hurry along because she has far to go. She is a totemic ancestress of Makəm, the senior subclan of Nggəla'angkw; and as she passes the houses of sisters' children of that subclan, she sets palm-fronds in the ground in front of their houses in farewell to her 'children'. Finally, the party reaches the end of the village, and Ndumwi, her net-bag, her brother and her dogs all vanish into the ground and the earth closes up after them.

The next day the initiators and the new initiates all parade through the village in their regalia. The novices stay in the enclosure for another day or two, receiving instruction in ritual procedures from their seniors. Once they are home with their families, the men must hunt and eat a wild pig before they can remove the initiatory enclosure. In the old days, it was not a pig, but a man of an enemy village.

As owners of the Ndumwi ritual, the men of Nggəla'angkw receive an especially severe beating. Ndumwi does not beat men of other groups too harshly because she is their 'mother' and pities them. But a special entitlement which the men of Nggəla'angkw have is that there are fewer restrictions put on their promotion into the Ndumwi ritual. Once one or two men of any non-Nggəla'angkw lineage have been initiated into Ndumwi, no more men of the same lineage may enter the Ndjəpas grade via this ritual until the previous initiates have died or retired from ritual life. No limit of this sort is put on the induction of Nggəla'angkw men. As a result, as the initiatory cycle continues, with performances of Ndumwi every four years or so, men of Nggəla'angkw come to comprise an increasingly large proportion of the third ritual grade.

In the past, this imbalance was redressed in a ritual called Maiyir, which belongs to Wuluwi-Nyawi and was the alternative initiation into the Ndjəpas grade. It seems to have been held about once a generation and to have closed the whole ritual cycle, taking the form of a mass induction of all the remaining Məndja Sə into the third stage. The original Ndjəpas retired, handing control of the ritual system over to the new ones, and the initiatory cycle returned to the state at which it had started a generation earlier: all the initiated men were now members of the third grade, the two lower grades were unoccupied, and a new generation of uninitiated males was ready for induction into the first grade.

Maiyir was last performed at Avatip in the 1920s, and by the 1970s the Ndjəpas grade had consisted disproportionately of Nggəla'angkw men for many decades, and pressure grew to stage Maiyir again. The Ndjəpas were dying off faster than they were being replaced; many second-stage initiates were middle-aged or elderly, some of them influential political figures, and these men were starting to demand promotion before they died. Two old ritual leaders, holders of the ritual offices called *simbuk*, had taken part in the last performance as young men; and it was felt that Maiyir should be held, and led by these men, before they died and their first-hand knowledge of the correct procedures died with them. In the end, it was decided that Maiyir itself was impossible to perform, because homicide and ritual cannibalism were integral features of it. Instead, a novel ritual, with the same initiatory function, was held in October 1978. It was essentially an augmented version of Ndumwi combined with some elements of the Maiyir ritual, and in it some 130 Məndja Sə men, almost the whole of the second grade except for a handful disqualified by genealogy, were promoted by forty-five initiators into the Ndjəpas grade.

Rules of promotion and the prerogatives of ritual status

A man's successive promotions in the ritual system are not, as they are in many male cults elsewhere in Melanesia, linked to the stages of his physical and social maturation. They are determined by his genealogical position in his subclan or, if his subclan is a large one, in his lineage. First of all, a man cannot enter any initiatory grade so long as it is occupied by any man of his father's genealogical generation in his own subclan. He must wait until they have all died or left that grade through promotion. Secondly, a man cannot be promoted ahead of any of his actual or classificatory elder brothers in his subclan. In the scarification ritual and in Maiyir, the two largest-scale initiatory rituals, all the men of the same genealogical generation within each subclan are, or were, initiated together. In the yam harvest ritual and in most performances of Ndumwi, they are inducted in small sets, in the course of several performances over many years, in the order of agnatic seniority of the descent lines to which they belong. The overall effect of this is to maintain a close correspondence, within each subclan, between its men's genealogical status and their ritual status. This ritual-genealogical status-ranking within the subclan is primarily generational: the differences in ritual status it maintains are primarily between genealogical 'fathers' and 'sons'. But it also maintains, to some extent, a ritual ranking of men by the genealogical seniority of their agnatic descent lines. That is to say, within the same generation, men of senior lines are the ritual superiors of men of junior lines for much of the initiatory cycle, and are never their ritual inferiors.

Because the villagers reckon agnatic kinship in a rigidly unilineal way, patrilineal ties between people are often quite out of kilter with their relative ages (see Needham 1966). Men are often the close classificatory fathers or elder brothers of men older than themselves. There tends to be, as a result, a wide age-range within each initiatory grade. Men of senior descent lines can find themselves in the highest ritual grade while not yet in their twenties; some genealogically disadvantaged men grow old and die as Nəmbanyanungkw, uninitiated 'children', never entering the men's cult at all. This is less common now than it was in the past, when men could only enter the first grade in a ritual held once a generation: a man had only two opportunities in his lifetime to be initiated into the cult, and if his genealogical position disqualified him twice, he remained uninitiated all his life. Whenever the ritual was held, fathers were therefore under considerable pressure to have all their sons, if they were genealogically qualified, put through the ritual even if they were infants. Many of the novices were therefore babes in arms. These were not scarified or subjected to the other ordeals, but they were considered initiated males after the ritual and formed a special category of unscarified first-stage initiates called Tumnggwa'ar. When the next initiation came around a generation later, the Tumnggwa'ar were expected to go through it again, before the other novices, to set them an example of courage. It was on this occasion the Tumnggwa'ar received their scars. But it was by no means unusual in the old days for a scarcely-weaned infant to be senior in ritual status to men sixty or seventy years his elders. In 1978, the uninitiated males at Avatip ranged in age from infants to men in their late forties. The youngest member of the second grade was a twelve-year-old boy, and its oldest members were in their seventies. Before the 1978 initiation, the age-range in the third grade was from about thirty upwards; after the initiation, from about twenty-five upwards.

In ritual, the authority of higher grades over lower ones is considerable and is strictly enforced by both supernatural sanctions, and by physical ones such as the threat of house-ransacking. But the hierarchy of ritual status does not, and in fact cannot, translate itself directly into authority in secular contexts:

A small but revealing incident took place one day in 1978, when a young man criticised some third-stage initiates for laziness at a house-building bee. Most of the men in the village were working on a new domestic house, but some of the more elderly Ndjəpas men had been doing rather little work, sitting in a nearby ceremonial house talking among themselves and occasionally shouting advice to the workers. An ebullient young uninitiated man of about twenty started criticising them loudly, accusing them half-jokingly of having come only to eat the yam soup and other food that the house-owner would later provide to thank the workers. The elders' response to this was striking. All the Ndjəpas men present, both those who had been working and those who had not, immediately left and returned to their own houses, and shortly afterwards the whole work-bee came to end in disarray. As they were leaving, the Ndjəpas men proclaimed that the youngster had 'shamed' their entire grade, and that it was necessary for them to withdraw immediately in case their Spirits harmed him. In other words, at one level their response was ostensibly 'solicitous' toward him; it was not they as conscious subjects who might harm him, but their Spirits, and they were acting only to protect him from the consequences of his egregious *faux pas*. But there was also an implicit threat in this too. The Ndjəpas felt deeply humiliated, and at least one of them assured me privately that they would now never permit him to be initiated into the men's cult and would keep him a noninitiate all his life. Later, there was also much talk in the village, fostered by certain hints dropped by the third-stage men, that when the next performance of a third-stage initiation came around they would work sorcery against him during the ritual. And indeed, when the initiation took place in October 1978, the young man took the precaution of being absent from the village for the whole period of the ritual.

In everyday contexts such as house-building, all the helpers are expected to contribute labour irrespective of their ritual seniority and not to claim any special exemptions from work. The young man's offence was not that he had challenged the privileges of his seniors, but on the contrary that he had reminded them that they *had no special privileges* in such a situation, and so had shamed them by calling public attention to their non-participation in the day's work. The *secular* authority of ritually senior men is curiously fragile; in everyday contexts it is vulnerable even to quite minor challenges and some-times, as in this instance, these men's only immediate response to such challenges is to appear to flee from them in humiliation and disorder. What special authority they are able to claim in daily life depends wholly on the coming of future performances of ritual, when their powers of coercion will, contextually, be very powerful indeed. Outside the setting of ritual, as I show in the next chapter, the men with political authority are the middle-aged and elderly who have earned the role of leaders by years of personal achievement in the debating system. High ritual status gives a man prestige outside of ritual contexts, but does not in itself directly give him authority, even over his family. For instance, in theory a third-stage initiate may never be struck by his wife or children; if such a sacrilege were committed against him, he could call the men of his *laki* (a ceremonial category I discuss shortly) to stage a ransacking of his house, which temporarily impoverishes himself along with his family. Not surprisingly, few Ndjəpas men abused physically by their wives and children report these occurrances to their fellow initiates.

Similarly, the Spirit of an initiated man is endowed with such ritual potency that he can make extremely powerful curses. The power of these curses increases with each successive ritual promotion, and he can use his power of cursing to enforce his authority over his household. But so great is his innate ritual power that his wife and children can also swear curses on it, to coerce *him*. If, for instance, he is lazy his wife can swear a conditional curse upon his eating any food she produces; his children too can do the same with any food they produce. They can withdraw their labour, laying conditional curses upon collaborating with him in productive work. These curses, which are a privilege of the wives and children of initiated men, and represent a considerable domestic sanction over their husbands and fathers, are called *wasunggwulna*. If the man failed to respect such a curse, some member of his household, including possibly himself, would be afflicted with sickness. Women and their children can be virtually self-sufficient if necessary, because they can fish, trade the surplus fish for sago at the barter-markets, and so obtain a more or less entire diet. A man cannot subsist adequately even in the short term without the co-operation of his wife, because the only food he can obtain by himself is game. A lazy or exploitative husband, if he is an initiated man, finds himself quickly reduced by his family to a kind of domestic pariah, begging food from other households and scavenging around his ward for fallen coconuts and edible leaves (see Harrison 1985a; 1985b).

I might say also that most Avatip men admit, in private, to having told their wives initiatory secrets. It is part of the ethic of married life, a compromise with the values of everyday domesticity, that a man is expected to make his wife privy to the ritual secrets of his initiation level, and so confer on her a kind of honorary, sub-institutional membership of his ritual grade. No harm can come of it, men say, so long as their wives keep the knowledge to themselves. The spirits invoked in the cult would visit sickness on a woman or her children (or indeed her husband) if she were to publicise her knowledge of male initiatory secrets. But the spirits, men say, have no interest in what people merely *know*, but only in their *actions*, and would only punish someone who actually broadcast initiatory secrets in public. In effect, the wives of ritually senior men have – and are expected to have – greater knowledge of the cult secrets than junior male initiates and, alongside the formal ranking of men by initiatory grade, there exists a shadowy, informal ranking of their wives as well.

Funerary rites

High ritual status entitles a man to exercise, in ritual, real coercive powers and to have, at the end of his life, an elaborate funerary ceremony. When a scarified man dies and his mortuary payment is made (this may be a year or more after his death) his co-initiates stage a visitation to the village by the Ndakwul Wapi spirits. His subclan's ceremonial house is enclosed and the area around it put out of bounds to women and noninitiates as the men play the flutes inside. The Ndakwul Wapi come to grieve and pay their respects at the dead man's *mək*, the big funerary effigy on which his mortuary payment is displayed and presented to his matrikin in his domestic house. Once the matrikin have come and collected the shells and cash, and the effigy is bare, the dead man's womenfolk cook a few packets of a delicacy called *ndjətəp*. This is a mixture of sago and grated coconut boiled in small leaf parcels, and the women hang these titbits on the effigy as an offering to the Ndakwul Wapi, who will visit the house during the night. When it is dark, the initiated men begin gathering in the dead man's ceremonial house. All women and noninitiates are warned to stay indoors and keep silent, and the dead man's house is abandoned. The spirits start emerging from various ceremonial houses, moving through the village and converging on the dead initiate's house. They are named spirits of his own subclan, and of his mother's and wife's subclans, all coming from their respective ceremonial houses escorted by initiated men. Each spirit is a pair of six-foot long flutes, played in antiphony by two men standing face-to-face and revolving in a kind of slow *pas-de-deux* as they go along. The men call out to the women and children in the houses they pass, warning them not to look outside in case they see the spirits and die. As they go along, the spirits strew *ndjambi mi*, the flowers and leaves of their subclans' totemic plants, to mark their paths for everyone to see in the morning. So as to convince the women and children hiding indoors, the men call loudly to the spirits by their names, telling them to move along, reminding them how long the village is, how far it is to the dead man's house. Some of the men, as they pass by their own domestic houses, call to their wives for areca-nut for the spirit to chew. Older wives will call back to the passing spirit from inside their houses, telling it to be on its way and that they have no areca-nut to give it this time, the weather having been unseasonably poor.

Each party enters the house in turn, and starts up an enormous din inside, to suggest a violent physical struggle to restrain the distraught spirit. They jump up and down on the wooden floor in unison, shouting for the benefit of women and children: 'Stop it! stop it! You might break the floor!' They take a few slats from the women's hearths, and palm-spathe platters, and scatter them around the house. The spirit decorates the effigy with its subclan's totemic flowers, takes the offering of *ndjətəp* (which will be eaten back at the enclosure by the initiated men of its subclan) and the men call to it to be on its way. It ties a parting bouquet of *ndjambi mi* to the house ladder, and retraces its steps to its ceremonial house, strewing flowers as it goes. If it passes a house where a sister's child of its subclan lives, it attaches *ndjambi mi* to the ladder in farewell.

Once the Ndakwul Wapi are back in their ceremonial houses, the women and noninitiates are told that the spirits are no longer abroad and that they may leave their houses if they wish. The dead man's household return to their house and put it back in order. The initiated men spend the rest of the night playing the flutes in the enclosure.

All scarified men, irrespective of their ritual grade, are commemorated in this way after their deaths, by having the spirits that 'gored' them as novices pay their respects at their funerary effigies. If they are third-stage initiates, Ndumwi comes to pay her respects as well, and a brief version of her eponymous ritual is carried out. Third-stage initiates are also commemorated in a ceremony called the Veimba'angkw, or 'spear ceremony', which is held on the day after their death. This is an entirely public, secular and intentionally comic event. All subclans are paired in sets, in such a way that their respective sisters' children have an institutionalised joking relationship and form what I call joking divisions. The Veimba'angkw is staged by the dead man's joking division and its opposite partner. The men of his division erect a framework of poles by his subclan's ceremonial mound, and put on it a variety of everyday utensils. Each of these objects represents an admired quality or achievement the performers are attributing to the dead man. Taken together, they are a kind of visual summation of Avatip ideals of manhood. They are:

- A sago-pounder, canoe-paddle, axe, adze, machete, fishing-spear: his general industriousness and productivity.
- A crocodile-spear, a wood-tipped spear for warfare and hunting: his prowess as a hunter and fighter.
- A piece of firewood: his physical strength.
- A food basket, a palm-spathe platter, a rope for climbing areca- and coconut-palms: his generosity with food.
- A set of tally-sticks: his generosity toward his kin with shell-wealth for their bridewealth, mortuary and other payments.
- A stoppered bamboo tube: his capacity to keep his ritual and mythological knowledge secret.
- A third-stage initiate's shoulder-bag: his status as a Ndjəpas.
- A mosquito-whisk (used in shamanic ritual): if he was a shaman, his prowess at protecting the village from malicious spirits sent by enemy villages.
- A string of white chicken feathers: to represent his generosity with the sexual favours of his kinswomen. Each feather is supposed to represent a kinswoman he has flattered and smooth-talked into having an affair with one of his friends or age-mates, or ritual initiators. This is an ability men highly admire in each other.

The men of his joking-division each take one of these items and parade in single file around the ceremonial mound, each one in turn giving a long peroration on whatever quality of the dead man the object signifies. They challenge the men of the opposite division, daring them, if they think themselves the dead man's equals, to come forward and take the objects. They tell them: whoever thinks himself as good a hunter as the dead man, let him come and take the spear; whoever considers himself as generous, let him come and take the food-basket. The joking partners accept these challenges with good humour, and respond to them in a deliberately ridiculous way by each taking an entirely inappropriate object: a young boy takes the firewood representing the dead man's enormous strength; a small, ugly old man disfigured with ringworm takes the feathers standing for his finesse with women; a non-shaman takes the shamanic fly-whisk, and so on. All this clowning is greeted with gales of laughter by the large audience of women, children, and men of uninvolved joking divisions.

The men of the dead man's division boast extravagantly of his achievements with an air of aloof, derisive indifference toward the antics of their joking partners; while the opposite division, for all the highly ironic way they do it, honour him too in their exaggerated displays of their own gross deficiencies. But there are, I think, complex undertones in this ritual. What the dead man's joking division are claiming for him is the attainment of an absurdly over-stated, unattainable ideal of manhood; and the opposite division, by making themselves ridiculous for the audience's appreciation, are tacitly ridiculing these claims. In a sense, they are ridiculing the ideal itself, and the entire notion that only third-stage initiates, men with the necessary genealogical credentials, can be 'real' men. This is not an interpretation the villagers agree with. They say the ceremony is to honour a dead Ndəpas and the personal qualities they associate with Ndjəpas status. But I suggest the ceremony both celebrates these ideals, and very slightly and subtly, satirises them as well.

Simbuks and the *laki* divisions

Every Avatip male belongs to one of five ceremonial divisions, called *laki*. These divisions are grouped into ritual moieties called Warəman and Mbanggwəs. Mbanggwəs consists of three *laki* and Warəman of two.

The Warəman moiety is the 'elder brother' of Mbanggwəs, and when any initiatory ritual is held the novices of the Warəman moiety are initiated first. Every initiatory ritual consists of two phases: the first inducting the senior moiety and the second the junior one. Nowadays, the two initiations usually take place on the same day. In the past, when initiation rituals tended to be larger in scale, the two initiations required two separate performances of the same ritual and took place several months apart.

Some other Sepik peoples, the Iatmul and Ilahita Arapesh being perhaps the best-known examples, have ritual moiety systems in which the men of the two divisions initiate each other, and each moiety stands as 'elder brother' to the other in alternate generations (Bateson 1958: 244–6; Tuzin 1980). At Avatip, the ritual moieties do not have a relationship of this sort. Warəman and Mbanggwəs novices are initiated by the combined men of both moieties of the next senior ritual grade. It is ritual grades that initiate one another, not ritual moieties. It is possible that Avatip borrowed the notion of initiatory moieties from the Iatmul, but discarded the principle of alternating reciprocity because of its incompatibility with the overall emphasis of Avatip ritual. The main relationships stressed in Avatip ritual are those of hierarchy and differential seniority, rather than symmetry and equivalence.

Each *laki* is headed by an hereditary office-holder called a *simbuk*. These offices, which are equal in status, are the paramount positions of authority in the ritual system. They are vested in lineages and in theory pass down their senior lines of descent. Before an heir to a simbukship can succeed to it, he must be of the highest ritual grade, and these offices are in effect an elite subcategory of that grade. A simbukship is inherited on its holder's death either by his eldest son or, if the son is not yet fully initiated, by the simbuk's younger brother. If all else fails, his sister's son assumes the office; he, however, cannot pass it on to his own descendants because it is the property of his mother's lineage, and on his death the office either returns to his maternal lineage or goes to another sister's son. The moiety affiliations of the five *laki*, and the lineages owning the five associated simbukships, are given in Table 6.

The role of simbuks is to oversee the progress of the men of their *laki* through the initiatory system, administering magic to them at each successive initiation to promote their growth, strength and fighting spirit. In the past, simbuks were war-magicians, carrying out fight-magic for the men of their *laki* before headhunting raids. Each simbuk keeps in his house a *sokapi*, or Iatmul fire-basin. These are large, decorated clay bowls in which Iatmul women make their cooking-fires, and are a perfectly ordinary part of the domestic equipment of a Iatmul household. To the Manambu, they are the most potent and dangerous of all ritual sacra. It may seem odd that the ultimate symbols of ritual power and status in Manambu society are the domestic fire-basins used by Iatmul women for cooking. But to the Manambu these are potent symbols of the 'female' powers of feeding and nurturance which men arrogate to themselves in ritual, and they are so because they are specifically *Iatmul* symbols of those powers. They are owned only by simbuks, and used by them only in their magical rites. They are the focus of all their magical powers, and the Manambu believe that it would be death for anyone but a simbuk even to approach a *sokapi*.

There are, however, two exceptions to this. One is the simbuk's hereditary assistant. These offices, like simbukships themselves, are vested in lineages and are governed by the same rules of succession. A simbuk's assistant has two responsibilities. Firstly, there are episodes in initiation rituals when a simbuk becomes ritually too potent to be approached or spoken to by men ritually junior to him. His assistant is immune to these hazards, and it is his task to

Table 6. *The initiatory moiety and* laki *organisation*

Moiety	*Laki*	Office-holding lineage	Subclans from which members are drawn
Mbanggwəs	Nyakawlaki	Yiraman (Valik subclan)	Valik, Yimal, Nyakaw, Sarambusarak, Nanggwundaw, Wanəkaw Maliyaw
	Ndjimbər	Tanggwai (Ambasarak subclan)	Ambasarak, Sarambusarak, Nawik, Wopunamb
	Warəman 'senior'	Waikisuwi (Nggambak subclan)	Nggambak, Valik, Yimal, Makəm, Wanəkaw
Warəman	Pukandu	Malikəmban (Maliyaw subclan)	Maliyaw, Nyakaw, Sarambusarak, Nanggwundaw, Yimal
	Warəman 'junior'	Kwaru (Kambuli subclan)	Kambuli, Wopunamb, Waranggamb, Nambul, Sambəlap

Warəman 'senior' and 'junior' are two separate *laki* which have the same name for historical reasons. They are called 'elder' and 'younger brother' to distinguish them, since they are held respectively by senior and junior Nggəla'angkw lineages. Both are distinct from the initiatory moiety also called Warəman.

communicate between the simbuk and the junior men and convey to them the simbuk's instructions. Secondly, when a simbuk becomes old and unable to carry out the more physically demanding of his ritual duties, he delegates these to his assistant.

The only other person immune to the simbuk's *sokapi* is his senior wife. If, for instance, a simbuk dies and the fire-basin needs to be transported some distance to the new simbuk's house, it cannot be carried through the village but must be taken by canoe by the new simbuk and his senior wife. While they are transporting it, the entire population of the village – women, children, and men irrespective of ritual grade – must hide in their domestic houses from the *sokapi's* dangerous power. The simbuk's senior wife actually plays an essential role in some of his most important rites, and he cannot carry out the full range of duties of his office without her. At the start of each agricultural year, the simbuks hold a ceremony to promote the growth of the coming yam crop. Because of its associations with yam-fertility the ceremony is inaugurated by the two Wuluwi Nyawi simbuks, but all five simbuks take part in it. Each simbuk and his senior wife prepare a meal of bespelled yam soup in their domestic house, and all the children born during the previous year are brought and fed by them to make them strong and promote their growth. All the village's children who undergo this rite in the same year form an age-grade. Age-mates of the same sex remain, all their lives, each other's close companions and commensals (see Harrison 1982).

The simbuk also sprays the children with a bespelled mixture of chewed areca-nut and ginger and, for the male children, this is their formal induction into a *laki*. *Laki* is the Manambu term for ginger, and each of these ceremonial divisions has a particular variety of ginger as its eponymous emblem and as a major ingredient in all the magic performed by its simbuk. Fathers generally enter their sons in their own *laki*, but these divisions, and the initiatory moieties as well, very largely cross-cut descent group structure.

Most Avatip subclans own specialised forms of non-lethal sorcery, known generically as *ndjambi*, which cause disfiguring sores or the paralysis of limbs. Men put these spells on their areca-palms and other fruit-bearing trees to protect them from theft, together with a knotted leaf to warn would-be thieves of the spell's presence. Simbuks own a particularly powerful spell of this sort, which can kill, as well as other sorts of lethal sorcery associated with their war-magic. They themselves are considered immune to all indigenous forms of Manambu sorcery, lethal and non-lethal. The spirit-beings they control, which are called Wakən Maiyir, protect them 'like the walls of a house' so long as they carry out their magical rites correctly. By being invulnerable to sorcery, except through their own misdoing, simbuks are in effect exempt from a major sanction which operates, as it does in many Melanesian societies, to maintain the political equality of adult males (Fortune 1932: 175–6; Mitchell 1978; Young 1971: 127). A similar mechanism promoting equality is the belief that anyone who killed a fellow-villager by sorcery would inevitably be killed in revenge by his victim's ghost. Simbuks, however, are immune – again, so long as they carry out their rites correctly – not only from sorcery but from the vengeful ghosts of anyone they themselves kill with sorcery. As one of my informants put it, 'a simbuk could kill me and I (i.e. my ghost) would never be able to take revenge'. These beliefs do not give simbuks authority in everyday contexts, in the sense of a right to command others and to expect their obedience. In secular life they have no more or fewer rights than other men; what they have are more powerful sanctions to defend these rights. Their food-gardens are better protected from theft, and ordinary men are especially reluctant to make adulterous advances toward their wives. Adultery is a very popular, if risky, pastime at Avatip, but men say they 'fear the wives of simbuks', and treat them with caution and reserve.

Male initiation

In short, simbuks are in some respects set permanently above the general egalitarian ethic which prevails in secular life at Avatip, and accorded a specially 'sacred' status. If anyone were to strike a simbuk, the men of that *laki* would punish the offender with a house-ransack. Any kind of physical insult or injury to a simbuk, the villagers say, lets loose the spirits he controls. It is a highly dangerous event for the entire village and could cause the simbuk himself to sicken and die, and it has to be redressed in a complex ceremony called 'covering up the Wakən Maiyir' (*wakən rambuna*). The most common mishap which occasions this ritual is when a simbuk is seen to capsize in a canoe. All the villagers have these accidents now and then and they are an occupational hazard of life on the river. If no-one actually witnesses the capsize, there is no danger and no need for the ritual. But if the simbuk's mishap is *seen* by someone, people say it is as if the *sokapi* itself had fallen in the water.

Essentially, Wakən Rambuna is an expensive feast mounted by the sim- buk's *laki* for the entire village. All the initiated men of this ceremonial division prepare, in the simbuk's ceremonial house, a large quantity of yam soup and meat, while their wives make sago pancakes in their houses. Once the food is ready, the third-stage initiates of the host division eat first, and then have some of the food taken to their wives and families (and also widows, in the case of dead members). They then call the men of the four guest divisions to come and receive their share. The divisions whose simbukships are owned by Wuluwi-Nyawi seat themselves on the ground to one side of the ceremonial house, and those with simbukships owned by Nggəla'angkw sit to the other side. The men of each division sit in a queue facing the building in order of ritual seniority, with the third-stage initiates at the front and the uninitiated members at the rear. The third-stage guests are served first. When they have eaten, or 'struck their teeth' (*nimbi viyanandi*) into the food, they are given a further serving which they pass to the second-stage initiates behind them; these men then eat, and so it continues until every grade has received, and eaten, food from the grade senior to it. Ideally, there should be enough for every man to take some home for his wife and children. At the ceremony I saw performed in June 1978, held by the Ndjimbər division, there was not, and the guest divisions complained later among themselves that the hosts had sent too much to their own families. At least one of these divisions made a careful tally of the food it got, and plans, when its turn comes to host the ritual, to humiliate the Ndjimbər men, by presenting them with exactly the same amount while giving generously to all the other divisions. In theory, the whole village should receive food: except for those men of the host division who are of less than third-stage status, and their wives and children.

This is the only ceremony in which the entire system of ritual categories is displayed at once. It is the men's response to a perceived threat to this system, and it is essentially, in its overtly diagrammatic layout and the complicated order of food-distribution, a publicly enacted restoration of the complete structure of ritual statuses throughout the total community. One of its notable features is the way in which differences in ritual status between men are extended, to a degree, to their wives and families: men of lower ritual status receive food *after* the wives and children of their ritual seniors. Like the wives of simbuks, women are partially equated in status with their husbands.

When a new simbuk takes office, there is an installation ritual in which he makes fire on the hearth of his ceremonial house, and a special funerary rite is held on a simbuk's death. All the initiated men gather in his ceremonial house and chant a long song from the days of headhunting, celebrating the simbuk as a homicide. Two third-stage initiates from each of the five divisions then dress themselves in fighting regalia and bespell themselves with war-magic, which makes them ritually dangerous to women and children. They then stage a mock raid on his house to 'capture' his body from his wailing womenfolk and other kin, who scatter as they burst in. They carry the simbuk's body to his ceremonial house and take it around the building's ceremonial mound where, in the past, the men of his division would bury the heads they took in war. Finally, they hand the body over to the burial party. The men who carry this out are called 'dogs' (*as*) and they imitate the baying of dogs when they rush the house: in the old days war-magicians seem to have been spoken of as standing to the fighters of their divisions, metaphorically, as hunters to their hunting dogs.

Simbuks make marriage alliances with one another, and their immediate agnatic kin groups are linked together in a highly exclusive network of affinal and uterine ties (see Figure 1). Simbuks do this for two main reasons. Firstly, they try to avoid receiving wives from men lower in status than themselves, so as not to obligate themselves and come under the authority of fathers-in-law who are their ritual inferiors. Secondly, simbuks are always concerned strongly with safeguarding the succession of their lineal heirs for, as I shall show later, frequent attempts are made to usurp simbukships and succession disputes are common. By marrying the sister or daughter of another simbuk, a man ensures that his heirs have simbuks as their maternal kinsmen, who can teach them the highly secret lore of the office should he die before doing so himself. The community is in this way divided, though the villagers do not openly acknowledge it, into two partly hereditary and semi-endogamous status-categories, as high-status kin groups ally themselves against potential challengers of, so to speak, 'non-simbukly' descent.

The attributes of this office, and the exceptionally high ritual status it has for the villagers, are reminiscent of some of the more purely ceremonial features of Oceanic chieftainship. In the Wakən Rambuna ceremony, there is perhaps even the faint echo of the economic 'redistributive' functions associated with chiefs. But though simbuks are acknowledged as paramount authorities in the ritual system, their office in itself gives them no political authority outside the

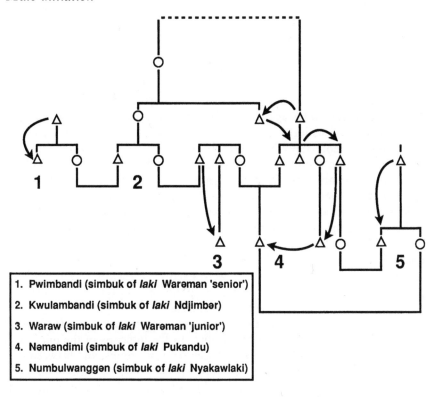

1. Pwimbandi (simbuk of *laki* Wareman 'senior')
2. Kwulambandi (simbuk of *laki* Ndjimbər)
3. Waraw (simbuk of *laki* Wareman 'junior')
4. Nəmandimi (simbuk of *laki* Pukandu)
5. Numbulwanggən (simbuk of *laki* Nyakawlaki)

Fig. 1 Affinal and kin ties between current and recent simbuks, showing lines of succession.

ritual sphere. Some simbuks assume office in their twenties, an age at which all men are political nonentities. To have political influence outside of ritual contexts a simbuk must, like any other man, achieve it by spending his middle years proving himself in the highly competitive day-to-day world of Avatip politics: which is to say, in the debating system. To men who have established themselves as political leaders, the 'ascribed' ritual authority of simbuks is, potentially, a threat to their own 'achieved' influence and prestige. There is a good deal of covert – and sometimes explicit – concern among non-simbuks that the latters' powers must remain confined to ritual. There are, for instance, legends known by everyone at Avatip of simbuks having been assassinated in the past by their own kinsmen for becoming 'despots' and exacting food, wives and other tribute from their fellow villagers under the threat of sorcery. The circumstantial details these stories contain suggest very strongly that they are based on real events. They may even be distorted accounts of unsuccessful attempts by simbuks to establish themselves in some sort of legitimately 'chiefly' role. But these speculations aside, the legends are quite clearly egalitarian 'counter-charters', laying down the limits of simbuks' powers and the penalties they can expect if they overstep them.

Conclusion

All of Avatip ritual organisation is pervaded by ascribed inequalities of status. Within the subclan or lineage, men's ritual grade membership is determined by their genealogical seniority. Within the clan or clan-pair, there is the ceremonial ranking, theoretically hereditary, of its descent groups. And within the total community, there are the hereditary simbuks, who comprise both a paramount initiatory grade and, together with their respective lines of succession, a society-wide ritual elite of close kin and affines.

This entire structure emerges into an approximation of full institutional reality only in the performance of ritual. Outside of ritual contexts, it exists largely as an ideology only; that is, as a conceptual or ideal system of social relations. Initiatory rituals are the periodic 'living' of it, by the whole community, in social action. If it were lived permanently, Avatip would probably be a small-scale ranked or chiefly polity of some type, such as exist in a number of other lowland Melanesian societies.

The ideology associated with the ritual system is a powerful one, for men at least, and motivates all of Avatip politics. In the intervals of the initiatory cycle, there is intense competition between descent groups, and between the men leading them, to be legitimised in future rituals, when the nascent outlines of hereditary stratification will briefly crystallise as real forms of action, as having high ascribed status. What prevents these structures from emerging fully, or permanently, is that competition for high status in ritual is institutionalised in the secular political life of the community. The disputes are carried out and resolved by means of established procedures which provide ambitious men with an institutionalised means of becoming important political figures. These men are the actual holders of power in secular life and are leaders by achievement. Some of them are also simbuks, or other men with ascribed authority in the ritual system. Many are men wishing to acquire such status for themselves and for the groups they represent. Structures of ascribed status are brought cyclically into existence in rituals, only to collapse again in competition between groups and their self-made leaders.

Conflicts of this sort are a recurrent, in fact integral, feature of social process in the community. But they become especially frequent and intense in the years leading up to a major initiation ritual. When preparations get underway for any major ritual, its senior and junior owners begin struggling for important positions in it, because the performance of the ritual will validate their order of ceremonial rank for many years to come. The incidence of these disputes, in other words, is tied closely to the phases of the generation-long initiatory cycle. The approach of a major ritual sets in motion a complex series of political conflicts within the group owning it; once the ritual has been held, and the rank order of its owners ritually confirmed and established for the time being, these conflicts abate, perhaps for many years, only to re-emerge as the next performance of the ritual comes around. In the following chapters, I turn to these cyclical processes of competition, to the procedures by which these conflicts are carried out, the strategies that groups and their leaders use, and to the long-term goals they are seeking.

6

Treading elder brothers underfoot

Introduction

In a classic paper comparing the political systems of Melanesia and Polynesia, Sahlins (1963) identified Big Men – financial transactors and entrepreneurs – as the quintessentially Melanesian type of traditional leader. But more recently a number of authors have suggested that Melanesian patterns of leadership are rather more diverse than Sahlins' argument implies (Allen 1984; Chowning 1979; Douglas 1979; Godelier 1986). In particular, it has become evident that the control of knowledge is an important basis of leadership in some Melanesian societies, and that leaders in these societies differ from the Big Men described by Sahlins. Lindstrom, for instance, has suggested an ideal-typical distinction between 'wealth-based' and 'knowledge-based' Melanesian polities, arguing that in the latter

[w]here men achieve power by knowledge alone, control of its production, exchange and consumption is (rather than merely serves) political praxis. (Lindstrom 1984: 305)

Avatip approximates very closely to Lindstrom's 'knowledge-based' type of Melanesian polity, and in this chapter I discuss the significance of ritual knowledge as the key resource of leaders in Avatip society, and the ways in which processes of political competition revolve around the transmission and control of this knowledge. The first part of the chapter deals with the transmission of hereditary mythology and magic within the subclan, and the implicit – and sometimes explicit – competition between subclan-agnates for the control of this lore. I then describe the way in which this knowledge is also transmitted between subclans along ties of marriage alliance, showing how this creates opportunities for ambitious men to extend their authority beyond their own descent groups.

My aim is to try to answer a question which Lindstrom's argument implicitly raises: that is, the nature of the relationship between knowledge and wealth as political resources. It is not enough to divide Melanesian political systems into different types. One must also seek whether underlying similarities between them exist, similarities that might lead to transformations of one into the other.

114

This stricture applies particularly to Godelier's (1986) important study of leadership among the Baruya. Godelier argues that Big Men are in fact an unusual and quite specialised variant of a more general category of Melanesian political figure, which he calls the Great Man. Great Men include not only the classic Big Men as described by Sahlins, but also war-leaders, ritual specialists, skilful hunters and perhaps other sorts of prominent individuals as well. Big Men, Godelier argues, only arise in those Melanesian societies in which the production and exchange of wealth, primarily as bride-wealth, is essential for the reproduction of kinship relations. Where it is not, as in those societies with marriage-systems based on sister-exchange, then other types of Great Men will operate.

But a problem with Godelier's argument is that it seems simply to fragment Melanesian leadership patterns into a collection of disparate types, and it is difficult to see any connection between the different sorts of Great Men he identifies, except that they are all in some sense men with influence or important reputations. If this variety of apparently dissimilar patterns exists, it is important, again, to try to discover whether common patterns underlie them.

The basic argument that I want to make is that ritual knowledge in Avatip society is, in effect, reproductive capital; like bridewealth and other affinal payments – or rather, *together* with them – it operates as a circulating fund of reproductive potential. I have argued that the division of ceremonial functions on which Avatip groups base their status is a transformation of the same structures which, in other Melanesian polities, give rise to Big Men: the essential difference is in the content or media of the political transactions, which at Avatip take the form of ritual knowledge and ritual services rather than material wealth. My argument in this chapter is that the power of Avatip ritual leaders is indeed based, like that of Big Men according to Godelier, on their control of wealth essential for social reproduction. It is simply that the nature of this 'wealth' is defined differently from those Melanesian societies in which Big Men prevail.

Teaching and learning esoteric myth

To earn a reputation in debating, a man must master the formal oratorical language used in debates, and learn secret mythology (*sakima'andj*) from established experts in return for gifts and services. Men who are important figures in debating are the political leaders in Avatip society, because of the key roles they play in conflicts between groups. It is they who mobilise groups to compete for ceremonial rights, and who represent their groups in those disputes.

Learning secret mythology is a prerogative of adult men. If a man is the last surviving male of his subclan or lineage, and there are no men able or willing to inherit his knowledge, he may teach it to his wife, or to his sister or daughter so that it does not die with him. There were two such women at Avatip in the 1970s, the last repositories of an extinct lineage's esoteric lore. In time, they expect to teach it to that lineage's inheritors. In practice, many men share their knowledge with their wives. But only men may act independently to seek out knowledge and establish formal learning relationships with experts.

Teaching and learning myth are thought to be potentially dangerous to the teacher, his pupil and to their close kin. All teaching takes place in privacy, either in the bush or, more commonly, in the pupil's house after he has had his household leave it for a few hours. The pupil must present his teacher with a payment, within the next few months, consisting usually of one shell valuable and the carcass of a wild pig. The teacher distributes some of the meat to the rest of his subclan, because the lore he has taught is the whole subclan's property. But the rest of the payment is his. The amount of myth taught for that payment is, within certain limits, a matter for the teacher to decide. For a small and minor magical spell, a single shell valuable is usually enough. For teaching an extensive and particularly powerful body of knowledge, such as *sokapima'andj*, the lore connected with the office of simbuk, the equivalent of a bridewealth payment is required. It takes many teaching sessions, spread over many years, for a man to become an expert in myth. On average, the total expenses involved are between five and ten pigs and the same number of valuables. In many cases, the teacher also gives the novice advice on debating technique. Two things are especially emphasised: the importance of keeping a level head and cool temper in debates, and the need to stick to one's argument in the face of one's opponents' attempts to create distractions with false or irrelevant issues.

The payments the teacher receives are not described as fees but as propitiatory offerings (*va'al*) to the totemic ancestors referred to in the myths and to the ghosts of the descent group to which the myths belong. Too long a delay of the offering would cause disorders in nature: floods, storms and the like, depending on the type of esoterica divulged. It would also bring affliction on the pupil's children, or on the pupil himself, his wife or even the teacher. The ghosts and spirits to which the offering is made are conceived as, in an important sense, immanent in the actual words, particularly the secret names, spoken by the teacher. The expression used to describe a payment for myth is 'he makes an offering to the myth he has received' (*kwurndəl sakima'andjək va'al andaka kwurnand*). If a man forgets any of the secret names he has learned, he can ask his teacher to impart them again and does not need to make a second payment. The learner's payments give him the permanent right to know the lore, and are not charges for the teacher's services.

The villagers say that a man who knows the secret names of totemic ancestors comes to have special, close ties with those beings. When a yam magician eats, the spirits of the yams eat with him. The spirits of rain invisibly share the meals of the rain-magician. An expert in myth and magic has spirits as his familiars and commensals, and their identities become to some extent equated with his. The accumulation of ritual knowledge is thought of as a kind of augmentation of the Spirit, in which spirit beings become added on to, or incorporated into, a man's own identity as supernumerary selves or aspects of the self and their powers of magical agency become *his* powers. Conversely, there is a strong notion that teaching knowledge involves an almost physical depletion of the teacher, a kind of exhaustion or diminution of his life-force.

This privileged contact with spirits is expected eventually to exact a price. Men with a great knowledge of myth are said to age rapidly and become senile before their time. The symptoms are palsy, asthma and confused, rancorous speech in debates: 'their minds no longer understand; they speak as though mad' (*mawul ma'an wak; kwam təna pək mbulanandi*). Once these aberrations start, it is assumed that the supernatural powers the expert harbours have begun finally to debilitate him. His political career is brought to an abrupt end by his juniors, who prevent him from ever again speaking in debates, and hustle him from the debating-ground if he tries to do so. The belief that leaders are destined for that somewhat Faustian end provides the pretext under which they can when necessary be legitimately removed and replaced by more effective successors.

About a fifth of all adult men never learn any esoteric mythology at all, because of the associated risks. There are many more who, for the same reason, never learn any more than an insignificant amount. Such men say they are poor hunters, and could not be certain of providing wild pigs quickly enough to forestall affliction falling on their households. To become an expert in myth takes courage, ambition, and prowess in the supremely 'male' occupation of hunting, and its reward, for a time, is personal prestige and authority.

Debating-'simbuks'

In debates these experts are called simbuk. This is an honorific extension of the term for the ritual officials discussed earlier. The villagers distinguish this metaphorical sense of the term from its literal one, saying that important debaters are really only 'like simbuks' (*simbuk kətək*), in that they too are leaders and important men. To distinguish them from these prominent debaters, 'real' simbuks are sometimes called *sokapindu* ('fire-basin men') or *lakisokapindu* ('ginger-and-fire-basin men'). The status of debating-simbuk, unlike that of simbuk proper, is not formally hereditary and is not an office. A man can be considered more or less of a 'simbuk' in debates and there are no fixed limits on the number of men eligible to earn reputations in debating.

Let me try to make quite clear the distinction between the roles of debating-simbuks, or orators as I shall sometimes call them, and the roles of men of senior grades in the initiatory cult. These roles are often, though by no means necessarily or always, held by the same individuals, but they are nevertheless quite distinct to the villagers and must be distinguished analytically. A man's membership in an initiatory grade is an ascribed and compulsory status determined in a more or less automatic way simply by his genealogical standing in his descent group. On his promotion into a particular grade, he learns various sorts of secrets relating to the rituals of that grade: for instance, that the Ndakwul Wapi spirits are actually bamboo flutes, that the Ndumwi spirit is impersonated by a kind of puppet, and all sorts of other secret details of correct procedure and protocol in the relevant rituals. This knowledge gives him considerable authority in actual performances of the rituals but, for reasons discussed in the previous chapter, this authority exists primarily in the context of initiatory rituals themselves.

The role of orator, on the other hand, is an achieved status open in principle to any adult man who wishes to seek it. The secret knowledge he must learn is entirely distinct from the knowledge of secret ritual procedures a man acquires in his initiations in the men's cult. An orator's knowledge is of secret cosmogonic *myths* and of the secret names of the totemic ancestors figuring in the myths, including the mythology of the creation of men's initiation rituals. That is, his special expertise is in the mythical 'charters' for the rituals and for the hereditary functions and privileges of subclans in the rituals. The mythology is never taught in the context of initiation rituals, and to learn it, a man must be an adept hunter, and act on his own private initiative to solicit knowledge from established orators in return for gifts of meat and wealth. In many cases, as I shall show, he must negotiate personal marriage alliances with such men in order to establish teacher–pupil relationships with them. An orator's central role is to use his knowledge of myth to engage successfully in disputes with rival groups over claims to ritual privileges. Finally, the knowledge itself is only a necessary condition, not a sufficient one, for recognition as an orator: an orator must be more than simply expert in myth, but actually efficacious in the competitive arena of debates and this, as I show in the following chapter, can require skill in bribing his opponents, subverting their allies and all sorts of other political tactics.

Older men say that in the past, access to secret myth was more restricted than it is now, and that there were fewer debating-simbuks. They speak of there usually having been only one such figure per subclan, and their descriptions of the traditional status of these leaders suggest that it resembled an office more closely than it does nowadays. An orator could expect his younger agnates to supply him with regular gifts of food, and with special help with tasks such as gardening and house-building. He was entitled to these privileges because of his role as repository of the group's myths and defender of the group's ceremonial rights in debates. If it is true that orators had these privileges, they do not have them nowadays; they do not receive, or expect to receive, food gifts or labour from their juniors.

Table 7. *Numbers of orators per subclan in 1978*

Number of orators	Subclans
0	Makəm, Nambul
1	Sambəlap, Nyakaw, Nanggwundaw, Wanəkaw, Nawik, Waranggamb
2	Nggambak
3	Wopunamb, Kambuli
4	Ambasarak, Valik
5	Yimal
6	Maliyaw, Sarambusarak

There is, in fact, circumstantial evidence to support my older informants' statements. Shell valuables have become far more easily obtainable than they were in the past, particularly since the 1950s, and the quantity of these valuables in circulation in the village has greatly increased. I might also mention that before pacification, the risk of ambush discouraged hunting, and limited the opportunities to hunt because of the need to first organise an armed party. Nowadays, hunting is free from these complications and has also become more efficient with the introduction of the shot-gun. In short, it is far easier nowadays for a man to obtain the wherewithal to learn myth; and it seems likely that it has become easier than it was in the old days for a man to earn the status of debating-simbuk. If the numbers of men competent in myth have increased, these men do not have the same monopoly of myth as their traditional counterparts presumably did, and therefore cannot command the same privileges.

In 1978 there were thirty-nine men generally acknowledged as debating-simbuks at Avatip. The number of orators per subclan varied from zero to six, roughly in proportion to the size of those groups.

The villagers consider it appropriate only for older men to be prominent orators. There are two other terms for orators, less commonly used than simbuk, and they are both synonyms for elderly men: *sapukwandu* (the old men, or elders) and *rəkasəp* (literally, 'the dry skins', referring to the dull skins of old men). Any young children a man has are supposed to be especially at risk from the hazards associated with learning myth. Young married men therefore tend to postpone learning much mythology until middle age, when their children are mature and more resistant to those dangers.

In 1978 the average age of the thirty-nine debating-simbuks was about fifty-three. Their estimated ages, and their age-statuses within their own lineages, are given in Tables 9 and 10, which show that debating-simbuks tend to be the oldest, or among the oldest, men of their lineages.

There is also an expectation that orators will be genealogically senior men of their lineages. Men of senior genealogical generations, and of senior patrilines,

Table 8. *Estimated ages of orators*

Age group	Number of orators
60–64	10
55–59	6
50–54	5
45–49	11
40–44	5
35–39	2
Total	39

Table 9. *Age-statuses of orators within own lineages*

Number of living male non-orators older than each orator within own lineage	Number of orators
0	21
1	4
2	9
3	5
Total	39

are the focus of greater expectations than their juniors. If such men do not fulfil these expectations, a nominal and sometimes sardonic respect still tends to be paid to their seniority:

Kumbwiwul, a man of about sixty, is the genealogically most senior man of his lineage. But he seems slow-witted and is quite ignorant of mythology. The orator of his lineage is Wundikas, his coeval and classificatory younger brother. Whenever Wundikas attends a debate, or a recitation of the totemic song-cycles which accompany many ceremonial events, he makes a point of bringing Kumbwiwul along and seating him on a large stool in a conspicuous position near himself and among the other prominent orators. But the incongruous attention paid to Kumbwiwul serves only to advertise his ignorance of myth, and places him in an unfavourable comparison with Wundikas. Wundikas permits himself a little private amusement at these scenes. He jokes that when he goes to debates in other villages, he is so solicitous of Kumbwiwul that he always takes him in the same canoe as himself: but really only so as to have Kumbwiwul paddle him there.

It is important for a debating-simbuk to teach his subclan's esoterica to as many of his subclan-agnates as are willing, in order to insure the lore against loss and to maintain the capacity of the subclan to defend itself in debates. But the sons of debating-simbuks, particularly eldest sons, are in a favoured position to inherit their knowledge. A leader tries to pass on as much of his knowledge as possible to his eldest son at an early age, or rather to the eldest of his sons who shows signs of having a good memory and an aptitude for public speaking. He may teach some of his knowledge to all of his sons who display these abilities. But it is the eldest son, all else being equal, who inherits the whole of his father's expertise. After the father's death, the eldest son then has a responsibility to teach his younger brothers. Leaders try to teach their sons before they marry, because that avoids the dangers which, once they marry, will threaten their children. Paradoxically, an unmarried youth is better placed to learn this lore than a married man a few years his senior. Once a man marries, it may be twenty years or more before he can start learning myth

Table 10. *Close agnatic ties between orators*

Close agnates who are/were debating-simbuks	Number of cases
F, B, FB, FBS	3
F, FB, FBS	5
F, B	3
FB, FBS	1
F	4
B	1
B, FB	1
FB	1
None of the above	4
Total	23

without risk to his children. Clearly, an effect of this belief is that by discouraging young married men from learning mythology, it reduces the challenge they could pose to their seniors. Unmarried youths are too young and too firmly under their fathers' control to threaten their authority.

In effect, leaders tend to prepare their sons from their teens to succeed to their status and, as a result, the future leaders of a subclan or lineage, or at least the sets of siblings from which they will emerge, are usually known well in advance, while the men are still in their twenties or thirties. I was unable to collect the full genealogies of all of the thirty-nine current debating-simbuks, but Table 10 gives the agnatic relationships of twenty-three of these men with previous or current orators of their lineages within the range of first cousin.

About two-thirds of these debating-simbuks are themselves sons of debating-simbuks. If a lineage has more than one orator, they are likely to be brothers or first cousins, usually with the senior of them being the pre-eminent figure and the teacher of his junior co-leaders. If he dies without teaching his sons, his juniors are expected to teach his sons before their own, so as to prepare the elder brother's sons to succeed to the leadership of the descent group after they die.

These patterns of inheritance are evident in Table 11, which shows that the most common sources from which orators learn their descent groups' myths are their fathers, and their actual and classificatory elder brothers and fathers' younger brothers. I should point out that some of the teachers were still active when these data were collected, so that they appear in the table both as teachers and as pupils; and that more teachers than pupils are represented, because some of the latter acquired their knowledge from more than one person.

There are a number of factors which tend to enable the close agnates of

121

Table 11. *Sources from which 23 orators learned
their own subclans' mythology*

Learned from [a]	Number of cases
F	8
eB	2
FeB	3
FFeBSS	1
Subclan 'eB'	1
FFFyBSSS	2
Subclan 'FeB'	1
FyB	6
FFyBS	2
FFFyBSS	2
FFFFyBSSS	1
ZH	1
FFZS	1
FFBDS	1

[a] These kin types in some cases include several
individuals.

Table 12. *Genealogical status of orators within own
lineages*

Number of living male non-orators genealogically senior to each orator within own lineage	Number of orators
0	25
1	4
3	1
4	1
7	2
8	4
10	2
Total	39

orators, especially their sons, to become experts in myth at relatively small
expense. When a man teaches his own son or brother, it is not right for him to
keep the payment of valuables, and he surreptitiously returns them to his
pupil. That subterfuge is supposed to escape the notice of the ghosts and
spirits. Secondly, unmarried men are allowed to learn myth for smaller
payments than married men, and often without any payment at all, because
they have no children to be at risk. Both conventions contribute to a tendency

Table 13. *Ritual status of orators*

Ritual grade	Total membership	Number of orators
Third (simbuks)	5	4
Third (non-simbuks)	43	22
Second	133	13
First and uninitiated	490	0
Total	671	39

for leadership of the subclan to remain, over the generations, under the control of certain patrilines.

Because promotion in the men's cult is determined by genealogy, there are close connections between agnatic seniority, ritual status and access to esoteric myth. In theory a man cannot learn secret myths concerning any initiatory rituals into which he has not yet been inducted. This rule is applied strictly only to the younger members of each initiatory grade. There are, for instance, many older second-stage initiates who have been taught all the secret myths concerning third-stage initiation, and some of them are renowned and powerful orators. But, 'officially', they do not have that knowledge, and it is more difficult for a ritually junior man than for a ritually senior one to gain a reputation as a debating-simbuk. The genealogical and ritual status of the thirty-nine debating-simbuks are given in Tables 13 and 14.

Clearly, there are many ritually senior men who are politically insignificant but, the higher a man's ritual status, the greater the likelihood of his being a debating-simbuk. This is especially so in the case of the men at the very top of the ritual hierarchy: the holders of the five offices of 'real' simbuk. Young simbuks are expected and encouraged by their kinsmen to become important orators, and are in fact usually advantageously placed by their kin ties to do so in time. Rising debating-simbuks tend to attach themselves to 'real' simbuks as sons-in-laws and the alliance network of these ritual office-holders has around it, as it were, a penumbra of ambitious orators linked into it by affinal and matrilateral ties. Simbuks gain in this way powerful allies, who can defend their mythological entitlements to these offices when they are challenged in debates. What the debating-experts gain, in turn, is admission to the high-status kin network of the simbuks and – in not a few cases – the possibility, or hope, of obtaining a simbukship for their own descendants.

Young simbuks therefore grow up among senior kinsmen who are either simbuks themselves, or established experts in myth and debating, or both simultaneously. From their late teens onwards, those men give them an extensive training in myth and groom them to earn themselves reputations in the debating system. Over the past two generations, there have been twelve simbuks at Avatip and all but two or three are, or became during their lives, major political figures as well as ritual ones.

The succession dispute over the Waikisuwi simbukship

But some of these men were not simbuks by hereditary right. They were men who usurped these offices from their rightful successors, and were able to do so *because* they had first become powerful orators. One such figure was the father of Pwimbandi. Pwimbandi himself was a man of about fifty in 1978, and one of the most important political figures at Avatip, being both a simbuk and one of the community's most renowned experts in myth and debating. He belongs to the junior branch of the lineage Waikisuwi of the subclan Nggambak. In 1978 Waikisuwi had fifty-seven members, twenty-two in its senior branch and thirty-five in the junior. Over the past three generations the size of the senior branch has remained more or less static, while Pwimbandi's branch has flourished. This trend seems likely to continue, because the adult men of the junior segment are comparable in age with their seniors but have nearly twice as many sons. The two branches have lived apart since the break-up of Old Avatip, the seniors based at Yentshanggai and most of the juniors at Yawmbak. Pwimbandi himself, however, lives at Yentshanggai, in a small, rather isolated ward of his own. He has had Kumbunwali, the ceremonial house of Nggambak subclan, built in his ward next to his own house. Because of its location, Pwindimi has the building virtually to himself, as a kind of private status symbol, and other men of his subclan sometimes complain that he treats it as his own personal property.

The simbukship he holds was held by the senior segment until two generations ago. It then lapsed into the junior branch, to Pwimbandi's father (see Figure 2). That is, Pwimbandi's father was not born a simbuk, but was a self-made orator who had taken over the simbukship in the course of a succession dispute, and this dispute was still continuing a generation later. In the mid-1960s Pwimbandi began bestowing large numbers of names associated with the simbukship upon the children of his segment. The seniors, growing alarmed at this, started asking him what his intentions were. Pwimbandi tried to allay their suspicions, telling them it was simply that his branch had had many children recently and therefore needed more names than usual.

But as the years went by, he began referring to his segment as a separate lineage, called Yambundǝmeli. He claimed it was incorrect to refer to it as part of Waikisuwi, because Waikisuwi was the name of the senior branch only. He denied the genealogical tie between the two groups and announced the existence of three previously secret human ancestors in the upper reaches of his pedigree. His subclan's totemic myths were also, he disclosed, incorrect on a number of small points. It was true that the simbukship was created by totemic

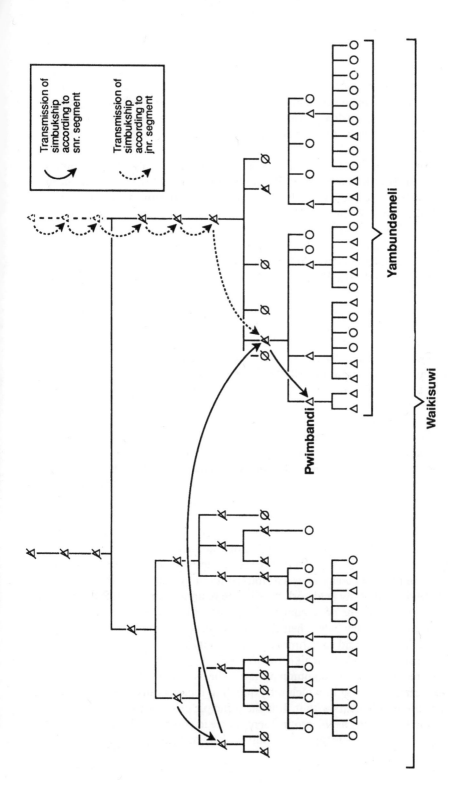

Fig. 2 Fission of the lineage Waikisuwi.

ancestors of Waikisuwi, just as the myths say. But these ancestors ceded the office, and all the names linked with it, to the totemic ancestors of Yambundəmeli, his own lineage. The office had been the property of his lineage ever since, and had passed down its most senior patriline for seven generations until himself. On his death, it would be held either by his younger brother or by his eldest son.

At this point the two groups began competing openly for the names connected with the simbukship. By the time I arrived, this contest had been going on for some ten years, and many of the two groups' children were namesakes. But Pwimbandi's party had gained the upper hand, as he presumably had foreseen, because it was reproducing at a faster rate.

The two groups were meeting once or twice a year to discuss their dispute, each side repeatedly demanding that the other relinquish (*kwutanggərana*, to bypass or avoid) the duplicated names. At one meeting I attended, one of the seniors asked Pwimbandi: 'Why are you trying to take all the important names and leave us with just a few worthless ones?' He insisted that the names of all the children of the two sides be counted publicly, and it was discovered that many of the children on Pwimbandi's side had seven or more names. Pwimbandi agreed under pressure to hand over certain names, but there were still a number of crucial ones that neither side was prepared to give up.

The meeting left the issue of the fission still unresolved. The seniors insisted they were all a single lineage under the name Waikisuwi, and that Pwimbandi should stop trying to secede. Pwimbandi responded by challenging them to tell him the names (which he had not revealed) of his three secret ancestors: how could his elder brothers be certain that the two groups are one lineage, if they are ignorant of the junior branch's ancestry? The point he was making in this challenge was a complex one. What he was implying was that the names of these ancestors were names used in the highly secret magic associated with the simbukship. In effect, he was reminding his seniors that none of them were capable of carrying out the duties of the simbukship because he alone knew the hereditary magic. Here, he was touching on the crucial issue in the dispute: the seniors were in a weak position because none of them had reputations as experts in myth, whereas he was a simbuk, an orator and an authority.

Until the end of my fieldwork the dispute remained unsettled. Sisters' sons and other allies of the protagonists played little role in the dispute for fear of exacerbating it. They bided their time, sometimes referring to the two groups as a single lineage and sometimes as separate ones.

The process by which Waikisuwi was fissioning seems, from other similar cases I recorded, to be a common pattern. The fission of a descent group is an asymmetrical process in which an expanding junior branch secedes, taking important entitlements with it. It is the principle of seniority that creates the asymmetry. As long as the group's seniors are in control of the group's secret lore and ritual entitlements, the group is likely to remain intact. But if these entitlements escheat to a junior branch, the scene is set for fission, because it is only by fission that the juniors can legitimise their new status. A factor tending to make these revisions of the structural *status quo* relatively easy to engineer is that an Avatip lineage has no permanent name. It is named after the senior sister's son of its most senior extant generation, so that every thirty years or so the name of the lineage perishes and is replaced by a new one. There is therefore an inbuilt amnesia (Barnes 1947: 52) in lineage structure and, potentially, any man who has a sister's son can hive off, like Pwimbandi, and found a lineage of his own.

Implicitly, close agnates are in permanent competition to control the hereditary mythological knowledge they in principle share. A man of a junior descent line who becomes an important orator by his own efforts, as Pwimbandi's father did, can take over hereditary entitlements such as simbukships. And he and his descendants must continue to prove themselves powerful orators if they are to keep the office.

At the same time they are competitors for reproductive viability. When open struggles break out between agnates for simbukships or other ceremonial prerogatives, as happens in processes of fission, the rate at which each side can lay claim to the associated personal names is constrained quite strongly by the rate at which it is reproducing itself. To be able to bestow a name, it must produce a child. Men cannot rename children who are named already, nor can they give their children inordinate numbers of names. Men are seeking to have their claims recognised as legitimate, and so avoid violating the rules of the naming system. If one side has numerical superiority over the other, as Pwimbandi's does, then it can make a greater number of legitimate 'moves' in the ensuing competition for names.

Marriage alliance and the transmission of myth

Every subclan allows all its magical and ritual specialisations to be learned and carried out by its male allies, most especially by its sisters' sons. The allies provide the subclan in return with several kinds of political support. The transmission of such knowledge between subclans through ties of marriage alliance is an important dimension of those groups' political relations. It is also a crucial element in the strategies by which ambitious men become important political figures.

Firstly, it can happen, particularly if a subclan is small, that its senior men die without having passed on all their esoteric knowledge to their agnates, and when this happens the subclan's allies are usually able to supply the missing knowledge. Because at least part of the subclan's hereditary mythology is always known by its allies, the lore is insured against loss. This is especially important in the case of mythology relating to the male initiation system. A subclan with few men may be unable to perform its hereditary functions in ritual, because it has no men of a high enough grade in the men's cult to be able to take part in the ritual. When that happens, the men's ritually senior sisters' sons can depute for them. The subclan can have its powers exercised on its behalf by its allies, until its own men are promoted into the relevant grade and become able to assume them. In the meantime, the sisters' sons keep the subclan's hereditary rights from lapsing to its juniors.

Secondly, allies give the subclan their political support by defending its rights in debates. The support of allies in debating can be crucial, again particularly to small and weak subclans. Some of these groups are defended in debates almost wholly by their allies, because none of their members know the relevant mythology.

One consequence of this, is that by marrying into a subclan of high ceremonial rank, a man can obtain important ritual powers for himself and for his sons. By marrying a woman of one of the senior subclans of Nggəla'angkw, a man of Wuluwi-Nyawi can acquire for himself and for his sons the power to interdict the fishing-grounds. His sons cannot pass this power on to their own descendants, because it is the hereditary property of Nggəla'angkw. But he and they can use this power during their own lifetimes, and it can make them powerful men, even though they may belong to a very junior subclan with few ceremonial powers. As a result, senior subclans tend to attract affines; ambitious men wish to bestow wives on them and to receive wives in return. Agnates, therefore, are not only rivals for ceremonial rank. They are rivals for the allies which ceremonial rank attracts; for the support that allies will give them in defence of their rank; and for the power to reproduce themselves and maintain their rank, which allies bestow in the form of wives.

It is quite acceptable for a subclan's allies to teach its esoterica to each other, and the transmission of this knowledge can continue indefinitely among these outsiders without any consultation with the subclan's agnatic members. But allies are under an obligation not to reveal it to anyone with no right to know it. For instance, a man may not teach the secret myths of his mother's subclan to his own agnates unless they themselves are also allies of that subclan. He cannot teach the myths even to his own son, unless the latter has renewed the alliance by marrying into his father's mother's subclan.

Rights to know myths are transmitted between subclans from wife-givers to wife-takers. Because each group preferentially has at all times sisters' husbands and sisters' sons in all of its marriageable subclans, and sisters' daughters' husbands in all subclans collateral with itself, so all these groups have men entitled to learn its secret myths. All subclans in the community are therefore linked in exchanges of secret knowledge, paralleling their links by marriage. Teaching these allies is referred to as 'giving mother's milk'. Sometimes it is called 'giving *ndja'am*'. Because this knowledge is taught in return for food and wealth, these goods flow from wife-takers to wife-givers in return for knowledge just as they do in return for women. But when a subclan's allies are called upon to teach its mythology back to the subclan's own members, no payment is made to them because they are simply returning the myths of another subclan to those myths' rightful owners. Secret knowledge moves between subclans against wealth, except when those messages are returning to their original sources.

The transmission of secret knowledge between subclans feeds back and has important effects upon the marriage system. The main reason the villagers give for the preference of descent groups to spread their alliances as widely as possible has to do with the political implications of communicating mythology between groups. If a subclan were to concentrate its alliances in only a few other groups, it would make itself vulnerable to those groups in debates, because its allies might support their own agnates and use their knowledge of the subclan's lore against it. If the subclan's own experts in myth were to die without passing on their knowledge, or important parts of it, to their agnates, the subclan could become politically dependent on its allies' descent groups for two generations. The allies could withhold the esoterica from the subclan's own members and so prevent the subclan from defending itself in debates without their support. During this period it would be the allies who carried out many or all of the subclan's ceremonial functions and, because they alone knew the relevant spells and mythology, their descent groups could permanently take over the subclan's ceremonial rights. It is therefore essential for a subclan to spread its alliances thinly and widely, so as to ensure that its allies are a dispersed category of men united by no other loyalties than their relationship with the subclan itself.

Viewing this system from the perspective of the individual, there are a minimum of four subclans whose secret lore a married man is entitled to learn: his own subclan, his mother's, his wife's and his wife's mother's. Every marriage a man makes gives him rights in the esoteric myths of two additional subclans, and marriage therefore plays an important role in succession to leadership and in the strategies which established leaders use to extend or consolidate their influence.

It often happens that a wife is bestowed on a leader specifically to gain his support in debates. Because it is expected that his sons will be debating-simbuks, the wife-givers' hope is that the marriage will eventually supply them with sister's sons who are orators and obliged to take their side in debates. The marriage can provide them in this way with valuable support for two generations. In many cases it is an orator who bestows his own sister or daughter, and the marriage creates an alliance between two patrilines of debating-simbuks lasting for two generations in the wife-takers' line.

The wife-givers teach their sister's or daughter's husband on the understanding, firstly, that he will eventually teach the lore to his son; and secondly, that the son himself will teach it back to his cross-cousins should they have been unable to obtain it from their own ascendants. In this way the wife-givers try to ensure that their descendants will become debating-simbuks even if they themselves should die before passing their knowledge on to them.

When an orator is recruited by marriage, it is not in fact necessary for him to learn his affines' esoterica in order to support them effectively in debates. What is important is that he possesses the secret lore of other subclans. It is that knowledge – of the myths of his affines' potential opponents – that makes him a valuable ally and formidable in debates. Up to a point, the more marriages a man contracts, the more expert in mythology he can become; and the more expert he becomes, the more he attracts bestowals of women.

Debating-simbuks tend, in short, to make alliances with each other: so as to recruit each other as advocates in debates; to learn the myths of other subclans from the acknowledged experts in those groups and so extend their own influence in the debating system; and to ensure the likelihood of their agnatic descendants succeeding to their own leadership roles. The effects of this, firstly, are that leaders tend to have a higher rate of polygyny than other men, and secondly that they tend to be close affines and uterine kin of one another, linked together in a somewhat exclusive nexus of affinal and matrilateral ties. Table 14 gives the relationships of twenty-six current debating-simbuks to those of their immediate affines and uterine kinsmen who were or are also leaders. The most common types of alliance relations between orators are between wife's father and daughter's husband, and between wife's brother and sister's husband.

It can happen that a debating-simbuk, especially if he is the leader of a small, declining subclan, has no subclan-agnates able or willing to inherit his knowledge. He therefore has to teach the whole of this lore to a sister's husband or sister's son, or bestow a wife on an orator specifically to teach him. The subclan's esoterica thereby pass entirely into the hands of its allies, and when this happens the subclan becomes dependent politically on these outsiders. The subclan becomes dependent on them for defending it in debates; for eventually returning its mythology to it; and for keeping this lore secret from groups – including their own subclans – which would use it against the subclan in debates.

The most influential leaders are men who are not only pre-eminent in their own subclans, but who have gained in this way a partial or complete monopoly of the secret myths of one or more other groups. They can turn against the groups which have entrusted their esoterica to them, and attack them in debates on behalf of their own subclans or of other subclans of which they are allies. But it is often politically more advantageous to them to remain the defenders of these groups, even – if they are not the sole leaders of their own subclans – in debates against their own agnates. By doing so they perpetuate, and publicly demonstrate, these groups' dependence on them.

Because leaders tend to have more wives than other men, and to be allies of a larger number of subclans, they are involved as principals in debates more

Table 14. *Affinal and uterine ties between orators*

Affines and uterine kin also orators[a]	Number of cases
WF, WB, MB, MBS, FZS	1
WF, WB, MB, ZH	1
WF, WB, ZH	1
WF, WB, MB	1
WF, WB	2
WF	4
WB	1
WB, ZH, FZS	1
WB, ZH	1
ZH, FZS	1
ZH, MB	1
ZH	1
MB	3
ZS	1
DH	1
None of the above	5
Total	26

[a] In some cases these kin types include several individuals.

frequently and have a greater freedom of choice as to which side to support. When a debate is about to be held, it is often a matter of intense concern to the two opposing groups which of them an important orator will support. Such a man often finds he can increase his standing in the debating system more by aligning himself with the weaker side; nothing furthers an orator's status more than defending a weak subclan singlehandedly against a strong opposing side. Small subclans, unable to defend themselves adequately on their own strength, can therefore usually find orators willing to rally to their support in debates. But the price they pay is the partial or complete loss of their political autonomy.

It is in the context of competitions for status between groups that leaders arise and exercise their distinctive role. But the interests of leaders are only partly identified with those of their own subclans. Their extensive alliance relations, and the crucial importance to other groups of their mythological knowledge, free leaders to a greater or lesser extent from what Sahlins called, in a different context, segmentary enclavement (Sahlins 1963; cf. A.J. Strathern 1971: 2). Men become leaders, not simply by opposing other groups on behalf of their own but, more importantly, and more subtly, by becoming their defenders; by showing themselves to be reliable and effective supporters of any group that might wish to recruit them by marriage and bestow esoteric knowledge on them. An important feature of politics at Avatip is the need of every group for external support – particularly small, declining subclans – because this opens up avenues for leaders to extend their influence beyond their own subclans.

The dispute between Makəm and Yimal over their prerogatives in the Ndumwi ritual

One group which has effectively lost the control of its mythological lore, and has become politically dependent on its allies, is the subclan Makəm. This is the most senior subclan of Nggəla'angkw clan-pair, and has many prestigious ceremonial rights, but it is a small group with only thirty-six members in 1978. The subclan immediately junior to it, Yimal, is the largest Nggəla'angkw subclan, and the second largest at Avatip, having 178 members.

If Makəm were to die out, Yimal, as its immediate junior, would have the right to inherit its entire ceremonial estate. It would be entitled to all the totemic ancestors of Makəm, its position in myth, and all its magical and ritual powers. These processes of succession are called *vasina*, or 'treading (the extinct group) underfoot'. People say that Yimal has been trying, for as long as can be remembered, to 'tread Makəm underfoot, steal its *ndja'am*, and stand as the most senior within Nggəla'angkw'. Many name-disputes are remembered to have taken place between the two subclans over the past two or three generations, all of them involving attempts by Yimal to dispossess Makəm of its prerogatives. Some of the disputes concerned the village's main fishing-lagoons, which have now largely passed into the ritual control of Yimal. Some were over the precedence of the two groups in the scarification ritual of first-stage initiation. Others have concerned their roles in the third-stage ritual, Ndumwi.

In these disputes, Makəm has been at a considerable disadvantage because there have been long periods when few or none of its men knew much of its hereditary mythology. A large part of this lore has come to be known by Yimal and by other, more junior Nggəla'angkw subclans. The last two Makəm men versed in their subclan's mythology died in the late 1960s. They were unable to teach it to their younger subclansmen before their deaths, because the latter were all too young (a common problem faced by small subclans), so they taught it to their allies for their safekeeping. Over the years, Makəm had bestowed a large proportion of its women on the powerful Wuluwi-Nyawi subclan Maliyaw, particularly on the Maliyaw lineage Malikəmban. As a result, many of the men of that lineage were affines and sisters' sons of Makəm and some of them acquired a very thorough knowledge of Makəm mythology. In the 1970s Makəm was the maternal subclan of the four most prominent orators of Malikəmban, and these men were virtually the only allies of Makəm

Malikəmban lineage   **Makəm subclan**

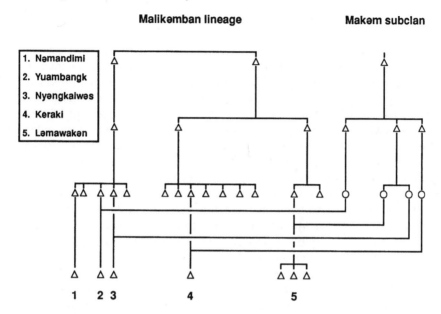

Fig. 3 Common maternal ties of some of the Malikəmban orators with the subclan Makəm.

who knew its secret mythology. Makəm was therefore almost totally dependent on these men for defending it in debates, particularly on the oldest and most knowledgeable of them, Ləmawakən, who at the time was one of the most redoubtable orators at Avatip.

There was only one Makəm man, Raminggawi, who showed promise as a potential orator. He was determined to put a stop to the gradual appropriation of his subclan's ceremonial rights by Yimal. But he was as yet unable to take part effectively in debates, since he was only in his late twenties, and knew little of his subclan's mythology. Ləmawakən was teaching him some of it, as he was obliged to do, but refused to impart much of it on the grounds that Raminggawi was still too young. Instead, Ləmawakən was teaching most of this lore to other orators of his own subclan who were sisters' sons of Makəm. The youngest of these men was in his mid-forties; and if he, rather than Raminggawi, should inherit Ləmawakən's expertise in Makəm myth, it is likely that Raminggawi and his subclan will remain dependent on the lineage Malikəmban for another twenty years or so.

It will be recalled that the most important initiatory ritual owned by the clan-pair Nggəla'angkw is Ndumwi, and that the key responsibilities in this ritual are shared by Makəm and Yimal. But because of its small size, Makəm has been unable to promote many men into the third ritual grade for some generations. As a result, many of the functions it shares with Yimal in the ritual are being gradually monopolised by Yimal. The men of Makəm and Yimal in theory share the right to use the secret percussion instrument which imitates the stamping feet of the Ndumwi spirit (two boards fastened together and slapped on the ground to make a loud bang). But when Makəm men are newly initiated into Ndumwi, Yimal men already initiated try to dissuade them from using this instrument. They may use it once or twice at the start of the ritual, so the Yimal men will tell them, in acknowledgement of their subclan's seniority; but then they should hand it over to the Yimal men and let them use it for the rest of the ritual. Similarly, Yimal men try to dissuade Makəm novices from playing the slit-drum shared by the two subclans, saying they should leave this responsibility entirely to Yimal.

For sixty or seventy years, Yimal has been the custodian of about ten Makəm names deriving from the myth of the creation of the Ndumwi ritual. Yimal had persuaded Makəm that it had too few members to keep these important names in continuous use, and therefore risked having them stolen by other groups. Makəm should let Yimal have them for a while, because Yimal would be better equipped to defend these names in debates. The Makəm men agreed to this, but on the understanding that it was a temporary measure only, and that when the Yimal recipients of the names died, the names would return to Makəm. By the time of my fieldwork, the Yimal individuals carrying these names were growing old, raising the question of who was going to bear the names next. The oldest of the present bearers, and the one expected to die soonest, was a woman in her mid-sixties called Yanggənmawai. Late in 1977 the leader of the Yimal lineage Silikindu gave this name to his younger brother's infant daughter, thereby breaking the undertaking made by his subclan two generations earlier. This greatly alarmed Raminggawi, who wrote immediately to an absent subclansman employed in a coastal town, telling him to name *his* newborn daughter Yanggənmawai. The Yimal leaders objected, and at this point an open dispute broke out between the two subclans over all the names which Makəm had entrusted to Yimal.

Before turning to this dispute, it is necessary to understand the stage which the ritual cycle had reached when the dispute took place. At the time, none of the Makəm men belonged to the third initiatory grade; Raminggawi himself had only reached the second grade. Several Yimal men were third-stage initiates, but of these only two were orators, and they were not the leading orators of their subclan. The effective leaders of Yimal, and the ones who played the central roles in the dispute with Makəm, were Kamiapan of the lineage Silikindu, and Walimbandi of the lineage Kwindjambangk, and both these men belonged only to the second ritual grade.

It was known that the Maiyir ritual, or some version of it, was going to be held within the next year or two, inducting the whole of the second ritual grade into the third. In other words, the three main protagonists in the dispute – Raminggawi representing the subclan Makəm, and Kamiapan and Walimbandi representing Yimal – were all second-stage initiates expecting shortly to be promoted into the final grade, after which they would become entitled to take part in performances of Ndumwi. Their respective subclans' prerogatives in the Ndumwi ritual were therefore an issue with intense personal significance for these three men. Once they were promoted, they would thereafter play key roles in Ndumwi whenever the ritual was held.

In February and March of 1977 mourning ceremonies were being held each Saturday at Yawmbak, in the house of a family whose daughter had recently died. It is usual on such occasions for name-disputes to be aired during breaks in the singing of the mourning-songs, and it was at the first of these gatherings at Yawmbak that the dispute between Makəm and Yimal was publicly opened.

The Yimal leaders acknowledged that the Ndumwi spirit was, genealogically, a totemic ancestress of Makəm. But they claimed she had been abandoned by the other totemic ancestors of her subclan in a subterranean ceremonial house. Ancestors of Yimal, hearing slit-drum signals emanating from under ground, then discovered and rescued her, incorporating her into their own subclan. Makəm had therefore lost all right to use her name, Ndumwikəsək. The slit-drum signals she played, which are the ones now used in the ritual to summon her to the village, also became the sole property of Yimal in this way, as did the secret totemic names of these rhythms.

All the other disputed names were, likewise, names of sacra shared by the two subclans in the Ndumwi ritual; for instance, Ndumwiwaləp, the name of the percussion instrument used to imitate the spirit's stamping feet. Because of the women and children present, none of these sacra could be referred to openly, and both sides took care to keep the discussion highly oblique.

Kamiapan and Walimbandi were almost the only speakers on the Yimal side. The speaker for Makəm was its sister's son, the orator Ləmawakən. Raminggawi spoke little, being too young and inexpert in myth. Apart from Ləmawakən, none of the two subclans' allies made speeches, for fear of escalating the conflict.

Relations between Ləmawakən and the Yimal leaders had been strained for many years. There was a long-standing and bitter name-dispute between their two subclans (see Chapter 8), and Ləmawakən and Kamiapan in particular had had many personal quarrels. But the main point is that Ləmawakən was a third-stage initiate, and at the time, was carrying out the hereditary functions of Makəm in the Ndumwi ritual whenever that ritual was held. In effect, the Yimal leaders were threatening to displace him from that key position in the ritual once they too became third-stage initiates. He was evidently using the present dispute to further his private quarrels with the Yimal leaders, but also had strong personal stakes in ensuring that his maternal subclan kept its hereditary seniority in Ndumwi. He made acrimonious speeches and tried to escalate the controversy by demanding a full-scale debate. Raminggawi wanted at almost any cost to avoid a major confrontation of this sort with his clansmen, but could not openly oppose Ləmawakən and remained in uncomfortable silence. For their part, the Yimal leaders tried to drive a wedge between him and his teacher. Adopting a conciliatory stance toward Raminggawi, they told him they had no argument with him. Their quarrel was only with Ləmawakən. Ləmawakən, they said, was notorious for stealing people's names and for his own ends had deceived Raminggawi into believing that Makəm had a right to the names. The myths that Ləmawakən was teaching him were 'all lies'.

The dispute continued in this way for two successive Saturdays. But on the third, just as the gathering was breaking up, one of the Yimal orators made a veiled threat of sorcery against Raminggawi. He ordered Raminggawi to give up the names and, when Raminggawi said he would not, added in a stage-whisper, 'therefore you will finish' (*ata kwusikəmənə*).

Raminggawi reported this to the village Councillor, who convened a meeting the next morning with Raminggawi and the Yimal leaders. Asked by Raminggawi and the Councillor to explain their threat, the Yimal men claimed they had all been intoxicated at the time with chewing areca-nut. They had not known what they were saying, and the matter should not be taken seriously. Raminggawi warned them that if any members of his subclan fell ill, the Yimal leaders would be taken to court at Ambunti and prosecuted for sorcery. Like all Avatip people, Raminggawi believed that only actual sorcery, and not sorcery threats, are against national law.

The dispute resumed at Yawmbak the following Saturday. A noisy argument broke out between Ləmawakən and Kamiapan, and the two men had to be restrained physically from fighting. With someone pinioning his arms, Ləmawakən shouted: 'I'm not your wife that you can shout at me like that. If I was still a young man I'd knock you down. Nobody shall steal my mother's brothers' names!'

The whole dispute was now starting to unnerve Raminggawi, and he offered to compromise with Yimal: the two subclans would share each name, one subclan using its male form and the other its female form. Ləmawakən objected, but the Yimal men agreed to the proposal, and they and Raminggawi then divided up the male and female versions of the names between them. This is the normal device used to call a temporary truce in a name-dispute, and does not settle the issue. Outsiders warned Makəm and Yimal that their dispute would inevitably flare up again in future years.

The following Saturday, Ləmawakən went to Yawmbak in the hope of reopening the dispute. But none of the Yimal men came. They had taken the diplomatic precaution of going on a week-long expedition upriver to buy nassa shells, saying they needed the shells for a mortuary payment their subclan was due to make.

Successorial rights and conflict between agnates

Close agnates are potential heirs of each other's ceremonial privileges, and in this respect they stand to profit from each other's extinction. A junior group, such as Yimal, does not wait for its senior to become extinct before asserting its successorial claims. It starts trying to take over its senior's patrimony if the latter shows any signs of decline. If these attempts are successful, they may in fact help to 'push' the senior group into demographic decline, because the rising ceremonial status of the junior group will tend to attract potential affines away from its senior.

Some seventy per cent of all name-disputes take place between groups related patrilineally; and the closer the agnatic relationship, the more frequent are these disputes. This chronic conflict between agnates is almost wholly the result of incessant attempts by junior groups to anticipate their seniors' extinction and take their ceremonial rank.

These attempts often meet with some success, and a junior group may gain some of its senior's entitlements while the latter is still very much in existence. When this happens, there are fairly standard devices which are used to account for it in myth. These devices figure in many of the myths of the clan-pair Nggəla'angkw. According to these myths, the ritual of first-stage initiation was created by the totemic ancestors of Makəm, but the first ancestors to actually perform it were those of the junior subclan Nggambak. Because of this it is Nggambak, and not Makəm, that has the right to inaugurate this ritual. Similarly, myth states that all the main fishing-lagoons of Avatip were the handiwork of Makəm ancestors; but these figures only outlined the lakes, and it was the ancestors of the junior subclan Yimal who actually dug them out and filled them with water. It is on the basis of that myth that the magical power over the lakes' fertility is now held mainly by Yimal.

An important feature of these sorts of mythological devices is that they always describe a set of totemic ancestors transferring from the senior to the junior group. The switch of subclan membership by these ancestors – and the corresponding transfer of the right to use their names – are the crucial 'charter' validating the succession of the junior group to one of its senior's entitlements.

Another feature of these devices is that they do not contradict the formal order of seniority between groups. Nominal respect continues to be paid to the precedence of the senior group, and this precedence is still preserved as dogma. Important prerogatives may be held by junior groups, but their seniors remain formally senior in the myths describing the transfer of these privileges. Mythological relationships of this kind between senior and junior agnates are regarded as an entirely acceptable and legitimate variant of the elder brother/ younger brother paradigm. They are referred to in debates as 'standing on the elder brother's shoulders' (*ma'am ndəkandə sa'anggwam təna*).

137

It was this device the Yimal leaders were using in their attempts to dispossess Raminggawi's subclan of its rights in the Ndumwi ritual. It seems to be a type of charter established only by means of protracted struggles over the control of names. The myths of Nggəla'angkw suggest that the juniors of Makəm have been gradually taking over its ceremonial rights for some generations, in processes of conflict much like the dispute I have just described.

When change takes place in the constitution of a descent group, it always involves a restructuring of the group's corpus of personal names. The fission of a lineage or subclan is signalled by the division of its names into two new, separate stocks. The 'treading underfoot' of a senior group by a junior one involves the fusion of two name-stocks into one. Both of these patterns of structural change take the form of a long-term political conflict within an agnatic group over the organisation of stocks of names. One party aims to divide a corpus which the other tries to keep together; or to amalgamate two stocks which the other wants to keep separate.

In these disputes, the final arbiters are the contestants' marriageables. If a junior branch of a subclan tries to secede, it can establish itself as a subclan only if its marriageables recognise it as one. It must persuade its marriageables that two distinct alliance-making units now exist, not one, and that these two groups have separate sets of allies. Above all, it must persuade them that the two groups have separate *ndja'am* and – the crucial expression of independence – may therefore marry each other's sisters' children.

For the secession to take place, the marriageables must redefine not only their real-life alliance relationships, but their mythological ones as well. I mean that their senior men must redefine the affinal and uterine ties of their own totemic ancestors. If they do so, it implies their assent to the seceding group's independence. Their fields of marriage, defined in myth, open to accommodate two subclans where there was previously one.

In short, when conflict occurs between agnates the two opposing sides are competing, implicitly, to have their rival versions of myth, and of the structural *status quo*, confirmed by their marriageables. Which version these affines choose to prefer depends in the long term, presumably, on which side they consider more valuable to have alliances with. If one group is larger and reproductively more successful than the other, and has gained important ritual powers, marriageable subclans are likely to see advantages in accepting its claims. When agnates compete for the control of names and totemic ancestors, each side is trying to demonstrate to potential affines both a greater demographic viability and a higher ritual prestige than its opponent; and, therefore, greater value as a group to intermarry with.

Conclusion

I should like to end this chapter by returning to the issues I raised at the start. In order to keep its ceremonial privileges a group must above all seek affines – that is, it must reproduce itself physically and socially – in competition with its own agnates. And, conversely, it must seek to maintain and augment its ceremonial privileges in competition with its agnates in order to attract affines and so reproduce itself. What a group's hereditary magic represents is an *imaginary* power to nurture and reproduce other groups, and an entirely *real* power to reproduce itself. As the case studies discussed in this chapter show, the strategies that Avatip leaders use to build their power and reputation are very similar indeed to those of Big Men: it is simply that they are working in a different transactional medium. Like the Big Men described by Godelier, the power of Avatip leaders rests on their control of the wealth essential for social reproduction: but the wealth consists of knowledge, names and magical powers. That is to say, Godelier's conception of what can constitute wealth is too limited.

In an earlier chapter I mentioned that bridewealth payments are small and relatively unimportant: what men seek from the marriages of their sisters and daughters is not bridewealth but sons- and brothers-in-law who are in permanent allegiance to them and under lifelong obligations to provide them with gifts, services, and political loyalty. A group's cosmological status represents its power to attract and create these relations. Like Big Men, Avatip leaders control wealth, but the forms of wealth with which they operate – hereditary names, spells and mythological lore – have possibilities of corporate, transgenerational continuity of a sort that material wealth never has in Melanesian society. A Big Man's networks of financial credit and patronage are prone to dissolve when he dies and new networks have to be built afresh by his successors. But what Avatip leaders are working within is a culturally defined universe of wealth that offers, potentially, a capacity to reproduce political identity and status across time and to carry implications of perpetuity.

That, as far as I can see, is the essential difference between Big Men and Avatip leaders: not that Big Men build their power on wealth while leaders at Avatip do not, but that these two sorts of Melanesian political actors build their power on forms of wealth having wholly contrasting orientations toward temporality.

7

The debating system

The answer to an enigmatic question is not found by reflection or logical reasoning. It comes quite literally as a sudden *solution* – a loosening of the tie by which the questioner holds you bound. The corollary of this is that by giving the correct answer you strike him powerless. In principle there is only one answer to every question. It can be found if you know the rules of the game . . . Often the solution depends wholly on the knowledge of the secret or sacred names of things . . . (Huizinga 1949: 110)

Introduction

In his examination of the social life of commodities, Appadurai identifies a class of transactional events that he calls tournaments of value:

Tournaments of value are complex periodic events that are removed in some culturally well-defined way from the routines of economic life. Participation in them is likely to be both a privilege of those in power and an instrument of status contests between them. The currency of such tournaments is also likely to be set apart through well understood cultural diacritics. Finally, what is at issue in such tournaments is not just status, rank, fame, or reputation of actors, but the disposition of the central tokens of value in the society in question. Finally, though such tournaments of value occur in special times and places, their forms and outcomes are always consequential for the more mundane realities of power and value in ordinary life. As in the kula, so in such tournaments of value generally, strategic skill is culturally measured by the success with which actors attempt diversions or subversions of culturally conventionalised paths for the flow of things. (1986: 21)

Examples of such tournaments of value include systems of ceremonial exchange such as the kula and potlatch, the medieval traffic in saints' relics (Geary 1986) and, in modern economies, art auctions and the markets in commodity futures. In all cases these are special, exclusive arenas of competition governed by an agonistic, romantic and gamelike ethos that sets them apart from the practicalities of everyday economic life (Appadurai 1986: 50).

In his classic study of Iatmul culture, Bateson (1958) refers to ceremonial debates in which men expert in esoteric mythology dispute the ownership of totems and ancestral names (see also Stanek 1983; Wassman 1982). Gewertz (1977b) has described a debate, apparently similar to those of the Iatmul,

140

among the Chambri, who are neighbours of Avatip. These verbal contests seem to be an important forum of politics among the riverain peoples of the middle Sepik.

In this chapter I describe the debating system at Avatip, showing that it is, very much in Appadurai's sense of the term, the principal tournament of value in the economy of Avatip; except that this is a ritual economy and the tokens of strategic value for which men compete in the tournaments are names and magical powers. Toward the end of the chapter I discuss some changes which this system has undergone in modern times. Finally, I draw some parallels between the debating system and the kinds of competitive feasts and ceremonial prestations made in what Lindstrom calls the wealth-based polities of Melanesia, arguing that debates and these transactions of wealth are, at the level of actual social process, very similar tournaments of value but are occurring in different kinds of culturally constituted 'economies'.

Disputing myths

Men claim that mythology never changes, and that someone who tried to alter myths or promulgate false ones would invite affliction by the totemic ancestors. But, in fact, myth is manipulated continually. On average, a completely new name-dispute breaks out at Avatip once a year, provoked by some group challenging a myth of another group with a newly-fabricated rival myth of its own. Mythology is therefore being constantly produced. Whether or not it gains currency depends on its proponents' success in the debating-arena.

Nowadays, some of the younger orators are semi-literate in Melanesian Pidgin and have begun recording esoteric names in private notebooks which they intend to pass on to their heirs. Some young absentees, on leave in the village, have recorded secret myths on cassette tape-recorders as a way of ensuring the preservation of their subclans' patrimonial lore. I doubt though that these innovations are likely to affect the debating system in any substantial way. If, a generation from now, orators brandish exercise books or tape-recorders at each other on the debating-ground, these are unlikely to be considered convincing forms of proof. The Manambu are quite aware that it is as easy to record lies on paper or on tape as it is to memorise them in one's head. As Freedman (1958: 69–72) showed for the written genealogies of Chinese lineages, a literate tradition by no means necessarily prevents the past from being manipulated.

What facilitates this constant innovation is the secrecy surrounding myth, and the small number of men who are authorities on it (see Barth 1987). A subclan has only a few men – either agnatic members or allies – recognised as experts in its mythology, and it is not difficult for such a small circle of individuals to revise this lore. When a new myth is put forward it is not, of course, presented as an innovation but as the disclosure of a myth which earlier generations had kept secret. The secrecy of myth fosters a pervasive belief or suspicion that 'behind' each known myth there are successively more secret and more 'true' versions, which senior men harbour and, from time to time, choose to reveal.

Even the supernatural sanctions against modifying myth are double-edged, and can work as much in favour of change as against it. When a large and expanding group attacks the claims of a small, declining one, its men argue that the reason their opponents are dying out is precisely that they hold to false mythology. Their own flourishing numbers, on the other hand, indicate ancestral favour and approval. In short, the sheer reproductive success of a group is taken as an index of the 'truth' of its mythological claims. Everything in this situation may persuade even the men who created the new mythology that it is authentic, and these men may well be, as Guiart (1972: 115) puts it, forgers with excellent consciences.

In general, men accept without question the lore set forth by the leaders of their own subclans and of subclans of which they are allies. But they often view the myths of other groups skeptically and readily suspect they are fraudulent. Men are capable at times both of credulity and cynicism in their attitudes to mythology, depending on their social relationships with the proponents of the myths.

As Bateson (1958: 127–8) observed among the Iatmul, men take great pride in their totemic ancestors, and like to boast of their exploits while passing ironic and disparaging asides on those of other groups. The men of the subclan Nambul, for instance, claim that their ancestors created the Sepik River by excavating a channel for it with digging-sticks. They admit that totemic ancestors of other subclans later did some digging of their own, but they were mere *parvenus* and only added a few unimportant finishing-touches. But the men of those subclans, when they are asked, emphasise a detail which the Nambul men tend to omit: that is, that when their own ancestors arrived on the scene, the river was only as wide as a man's finger, 'a mere trickle of urine', and it cost them enormous effort to widen it to its proper size. Even when a myth is relatively fixed and agreed on, it still offers scope for the play of nuance. A stress laid on some details, a de-emphasis of others, allows each subclan to present itself in the most impressive light, and to disparage other groups without actually contradicting them.

It is a small step from this to an actual dispute over mythology. What defines a formal dispute is that it involves a conflict over the ownership of one or more of the named ancestors appearing in the myth, and over some magical or ritual prerogative for which the myth is the charter.

The closest the Manambu ever came to having a name-dispute with Europeans happened in the village of Yuanamb in the early days of the Australian administration. One of the first missionaries to visit their village, the Yuanamb people say, assembled all the villagers and told them the story of Genesis by means of an interpreter. During the course of this, one of the village leaders became increasingly agitated and, at the end, rose and made an outraged speech. Atam, he told the missionary, was the name of a figure in his own subclan's origin-myths. The missionary had no right to make up fraudulent myths concerning Atam and treat that ancestor as his. 'Why', he demanded, 'are you trying to steal my ancestor?'

When some group challenges the mythological claims of another group, it does not present a radically different myth. Often, its version is identical in its essentials to its opponents' version, the only difference being that the figures appearing in it are claimed by the challenging side to be their own totemic ancestors. Usually, the challengers' strategy is to present a myth following their opponents' version closely, but distorted in such a way as to change, subtly but fundamentally, its implications. The challenged group are confronted with a myth that is recognisably their own, but modified so that its purport is to disinherit them of the disputed prerogative and entitle their challengers to it.

The attempts by the subclan Valik to gain control of the ceremonial house Kamandja'amb

Many subclans have long-term strategies in name-disputes, and have been pursuing specific goals consistently for generations. One such group is the Nggəla'angkw subclan Valik, whose major long-term goal has been to take control of the important ceremonial house of the declining subclan Makəm. This building is called Kamandja'amb. It is ritually the most important of the Nggəla'angkw cult buildings, and is maintained as the largest and finest of them. It is the usual venue for performances of Ndumwi. According to myth, Makəm and the subclan Nambul are the oldest descent groups at Avatip and their ceremonial houses are the two most prestigious in the whole community and the most senior in myth. These buildings are known respectively as the 'canoe-stern' (*tamaval*) and 'canoe-prow' (*malval*) of the village and are the homes of the community's two tutelary spirits, Təpəyimbərman and Kwa-sa'am. These beings, totemic ancestors of Makəm and Nambul respectively, keep watch over all of Avatip and are invoked with sacrifices in times of crisis.

For as many generations as can be remembered, Makəm has had no ward of its own, and most of its men have lived in the ward of Valik, the subclan fourth after Makəm in seniority within Nggəla'angkw. Ever since, Kamandja'amb has stood in the Valik ward, and the men of that large subclan have been in effective control of the building. All decisions relating to the running and maintenance of the house are in practice made by the senior men of Valik. Because of its small size, Makəm has often been for long periods without fully initiated men. Although Makəm is the hereditary owner of Kamandja'amb, there have often been periods when none of its men could actually enter or approach the building.

The ownership of the building by Makəm is still nominally respected. Whenever the house is rebuilt or repaired, a Makəm man must lay his hand to the work first, so as not to offend the building's indwelling spirits. He must break the ground when a new post-hole is dug, strike the first – and only the first – axe blow when a tree is felled for a post, and so forth. But he is expected to leave the rest of the work entirely to Valik men, with their greater manpower.

Since Valik is the junior subclan in the same clan as Makəm, it does have reversionary claims, if rather remote ones, in its senior's ceremonial estate. But it seems to have 'jumped' the successorial queue so far as the management of Kamandja'amb is concerned, pre-empting two other more senior subclans which stood to inherit control of the building. This situation has little validation in myth. Valik has no significant mythological ties with Makəm and, in particular, plays no role in the myth of the creation of the building. Most of the names associated with the house are owned either by Makəm or by Yimal. Valik owns only one such name, Ndjikinanggi, the totemic name of the cross-pieces (*ndjiki*) supporting the floor of the loft. Makəm allowed Valik to have this name a generation ago, in recognition of its help in maintaining the building.

The Valik leadership have been trying for generations to have their control of Kamandja'amb sanctioned in myth. Their particular motive for doing so is that Valik owns the simbukship of the *laki* Nyakawlaki, an office said to have belonged, in the distant past, to the Wuluwi-Nyawi subclan Nyakaw. According to legend, Valik 'stole' this simbukship from Nyakaw or, in other versions, 'married' its fire-basin. The fire-basin itself, and all the spirit-beings associated with this office, are still admitted even by the men of Valik themselves to be, by genealogy, totemic ancestors of Nyakaw. A simbukship must be associated in the organisation of ritual with a specific ceremonial house in which the simbuk and the men of his *laki* carry out their rites. Valik simbuks perform their rituals in Kamandja'amb, but this is anomalous because neither the simbukship, nor the cult house linked ritually with it, are actually vested by myth in the subclan Valik itself. What the Valik leadership have in effect been trying to do, is to make their ritual office fully legitimate by having it redefined in myth as the simbukship of the most important of their clan-pair's ceremonial houses.

Valik has carried out many name-disputes as part of this long-term strategy, most of them concerning the ownership of various parts of the building. None of the disputes have been with Makəm itself. Valik has always been one of the strongest supporters of the patrimonial rights of Makəm, because any threat to the important status of Makəm in myth and cosmology is, indirectly, a threat to itself. Over the past few generations, Valik has repeatedly had to teach Makəm myths to that subclan's men, to enable them to defend

144

themselves against the constant encroachments on their ritual privileges by Yimal. In its own name-disputes the strategy of Valik has been to attack subclans linked in myth with Makəm, with the aim of displacing these groups and acquiring these ties for itself. The men of Makəm have remained neutral in these disputes, not wishing to antagonise any of the parties involved.

The most important of these attempts by Valik to strengthen its mythological links with Makəm and its ceremonial house, has taken the form of a long-standing dispute with the subclan Waranggamb over the ownership of the name Wasakwuapan. This dispute concerns the myth of the founding of Avatip. I describe the myth more fully in the next chapter, in the context of a different name-dispute, but the details of it relevant to the present dispute are as follows.

Makəm and Nambul are the two oldest subclans at Avatip because each, according to myth, had a totemic ancestor existing at the site of the village at the beginning of the world, while the site itself still lay under primordial water. Both of these ancestors were completely immobilised in mud and disfigured by skin ulcers. They were discovered in this state by a succession of ancestors belonging to various other subclans, some of whom eventually extricated them from the mud and cured their sores. This enabled them to marry and beget children. The Makəm ancestor was rescued by a figure called Wasakwuapan, who is claimed as a totemic ancestor by the subclan Waranggamb, and in gratitude to Wasakwuapan he let him adopt a number of his children. The adoption of these children is a secret detail of the myth, because the 'children' are actually highly secret and extremely important ritual sacra which are stored in the loft of Kamandja'amb, and on the basis of this myth the rights to use them in ritual and to bear their names belong to Waranggamb.

Privately, most men who are not involved directly in the Wasakwuapan dispute consider the claims of Waranggamb authentic, and all other indications are that the Waranggamb version of the myth is considerably older than the rival myth of Valik. The Valik myth is almost identical, its main difference being the simple but crucial one that it portrays Wasakwuapan as a Valik ancestor.

The debates over this name have focussed mainly on a single episode in the myth. When Wasakwuapan arrived at the village site, the Sepik River was being created by two other totemic ancestors, who belong to descent groups uninvolved in the Wasakwuapan controversy. These two figures were travelling downstream past the village, opening a channel for the river as they went, and they called out to Wasakwuapan and asked his name. He shouted (*wasakwunand*) his name in reply (hence Wasakwuapan, or 'strong shout'). Waranggamb and Valik agreed in the debates that they both have an ancestor who shouted in this way. But each subclan has tried to show that its own ancestor shouted first and is therefore the 'true' (*mwia*) Wasakwuapan. In these arguments, Waranggamb has been able to make the more convincing case. At Old Avatip its ward was upriver from the ward of Valik and therefore, so its orators have pointed out, the two figures who created the Sepik must have encountered their own ancestor first.

The two subclans have debated Wasakwuapan many times, always inconclusively. The name was first debated before the arrival of Europeans on the Sepik, and was most recently debated three times in close succession during the 1970s. One incident in this protracted dispute gives a curious sidelight on debating as a method of dispute-settlement. In the early 1950s the two groups apparently became so exasperated with each other that they took their dispute to the sub-district headquarters at Ambunti to be adjudicated by the *kiap*, or patrol officer. The officer heard the case, and was persuaded by the Waranggamb men that the name was rightfully theirs. He told Valik to call their children something else, and sent everybody home with a warning to keep the peace. But once back at Avatip, Valik ignored his ruling, on the grounds that *kiaps* are no authorities on myth. After this egregious failure of the European legal system to deal with name-disputes, none have ever again been brought before it.

Small-scale and full-scale debates

The formal procedure for resolving a dispute of this sort is a debate, or *saki*. Occasionally, other types of disputes, unconnected with myth and personal names, do break out between groups, and debating, or a technique similar to it, may be used to settle them. But the debate as an institutionalised dispute-settlement procedure is adapted specifically to resolving conflicts over myth and the ownership of totemic ancestors. Staging a debate is called *saki mbulana/viyana*, 'debate speaking/hitting'; or sometimes *ka'aw mbulana/ viyana*, 'cordyline speaking/hitting', in reference to the cordyline leaves which orators hold when speaking in debates.

When two groups dispute the ownership of an ancestral name, they do not lay claim to the name in a merely hypothetical way. Rather, each actually bestows the name on one of its own infants, and it is the existence of namesakes in the two groups that publicly signals the start of the dispute. Although a debate is an entirely public event, few of the men involved know the disputed mythology fully. Most adult men are familiar with its general exoteric outlines. But some of the audience, especially younger people, may be quite unaware of the ceremonial prerogative being disputed, particularly if it is an hereditary responsibility in male initiatory ritual. By a kind of public fiction, debates are represented as disputes purely over the ownership of personal names. But almost everybody knows that other, deeper and more important issues of some kind are always at stake. In debates all references to myth are made in a highly condensed and oblique way, full of allusion and innuendo. The listeners' understanding of these references, and their awareness of the actual ceremonial right being disputed, depend on their ritual status and expertise in myth.

About half of all name-disputes take place between close agnates, and are a part of long-term changes, such as fission, taking place in group structure (see Table 15). The remainder are disputes between marriageable subclans, or between groups related distantly by agnation such as subclans of different clans of the same clan-pair. These are rarely connected with processes of change in group structure. A dispute between close agnates tends to involve a relatively small number of groups and individuals, but a dispute of the second sort usually involves in one way or the other the whole adult population of the community. For that reason I shall call the two types minor and major name-disputes.

In a minor name-dispute, attempts to reach a settlement are made in public but informal disputations such as those illustrated in the previous chapter or, if these fail, in what I shall call minor or small-scale debates. Close agnates usually try to preserve a show of amity among themselves, and there are loosely-defined supernatural sanctions against them holding formal debates against each other. The main diacritical features of a small-scale debate is that it is held indoors, either in a domestic house or, if feelings are running high, in a ceremonial house. Major name-disputes, on the other hand, are usually carried out in what I shall call major or full-scale debates. A full-scale debate is held in the open air in the cleared area in front of a ceremonial house. It involves outlays of food and wealth, and is conducted with much ceremony and formality.

Whether a major or minor debate is held is also influenced by the history of relations between the opposing groups. If a name-dispute between close agnates continues for several decades, it may escalate to a stage where the two sides hold full-scale debates against each other. On the other hand, a name-dispute which breaks out between two marriageable subclans whose relations have previously been amicable, may be carried out initially in small-scale debates.

Table 15 gives the incidence of conflicts over personal names at Avatip over a period of about forty years ending in 1979. The figures are certainly incomplete, especially in the case of disputes involving only small-scale debates or informal disputation, and the more so the longer ago they occurred. I should also say that some of the name-disputes began before 1940, some in pre-contact times.

During that forty-year period, sixty-seven major and minor debates are remembered to have taken place, giving an average frequency of about one every seven months. Of those debates, fifty-one were between agnates, as were twenty-six of the total of thirty-six name-disputes I recorded for the same

Table 15. *Name-disputes at Avatip, c. 1940–1979*

	Number of name-disputes	Number of names involved	Number of debates held
Within the clan			
Senior Nggǝla'angkw clan			
Makǝm vs. Yimal	3	15	6
Yimal vs. Valik	1	1	1
Valik vs. Nggambak	2	3	3
Nggambak (internal)	1	c.20	0
Junior Nggǝla'angkw clan			
Wopunamb vs. Kambuli	1	1	1
Kambuli (internal)	1	1	2
Nambul-Sambǝlap clan			
Nambul vs. Sambǝlap	1	1	1
Nyawi clan			
Nyakaw vs. Ambasarak	1	2	3
Nyakaw vs. Sarambusarak	1	1	1
Nyakaw vs. Wanǝkaw	1	2	2
Ambasarak vs. Sarambusarak	1	1	1
Sarambusarak vs. Wanǝkaw	1	1	1
Ambasarak vs. Wanǝkaw	1	1	1
Wuluwi clan			
Maliyaw vs. Nanggwundaw	1	5	5
Totals 14	17	c.55	28
Within the clan-pair			
Nggǝla'angkw clan-pair			
Yimal vs. Wopunamb	1	1	1
Yimal vs. Kambuli	1	1	1
Valik vs. Waranggamb	1	1	5
Wuluwi-Nyawi clan-pair			
Nyakaw vs. Maliyaw	1	1	4
Maliyaw vs. Ambasarak	1	1	1
Maliyaw vs. Sarambusarak	2	3	9
Maliyaw vs. Wanǝkaw	1	1	1
Wanǝkaw vs. Nawik	1	1	1

Totals	8	9	10	23
Between marriageables				
Makem vs. Maliyaw		1	1	1
Yimal vs. Ambasarak		1	1	3
Yimal vs. Maliyaw		1	1	3
Nggambak vs. Sarambusarak		1	1	1
Nggambak vs. Nawik		1	1	1
Valik vs. Ambasarak		1	1	2
Valik vs. Sarambusarak		1	1	1
Valik vs. Sambəlap		1	1	1
Nambul vs. Sarambusarak		1	1	2
Sambəlap vs. Wanɛkaw		1	1	1
Totals	10	10	10	16
Grand totals	32	36	c.75	67

Table 16. *Ranking of Avatip subclans by involvement in name-disputes,*
c. *1940–1979*

Subclan	Number of subclans disputed with	Number of name-disputes	Number of names involved	Number of debates held
Maliyaw	7	8	13	24
Yimal	5	8	20	15
Sarambusarak	7	8	10	16
Valik	6	7	8	13
Ambasarak	6	6	8	11
Wanəkaw	6	6	6	7
Nyakaw	4	4	5	10
Nggambak	3	4	5	5
Makəm	2	4	16	7
Sambəlap	3	3	3	3
Nambul	2	2	2	3
Wopunamb	2	2	2	2
Kambuli	2	2	2	2
Nawik	2	2	2	2
Nanggwundaw	1	1	5	5
Waranggamb	1	1	1	5

period. These conflicts are, in short, more than twice as frequent between agnates as they are between marriageables, and they are more common between close agnates than distant ones.

Of the thirty-six name-disputes, I was able to ascertain at least in outline the issues at stake in twenty-five (involving a total of sixty-one personal names). Sixteen were connected in one way or another with the ritual system, four of these sixteen concerning rights to simbukships. Of the other nine name-disputes whose issues I recorded, five concerned land rights, and four the ownership of magic.

Table 16 gives the ranking of Avatip subclans by their involvement as principals in name-disputes (disputes internal to the subclan are omitted in this table). This is a reasonably accurate indication of their relative dominance of Avatip politics. As one can see, every subclan has been involved as a principal in at least one name-dispute and two debates over the past forty years. Also, the frequency with which a subclan is involved in name-disputes is roughly proportional to its size, as can be seen by comparing Table 16 with the sizes of Avatip subclans given in Table 5. Large groups are better equipped than small ones to initiate name-disputes and engage in debating. They and their allies are likely to have more experts in myth, can more easily defray the expenses of a debate, and have the demographic resources with which to lay claim frequently to the personal names of other groups.

To illustrate the processes by which name-disputes are resolved in debates, I

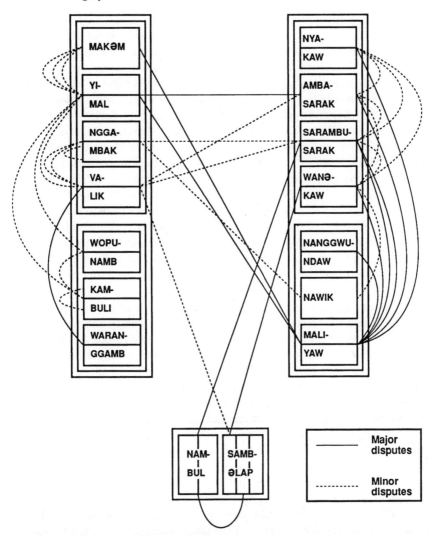

Fig. 4 Name-disputes at Avatip, *c.*1940–79.

shall refer now and then in this chapter to a major dispute which began in the early 1970s between the subclans Maliyaw and Sarambusarak, the two largest subclans of the clan-pair Wuluwi-Nyawi, over the ownership of storm-sorcery.

This dispute is described in Harrison 1989, where Maliyaw is spelt Maliyau, and the subclan Sarambusarak is referred to as Sarak, an abbreviation commonly used by the villagers. Maliyaw is the largest and politically dominant subclan in the community, and this dispute was only one episode in

151

a long-standing and complex political struggle between Maliyaw and many other subclans, both within Wuluwi-Nyawi and outside it, for certain key ritual prerogatives and for dominant positions in the ceremonial system.

The subclan Sarambusarak owns sorcery for summoning up thunderstorms, which is regarded as a very powerful weapon capable of obliterating the village and is held in great fear even by its owners. According to legend, it was a man of Sarambusarak who used this sorcery to destroy Asiti, the original home of all the Manambu. Sarambusarak also claim to have used it some years ago during a land dispute with the village of Malu, to smash the canoes of Malu with 'lightning-stones' as they lay at their moorings. In myth, the sorcery originated in a men's cult-house in the sky called Nyapal, belonging to the subclan Nyakaw, the senior subclan of Wuluwi-Nyawi. A totemic ancestor of Sarambusarak, called Manggalaman, flew to Nyapal and obtained the sorcery there, and ever since, Sarambusarak men claim, the sorcery has been the joint property of Nyakaw and Sarambusarak. In particular, the rights to use the name Manggalaman, and all the public and esoteric names connected with that figure, have been the property of their subclan.

The sorcery figured importantly in the old Maiyir ritual of third-stage initiation. There was an episode in this ritual when the women and noninitiates were made to leave the village, and the initiators then stripped all the palms and trees around the initiatory enclosure of their leaves, telling the women on their return that they had caused this devastation with the lightning-sorcery. What appears to have made this dispute break out when it did, were the preparations that Wuluwi-Nyawi were making to resurrect this ritual within the next few years. The initiatory cycle had reached a stage at which Maiyir, or some version of it, had to be performed in the near future. As it turned out, the ritual in the end performed in 1978 was not Maiyir, as I explained in an earlier chapter, but a version of Ndumwi incorporating some elements of the Maiyir ritual. But, at the time, Maliyaw and Sarambusarak had, in effect, begun a struggle for an important and highly prestigious role in the planned initiation.

In 1972 the senior men of Maliyaw began trying to dispossess Sarambusarak of the sorcery. They bestowed the name Manggalaman on a newborn child of their subclan, immediately provoking Sarambusarak into naming one of *their* children Manggalaman, and for several years the two groups quarrelled bitterly over the ownership of the name, each accusing the other of having 'stolen' (*lukwu kwurna*) it. After many delays caused mainly by the absence of certain key orators from the village, a full-scale debate took place in 1976, which produced no settlement, and a second in November 1977. Manggalaman, so the men of Maliyaw argued in these debates, was a totemic ancestor of their subclan. They acknowledged that Sarambusarak may also have had an ancestor who visited Nyapal; but if so, that figure did so after their own, did not obtain storm magic, and was not called Manggalaman.

The debating system

Winning a debate: names with a single face and names with two faces

An important feature of a debate is that there is no third party with power to arbitrate or adjudicate. There are neutrals, who usually have an interest in seeing the dispute carried out peacefully, but all they can do to achieve this is to try to guide the discussions from time to time and defuse tensions. Although there is no presiding authority, full-scale debates do not normally lead to the compromise outcomes usually associated with bilateral or mediated settlement processes (Gluckman 1955b; Gulliver 1963; Nader and Todd 1978; Roberts 1979). These debates end either inconclusively, or else in a decisive win for one side, with the losers forced to rename their child and to give up their claims to the disputed magic. The crucial, decisive episode comes at the end, after many hours of argumentation and oratory, and is a ceremonial contest between the two sides in esoteric knowledge. The rules of this contest are explicit and quite simple: to win, a side must prove that it alone knows the secret names relating to the disputed ancestor. By doing so it proves, by implication, that it alone is capable of performing the associated magic. The names, in which that magical power is inherent, are those of the disputed ancestor, and of that figure's father, mother and mother's brother. In major name-disputes, the two sides usually harbour quite different versions of those secret names, and consider each other's versions to be entirely spurious. The disputed name is described, idiomatically, as having 'two faces' (*mutam vəti*). The aim of each side in the contest is to have their own versions publicly recognised as the genuine ones.

Because of its highly secret nature, the contest is carried out entirely in whispers and involves only the most senior men of the two sides. An orator from each side comes forward, and the pair meet in the middle of the debating-ground. One of them whispers in the other's ear what he suspects is one of the secret names harboured by the opposing side. If he is wrong, his opponent simply shakes his head, and announces 'no' (*ma'a*) to the audience, to let them know it was a miscall. He must then swear an oath of purgation, otherwise he might lie, claiming a miscall when the name uttered was in fact correct. The oath is sworn on a *kapi*, a shell necklace worn only by men of the Ndjəpas ritual grade, hung on a stake nearby. A *maiyira sa'al*, as this type of oath is known, is the most powerful of all oaths, supposedly killing a perjurer in a matter of days.

It is then the turn of the other side. The same interrogation takes place with the roles reversed, either by the same pair of men or by a new pair. And so it continues, each side taking it in turns to try to prove it knows the other's magic names. One pair of men after another meet in the middle of the debating-ground; one whispers a word to the other, who shakes his head, lays his hand upon the oath, and they both walk back to their seats. The secret name of the disputed ancestor is usually dealt with first, and the two sides then turn their attention to the names of the other three ancestors. The contest is called *nduand wandanand*: 'they utter [the name of] the man'.

A variety of outcomes is possible. Often there is scope for both sides to claim partial victory. One side, for instance, might utter its opponents' version of the ancestor's mother's brother, while the latter show themselves to have discovered its own version of the figure's father. This is a common outcome, but does not settle the dispute and further debates will normally be staged. But if one side can prove itself acquainted with its opponents' entire set of secret names, and show its opponents to be totally ignorant of its own, it wins the dispute decisively. The question, from the point of view of the audience and all third parties, is which side actually *has* the magical powers in dispute. It is not so much a question of legitimacy, of which side 'ought' to have those powers, but a question simply of fact. To them, the winners must by definition have those powers because, whichever set of names is the genuine one, the winners are the only ones possessing *both* sets. And so public opinion, as it were, hedges its bets: the winners may not be in rightful possession of the magical power but, one way or the other, they are certainly in actual possession of it. The losers' claims to the disputed ancestor, and all the associated names and magic, are no longer recognised. Privately, the losers may indeed continue to nurse those claims among themselves, and hope for some future opportunity to win the magic back. But in the meantime, they cannot voice those claims publicly and must give up using the disputed name, because the winners hold a powerful sanction: they could publicly expose the losers' secret name-set, and so make it impossible for them ever to win the magic back.

Of the 67 small-scale and full-scale debates I have recorded, 17 – about a quarter – were won in this way, the rest ending inconclusively. For reasons to do with the nature of most minor name-disputes, these contests do not occur in some small-scale debates. In name-disputes between close agnates, the challengers usually agree that the disputed ancestor is, by genealogy, an ancestor of their opponents. They simply claim that the figure, and all his associated names and magic, were ceded to their own descent group in mythical times. There is no disagreement over the secret names and filiation of the ancestor. The disputed name is, as the villagers put it, one with 'a single face' (*mutam nakamwi*). In these sorts of disputes, the sanction of exposing one's opponents' secret names cannot work, because the two sides share the same versions of those names and so cannot convincingly threaten each other with exposing them. Minor name-disputes tend therefore to be rather more difficult to settle than major ones, and their outcomes tend to depend more on the kinds of long-term demographic processes which I illustrated in the previous chapter.

Personal and group alignments in debates

The men of the two opposing subclans, together with the men of any totemic-sibling groups their subclans may have, and who automatically support them in debates, are called the *sakindu*, or debate-men. I shall call them the principals. The principals are supported by their allies, who are expected to contribute food and wealth to help them defray the expenses of a debate. Allies expert in myth are also expected to provide oratorical support and, most importantly, to take part in the contest in magical knowledge. The closest allies of the principals are their collective sisters' sons. Men take a pride in defending their mothers' subclans vigorously in debates, and if fights happen they are most likely to break out among the sisters' sons of the two sides. The principals, for their part, treat their sisters' sons with a kind of ostentatious solicitude, making sure they are well supplied with food and areca-nut, and setting up next to each of them a sago-leaf shade as the debate progresses into the hottest part of the day. Some of the sisters' sons, especially the eponymous sisters' sons of the lineages of the principals, are heavily decorated and made to sit in a conspicuous position on an upturned canoe. The canoe (sometimes a plank split from an old canoe is used) is the symbolic focus of each side and in the context of debating is called a *mba'ar*. *Mba'ar* is also, by synecdoche, the term for a debating-side.

A second category of supporters are sisters' husbands, who are known as *kwa'ar*. This is not a kinship term but the word for a woman's skirt. Etymologically, it may be connected with the term for sister used by male speakers, *ndjəkwa'ar*, which seems to mean 'skirt-fastened', or in other words a prohibited sexual partner. The term *kwa'ar* is only used in the context of debating. It has slightly mocking and derogatory overtones, and sisters' husbands are generally regarded as a rather second-class category of allies. They are often said not to know the myths of the *sakindu* and to support their affines only because their wives have threatened to refuse them their sexual services if they did not. Men often make these accusations against their opponents' *kwa'ar* in debates, especially the humiliating charge of uxorious-ness, and sisters' husbands tend to be in an uncomfortable situation, obliged to support their affines yet a favourite target for the raillery of their opponents.

The third and least significant category of allies are sisters' daughters' husbands (*nanggwund*; pl. *nanggwundangkw*). They have the weakest ties of all to the *sakindu*. There are usually few of them, and sometimes none at all, because they have been affiliated to one side or the other by stronger obligations – to their own subclans or to those of their mothers or wives.

All adult men in the community take part in a full-scale debate. Many of them are neutral, because they have no ties to either side or, much more commonly, because they have ties to both. Men may stand as sisters' sons to one side, for instance, and as sisters' husbands to the other. Men in these sorts of intermediate positions make a point of contributing food and wealth to both sides. If they are orators, neutrals are expected to play mediatory roles.

The wives and unmarried daughters of the principals, and of their allies, cook a meal for their side and serve it around mid-day. Although women do not speak in debates, they have a strong sense of involvement and show uncompromising loyalties to their own sides. My impression is that, to women, personal names are more closely bound up with notions of personhood or selfhood than they are for men. For the men, at least the more senior ones, the main significance of the disputed name is its functions in cosmology and ritual; but what seems more significant for the women is that it is specifically *their child* whom the opposing side are trying to 'de-name'. What the women see themselves as acting to defend, and perceive their opponents as attacking, is the actual personal identity of the child. The women decorate themselves and dance during the later stages of a debate and, in the past, it was common for the two mothers whose children bore the disputed name to duel with fighting-sticks. Sometimes this would turn into a full-scale brawl with sticks between all the women, and unarmed fights still break out nowadays.

Subclans collateral with those of the principals are expected to support them, and men use a simple segmentary model to describe the way this should occur. In a debate between subclans of different clans of the same-clan pair, for instance, the two whole clans would stand opposed to each other. In a debate between a Wuluwi-Nyawi and a Nggǝla'angkw subclan, the two entire clan-pairs would confront each other as blocs. But, in practice, the alignment of groups is rather more complex. Firstly, the importance of ties by marriage prevents a simple segmentary pattern (see Gluckman 1955a). In debates between Wuluwi-Nyawi and Nggǝla'angkw subclans, many men – except the principals themselves – side with their wives' or mothers' subclans against their own agnates. Men with these divided loyalties avoid appearing to support one side exclusively, and tend to act as conciliators.

The alignment of groups is further complicated because it is not only determined by clanship but also by totemic and other links, and the actual configuration of groups in a debate is usually a compromise between a number of inter-group ties of different kinds operating simultaneously. Figure 5 shows the alignments of groups in the debates which took place between the subclans Maliyaw and Sarambusarak in 1976 and 1977 over the name Manggalaman. Sarambusarak belongs to Nyawi clan and Maliyaw to the clan Wuluwi and so, if a purely segmentary logic had been followed, all the Wuluwi descent groups would have sided with Maliyaw, and all those of Nyawi with Sarambusarak.

This was in fact rather far from being so. Firstly, some of the men of the subclan Nawik supported Sarambusarak against their own clansmen. The reason for this was that a simbukship owned by the Nyawi subclan Ambasarak had at the time been held for some twenty-five years by Kwulambandi, a man of Nawik. In the early 1950s a struggle had taken place within Ambasarak over the succession, and had enabled Kwulambandi to step in and assume the office himself. Like the father of Pwimbandi, to whom I referred in the previous chapter, he was a self-made orator whose expertise in myth had enabled him to take the simbukship away from its rightful line of successors. He held it until his retirement from an active role in the ritual system after the major initiation ritual in 1978, a year after the final debate over Manggalaman, and the office then returned to Ambasarak. But in the meantime, Kwulam-bandi had learned much of the secret lore of Ambasarak. He became the major orator representing that subclan in debates, and for that reason he and some of his close agnates and allies sided with the clan Nyawi in the Manggalaman debates.

A second departure from a segmentary paradigm is that Ambasarak itself, together with its allies, divided during the debates, some men siding with Maliyaw and others with Sarambusarak. The reasons for this were again historical rather than structural. Some generations ago, Ambasarak very nearly became extinct, and all its secret myths and magic came into the possession of Maliyaw. Later, Ambasarak grew again and Maliyaw returned all its hereditary lore. Maliyaw men no longer know that lore, but Ambasarak has ever since been regarded as in debt to that subclan and expected to give it support in debates.

Ceremonial and totemic relationships also played an important role in the Manggalaman debates. The Nyawi lineage Mbwindimi and its allies sided with Maliyaw against its own clan, because it belongs to the yam harvest ritual association led by Maliyaw (see Chapter 8). Maliyaw were claiming that it was their own subclan, and not Sarambusarak, that shared the ownership of the storm-sorcery with Nyakaw. These claims were lent credibility by the fact that Nyakaw does have stronger totemic and mythological links with Maliyaw than with Sarambusarak, in connection with the membership of Mbwindimi in the ritual association which Maliyaw controls. Nyakaw maintained a careful neutrality in the Manggalaman debates, as groups in such a position usually do. Mbwindimi officially aligned itself with Maliyaw, and the other Nyakaw lineage with Sarambusarak, but both tried to play mediatory roles.

Turning to groups outside Wuluwi-Nyawi, the Nggəla'angkw lineage Kwaru supported Maliyaw because the two groups are totemic-siblings. The Nambul-Sambəlap lineage Makapangkw has totemic-sibling relationships with both Maliyaw and Sarambusarak, and therefore divided itself in the debates, some men and their allies supporting one subclan and others supporting the other. When a descent group has ties to both sides and divides itself in this way, it does not necessarily divide itself by a segmentary principle. Rather, its men meet before the debate and decide how best to allocate themselves in such a way that their varying expertise as orators is more or less equally shared between the two sides. There is a strong notion that the two sides in a debate should be evenly matched, both in size and in the quality of their orators.

The full-scale debate

Once the two sides have agreed to a debate they may be able to hold it within a week or two if they have no other commitments. A full-scale debate is held in front of the ceremonial house of one of the two subclans, and they must

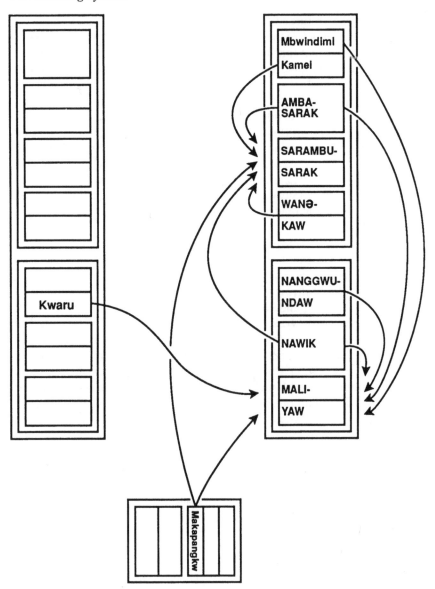

Fig. 5 Alignments of groups in the debates between Maliyaw and Sarambusarak over the ownership of the name Manggalaman.

therefore agree on the venue. A debate may run for more than twenty-four hours without a break, and in the week or so before the debate the principals and their allies must get ready enough provisions to be able to feed their sides for however long the debate lasts. Each side spends perhaps K20–K30 on store-bought foods, such as rice, tinned fish and meat. Coffee, tea and sugar are made ready to keep awake any somnolent orators. One or two wild pigs are caught and the flesh smoked, and large stocks of areca-nut and betel pepper prepared. All men, the villagers say, work for their *ndja'am*: even if they are not orators, they can contribute wealth and food to the defence of their subclans' ceremonial entitlements. Each side requires two domestic pigs as sacrificial offerings, one to be killed before the debate and the other afterwards, at a total cost of some 70–100 shell valuables, or between K200–300 in cash. Finally, about twenty or so valuables are needed as payments to supporting orators (see below). The expenses involved in mounting a debate are not especially large but they are enough to discourage the two subclans from committing themselves to a debate before their leaders have tried to solve their dispute in informal negotiations.

The day before the debate, each side gathers in one of its domestic houses for an event called *vei kwulapuna*, or 'delivering the apical ancestor'. Starting in the morning, and continuing all through the night, the men chant the long song-cycles (*saki*) connected with the subclan's origin myths. The first songs concern the birth of the subclan's founding ancestor (hence 'delivering' him) and the births of his sons, the founding ancestors of the subclan's lineages. The later songs describe the exploits of their descendants, the totemic ancestors figuring in the mythology to be disputed in the debate. Orators sit in the place of honour in front of the central post at the fore of house, with the less prominent men in a circle around them. Youths and young men who have not yet memorised the song-cycles accompany the chanting by keeping beat on hand-drums, and the women decorate themselves and dance at the rear of the house. The women serve food during the night, and everyone is kept supplied with areca-nut to keep them awake.

Every so often the men take a break from their chanting to reiterate their mythological claims and rehearse the arguments they plan to use in the debate. While *vei kwulapuna* is meant to foster an *esprit de corps* in readiness for the debate, it is also meant to ensure that all the men understand their side's version of the disputed mythology and the arguments that will be used to support it, so that no public disagreements occur between them during the debate itself.

The references the songs contain to secret myths make necessary a propitia-tory sacrifice to the totemic ancestors. The singing ends around daybreak, a few hours before the debate starts, and a domestic pig is killed and singed in front of the house, taken indoors and butchered, and its blood is sprinkled on the house-posts and the men's seating-places. The principals present one shell

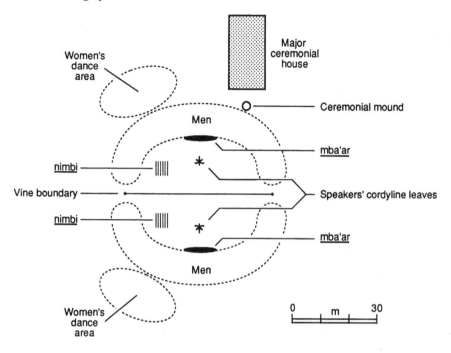

Fig. 6 Layout of a full-scale debate.

valuable to each guest orator, in appreciation of their help with chanting the song-cycles. These valuables are called euphemistically 'areca-nut for putting in the shoulder-bag' (*ma'as vanggavanggak kwasembi*). Sometimes, if the recipients value a reputation for generosity, they pass the valuables on to other men of their lineage or subclan, but as often as not they keep them for themselves. The gathering breaks up as men leave to refresh themselves with a wash in the river, each as he goes receiving a raw portion of the sacrificial meat.

Men begin assembling at the debating-ground in the early morning. The two sides seat themselves, on stools or on the ground, facing each other in two semi-circles about fifty metres in diameter (see Figure 6). Several hundred men usually attend a debate, sometimes including supporters from other Manambu villages. Men who are neutral or semi-neutral generally seat themselves at the ends of the semicircles, to avoid seeming to favour one side exclusively. In the middle of each semicircle sit the main protagonists, the *sakindu* and their sisters' sons.

Just in front of each side, elaborate arrangements of spears and arrows are set upright in the ground, heavily decorated with totemic bird-plumes and leaves. Scores of small sticks, each capped with a round, orange fruit called *mbandi*, are arranged in rows alongside them. These arrays are called *nimbi*

160

('arrows') and are partly a genealogical diagram, each spear, arrow and stick representing a specific totemic ancestor, and the whole arrangement representing the kinship and affinal relationships among them. Four of the decorated arrows are particularly important. These represent the disputed ancestor, his father, mother and mother's brother. When an orator wants to test an opponent's knowledge of myth, he will point to one of the spears or arrows, saying it is the father of the disputed ancestor and challenging his opponent to utter the figure's secret name. The decorations of the spears and arrows all refer to episodes in secret myths, and the men too – especially the principals and their sisters' sons – decorate themselves with leaves, bird-plumes and face-designs having special esoteric significance.

An Australian missionary told me he once tried to use *nimbi* as a way of illustrating the genealogy of Christ to a group of men in one of the Manambu villages. The men found it extremely interesting, but asked the missionary if he would also tell them those ancestors' secret names. Thinking he had inadvertently raised 'cargo-cult' hopes, the missionary brought the demonstration to an abrupt end and never again tried that technique.

Nowadays, a debate is opened by the Councillors of Avatip, the elected officials representing the community on the Ambunti Local Government Council. They warn the two sides to follow the proper etiquette of debating and not to fight. In the past, it was common for brawls to break out during debates and, as a modern innovation, a length of cane is stretched across the debating-ground at chest height between the two sides and the men are forbidden by the Councillors to cross it. Once the debate begins the Councillors hold their official roles in abeyance, so long as there are no breaches of the peace, and take part in the debate like any other men.

The debate proper starts with a little ceremony called *mba'ar səna*, or 'beating the *mba'ar*', in which each side formally announces its identity. An orator from one side recites lists of the totemic names and mythological epithets of his *mba'ar*, while someone beats slowly on the upturned canoe with a drum-beater. The other side, in the same way, proclaim the identity of their *mba'ar*, and then the debate begins.

In some respects, the villagers regard debating as a type of sport, or game in Huizinga's (1949) sense of *agon*, the contest of skill played by set rules and for specified stakes. The villagers value skill in oratory and disputation, and enjoy witnessing two subclans pit their skills against each other. The debating-ground has a colourful, carnival-like appearance, as each side tries to present as impressive a visual spectacle as possible. Sometimes, men act out an episode from myth in order to emphasise their claims, using 'props' and a few assistants from the audience, and the debate becomes a kind of competitive theatre. Men describe the acts of their totemic ancestors always in the first person and the present tense, as though trying to re-create the mythical past on the debating-ground. A speaker does not say, for instance, 'my ancestor created (*wunandə nggwa'al takandənd*) such-and-such a mountain', but 'I am creating (*wun takatuwand*) that mountain', or even 'I am (*wunandəwun*) that mountain' (see Harrison 1983). When the subclans Maliyaw and Sarambusarak debated the ownership of the ancestor Manggalaman, many of the speakers claimed, as the debate became heated, to have *become* Manggalaman, saying to their opponents 'I am Manggalaman' (*wun Manggalaman andəwun*), as though they were at that moment their own totemic ancestor in the act of performing his cosmogonic exploits. If some sorcery power is in dispute, the two sides may threaten each other with using it to obliterate each other during the debate itself. For instance, before the second Manggalaman debate, some of the younger and more hot-headed Sarambusarak orators had threatened to use the storm magic in the debate and call down a destructive hail of 'stones' on all the participants. The debate began in an apprehensive mood, and everyone scattered for shelter as rain-clouds appeared around midday and a heavy downpour interrupted the debate. But after an hour or so the weather cleared and, when the debate resumed, the senior leaders of Sarambusarak announced they had managed to restrain their more volatile juniors from using the sorcery to its full effect.

The villagers are very conscious of the risk of a debate disintegrating in violence, and an important way in which a debate is kept under control is its highly stereotyped and ritualised style. Speaking, for example, is accompanied by fixed, dance-like actions (cf. Burridge 1957). On the ground in front of each side are placed a few bundles of cordyline leaves (*ka'aw*). When a man wants to speak, he goes forward and picks these bundles up with a big flourish. As he speaks, he stamps the ground, holding the leaves in one hand, while with his free hand he takes the bundles one by one and tosses them to the ground in front of him as he makes each point. When they are gone, he crouches down, gathers them up and springs to his feet, still speaking all the while, and keeps repeating this sequence of actions until his speech is finished. The performance is done in a deliberately dramatic way meant to impress the spectators with the speaker's fighting-spirit.

Men sometimes accompany their speeches with theatrical displays of anger, raising an arm behind them as if preparing to throw an imaginary spear at the opposing side. But anyone who seems really to lose control of himself is despised. Men say that such men are like women. It is the way of women to lose their tempers in an argument, while men – so they themselves like to claim – settle their disagreements by patient discussion. Men who become violent also lay themselves open to the charge of being ignorant of mythology. Only ignorant men resort to empty vituperation and threats of violence, because they have no other way to take part in the debate. Men who know mythology may put on a show of anger but, so people say, this is deliberate and they are always in control of themselves (see Read 1959).

So long as a speaker holds the cordyline leaves he is entitled to an uninterrupted hearing. Heckling is very uncommon and only occurs when a fight is about to start. When a speaker makes a telling point, his side may show their approval with a kind of concerted cheer called *sənggwur tuwəna*, while the other side show their disapprobation with a similarly unanimous jeer, a nasal, neigh-like mass shout of derision known as *wandjəmbeina*. Speeches tend to be short, usually lasting less than five minutes, and when a speaker finishes he drops the cordyline leaves where he found them and returns to his seat. It is then the turn of his opponents to speak. It is one of the most basic conventions of debating that the two sides take turns to give speeches.

Many of the conventions of speech used in debates are meant to temper animosity and maintain an atmosphere of high formality. Orators rarely address each other by name but address their speeches to lineages, or call their opponents by their subclans' hereditary address-forms, which are courteous epithets, sometimes flowery, referring to the renown of their totemic ancestors. Speakers try to conduct the debate above a merely *ad hominem* level, and to keep it set in the more abstract and impersonal context of relations between corporate groups. If speakers do address one another directly, they do so by each other's bereavement names, expressing compassion and respect. Nor are kin terms used except in relation to whole lineages or subclans. A man might address a lineage junior to his own as his 'younger brother', treating that group as a kind of jural person. In the same way, he might address his wife's lineage or subclan as his 'child', a figure of speech identifying his children with their matrikin.

As the debate proceeds these courtesies act as a kind of barometer of the degree of control being kept over the affair. If men start seeming to dispense with them, it can indicate an impending brawl, and act as a cue for neutrals to step in and restore decorum. Having no authority over the proceedings, neutrals use a variety of informal diplomatic techniques, not the least of which is humour. As someone once told me:

> When the two sides are beginning to get angry, someone comes forward smiling as he speaks, and makes a joke. Everyone laughs and their minds are good again (*mawul viyakət tana*). He knows that men cannot fight when they are laughing.

The speeches made in debates are broadly of two kinds, which differ in style and content. The first are those dealing directly with the disputed mythology. These have a highly formulaic style, specific to debating. They use a specialised vocabulary, and are filled with totemic names, elaborate mythological epithets, and condensed references to recondite details of myth, all expressed in a relatively limited set of syntactic forms and intonational patterns. To be able to use this style successfully requires much experience in debating and an extensive knowledge of myth. Younger people have difficulty even under-standing speeches given in the formal debating style. In these respects, and in all its linguistic characteristics, it resembles what Bloch (1973: 13) calls the language of traditional authority: formalised language used by holders of authority as a medium of social control.

Very often, the arguments made in the formal debating style concern the etymology of the disputed name. In the Manggalaman debates, for instance, the subclan Maliyaw supported their claims to own the name with the following etymology. One of the totems of Maliyaw is the *ma'angk* tree (*Homalium foetidum*), which is personified in the myths of that subclan as an ancestor called Manggandimi, with the crown of the tree as his head-dress. Maliyaw argued that Manggalaman was the personification of that head-dress, and that it was he, their own totemic ancestor, who acquired the storm magic from Nyapal. They claimed that *Mangga-* derived from the word *ma'angk*, on a parallel with the name Manggandimi; while *-laman* came from *lamana* (to glow or shine) and referred to the bright red leaves of the tree. Only their own subclan, they said, was entitled to have the word *ma'angk* in its names, and for another subclan to do so was a disgraceful affront. They accused Sarambusarak of trying to steal the tree from them, inquiring of them sardonically whether they did not have enough totems of their own.

In the first debate Sarambusarak tried to counter this argument with an alternative etymology. *Their* Manggalaman, they explained, flew to Nyapal holding firebrands in his hands and feet; *-laman* referred to the glowing of the firebrands, while *Mangga-* derived from the word *ma'an* ('leg'). But the audience were skeptical of that etymology, and in the second debate Sarambusarak tried a different tactic. They agreed that *Mangga-* resembled the word *ma'angk*, but argued that the resemblance was accidental: *Mangga-* was 'only a word' (*ma'andja ndəka*) and meant nothing. They emphatically reiterated that they acknowledged the tree to be a Maliyaw totem, and recounted lists of the names of their own totemic trees at great length to prove they had more than enough of their own and had no motive to steal the totems of other subclans. There was only one genuine *ma'angk*-ancestor, called Manggandimi, they told their opponents, over whom there was no dispute. But Manggalaman was an ancestor with the form (*səp*; 'skin') of a man, not the form of a tree. The dispute had nothing to do at all with the *ma'angk* tree and the Maliyaw side were notorious thieves of others people's names and deceitfully trying to 'put the name inside their worthless tree' (*kuvəra'ap kwaləmir kawlana*). The orators of Sarambusarak also pointed out that their subclan owns several names containing *Mangga-*; if Maliyaw claimed ownership of all such names, why then, to be consistent, was it not also laying claim to those?

The second type of speech tends more to concern the current state of relations between the two opposing sides. One subject it especially concerns is the history of the use of the disputed name. When a group tries to usurp a name, its opponents will naturally demand that it explain why, if it owns the name, it has never before used it. The challenged group will describe the 'pedigree' of the name, showing how it passed down the generations among their forebears, telling their opponents to offer similar evidence of having used the name in the past. They will demand to know why the two subclans have never disputed the ownership of the name before, asking their opponents rhetorically whether their forefathers had no ears and were unaware another subclan was using the name.

These are questions which the challengers can counter with any of a number of fairly standardised ploys. They might reply that it is true that their forefathers never used the name, but it was because their subclan had been too small to have a bearer for it. Or it was because their forebears were ignorant of their own myths and unaware they owned the name, their subclan only recently having 'reacquired' the mythology showing the name to be theirs. They might argue that their ancestors were unaware that another subclan was using the name, because it had always been bestowed as a secondary name, and so was rarely spoken and, in any case, all those previous bearers lived in distant parts of the village. The opposing side may be able to present evidence disproving these claims, resulting in mutual accusations of lying, and challenges to swear oaths of purgation, flying back and forth between the two sides.

These sorts of arguments are made in everyday speech, and even very junior men can take part in them if they have important evidence. The two speech-styles tend to alternate with each other throughout the debate. A junior speaker might present evidence that one of the opposing orators is lying, and the orator then side-steps this with a string of formulae in the formal debating style, dismissing his accuser with the sheer weight of authority which that style conveys. The attempts by the two sides to out-manoeuvre each other verbally result in the debate constantly shifting back and forth between its two basic frames of reference: the world of the totemic cosmology, and the world of contemporary political relations.

Around midday, the women and youths serve their sides with food and areca-nut, as the debate continues uninterrupted. Orators, especially the principals themselves, are expected to disdain the food, their minds being fixed so wholly on the debate. If they were to show an appetite their opponents might accuse them mockingly of having come to the debate just for a meal. They do, however, chew areca-nut incessantly in a slow, ostentatious manner suggestive of implacability and controlled aggression, and become highly intoxicated. By the end of the debate, these men will have had no sleep and little food for forty hours or more, and some of them will be semi-delirious. While areca-nut does suppress fatigue and hunger, the stamina of those elderly orators is impressive.

By late afternoon, it usually becomes clear that neither side is prepared to give ground, and men begin to exhaust their arguments. Neutrals proclaim that the time for argumentation is over, and call on the two sides to begin testing each other's knowledge of the secret names so that the dispute can be settled without further ado. The two sides begin taunting each other, each challenging the other to try to 'see' (*vəna*) its esoteric names. Men boast that they know all their opponents' fraudulent names and are getting impatient to utter them.

The test may last an hour or so. While it is taking place the atmosphere is tense, and it is during this phase of the debate that there are the greatest risks of a brawl. The outcome of the whole dispute depends on nothing more than a few whispered words, and if one side tries to whisper out of turn, or someone announces a miscall but refuses to make the oath, a fight may break out.

It is rare for the contest to end in a decisive win for one side. Many names have been in dispute for generations, repeatedly debated without any conclusive settlement being reached. If the contest is inconclusive, the debate effectively ends and turns into a purely ceremonial display. The two sides start to chant their song-cycles to the accompaniment of hand-drums, while the women decorate themselves and dance. Each side ostentatiously ignores the other, trying to drown its rivals' songs with its own. Any orators able to make themselves heard make arrangements for the name to be debated again at some future date, or turn their attention to other unrelated name-disputes or pending debates.

But sometimes one side demonstrates knowledge of one or more of the secret names harboured by the other side. During the second Manggalaman debate in 1977, after the test had been going on for half an hour or so, one of the Maliyaw orators correctly whispered the Sarambusarak version of the secret name of Manggalaman. There was uproar on the Sarambusarak side, with men shouting outraged demands to know how he learned the name, and many wanting to brawl. After much prevarication, he announced that he learned it many years ago from one of the leaders of Sarambusarak itself, and named a long-dead orator of that subclan as his source. No-one on the Sarambusarak side believed him, and they tried to make him swear an oath. He refused, despite intense pressure from his opponents, making it quite obvious to everybody that he was lying.

Sarambusarak accused him of having learned the name 'yesterday'; of having, in other words, secretly bribed one of their own supporters to disclose the name shortly before the debate. Bribery, I might say, is a common tactic, and a shell valuable can often induce a supporter – most often an affine – to reveal secret names. Suborning one's opponents in this way is known idiomatically as 'pulling the headrest aside' (*kasuwina kumbutəkər*), suggesting an orator being secretly awoken at night by having his wooden pillow slipped from under his head, and being offered a bribe by some furtive visitor from the opposing side. Cheating of this sort is by no means disapproved of; on the contrary, it is admired as a sign of strength and political efficacy if a group can carry out such tricks successfully.

The test was resumed with feelings running high, the two sides turning their attention to the father, mother and mother's brother of Manggalaman, but neither group was able to make any headway in respect of those ancestors. Sarambusarak then demanded an indefinite number of tries at the Maliyaw version of the secret name of Manggalaman, to compensate for having had their affines suborned. They wanted, they said, to keep uttering all Maliyaw names they knew or suspected to have esoteric significance – to 'harvest the names like spinach' – until they hit on the right one and restored equality between the two sides. As a conciliatory gesture Maliyaw allowed them a few tries, but these were unsuccessful and Maliyaw then called for the test to end: the two sides had already spoken so many dangerous names, they claimed, that they risked causing sickness and disturbances in the environment if they continued any longer.

Neutrals began calling on Sarambusarak to drop their claims to Manggalaman and concede defeat. They agreed that Maliyaw probably did bribe someone, and rebuked the Sarambusarak men for not having had the sense to do the same themselves, telling them to cease prolonging the debate with pointless recriminations and allow everyone to go home. But the Sarambusarak leaders insisted that all that Maliyaw had discovered of their magic was a single name, learned by bribing someone, and that they could continue to use the name Manggalaman, and the gathering dispersed, late at night, with the Sarambusarak men consoling themselves with the prospect of discovering the traitor in their midst and finishing him off with sorcery.

A few days later, the leaders of Sarambusarak promulgated a rumour to the effect that they had just discovered, by bribing a supporter of Maliyaw, all the esoteric names connected with their opponents' fraudulent ancestor; and that when the name was next debated they were going to defeat Maliyaw totally. I suspect that was bluff. But, in the meantime, it had its intended effect of discouraging Maliyaw from exposing the esoteric name of their own 'real' Manggalaman, at least so far as I know. This sort of bluffing is always possible if one side has only discovered some of the other side's secret names, and not the full set, because it is understood that the name will have to be debated again.

A full-scale debate rarely ends before nightfall, whatever the outcome. Before leaving or, if it is already very late, the next morning, each side sacrifices on the debating-ground a domestic pig to the totemic ancestors referred to during the debate. This is to ward off sickness or misfortune that might result from the uttering of their secret names. As with the pig sacrificed before the start of the debate, each side distributes the meat among its own supporters.

Conclusion

Some Melanesian societies have been described as seeming to relish litigation and dispute, and to treat conflict as intrinsic to social life (Chowning 1974: 153;

Goldman 1983; Young 1974: 41). A similar observation could be made of Avatip. Debates are an essential feature of relations between subclans, and to the villagers it is part of the definition of subclans that they are organisations for debating and must constantly test each other's capabilities in the debating arena. Far from debates being in any way out of the ordinary, the villagers would think something was wrong if a year or two went by without any taking place.

Debating is a forum in which men and groups compete within institutionalised rules and by a fixed ceremonial procedure. Like the competitive food-exchanges of the Goodenough Islanders described by Young (1971), it makes appeal to a wide range of shared social values. Name-disputes can result in brawls and sorcery-feuds, and a large amount of energy in a debate is directed simply toward preventing the event from turning into a fight. But the esoteric, stylised and game-like qualities of debating set it apart from, and above, ordinary practical affairs. The antagonisms played out in debates are supposed to stay confined to the debating arena and not to overflow into the world of day-to-day social relations. This was a point made by the Councillor of Yentshanggai, during a speech opening the second Manggalaman debate, in which he compared debating to a football match:

Debating is just a kind of game. It isn't something to get angry or fight about. These two sides are going to kick off now, and they are going to fight only with words. You people on the sidelines mustn't try to kick the ball, because that's the way fights start. When the debate is over, the quarrel will be completely finished. Then tomorrow we can all go back to being brothers, sisters and uterine kin again, chewing areca-nut in peace together.

What makes it possible, indeed what makes it necessary, to maintain the public fiction that debating is 'just a kind of game', is the secrecy of its real issues. Debating is the behind-the-scenes politics of men's initiatory ritual being fought out, paradoxically, entirely in public, but in the disguise of a verbal sport. It is not only women and children who supposedly do not understand the issues at stake in a name-dispute, but many of the adult men as well. Few of the men involved in a debate even speak. The main speakers are the established or aspiring leaders of their subclans, men qualified by age, oratorical ability and knowledge of myth. A debate is a confrontation between whole subclans, but it is more immediately a personal contest between their leaders, with their followers providing the audience. Knowledge alone is not a sufficient pre-condition of leadership, because a knowledgeable man who is ineffectual in debating, easily outmanoeuvred in argument or too ready to concede defeat, will be ousted by more effective men of his subclan. It is in the debating-arena that men's capacity to act as leaders is judged by their followers and by others.

Important speakers, whatever side they are on, implicitly have a common interest in maintaining their high status. While the main rift in a debate is between the two opposing subclans, there is another, more submerged one cross-cutting this and to some extent mediating it: between the orators of the two sides, linked, as they often tend to be, by close affinal and uterine ties, and men who are their followers and audience. Orators of opposing sides often tacitly support and reinforce each other's status, for instance by refusing to recognise other members of each other's subclans as qualified to speak or, especially, qualified to take part in the uttering of secret names.[1] There is at least latently an element of co-operation between opposing orators as well as competition, and this is one factor serving to keep debates under control and preventing them from turning into brawls. Leaders have strong stakes in upholding the ideals of proper conduct in debating, as well as greater opportunities than ordinary men to exemplify them.

Older men say that there were fewer disputes over names in the old days. When disputes did break out, the leaders of the two sides would often settle the dispute privately among themselves, so that there was no need to involve their whole subclans in a debate. And when debates were held, the small numbers of orators made the debates easier to settle. Men speak deploringly of the increased numbers of speakers and aspiring orators, a democratisation of the debating system which they say has made debates more frequent, longer and more difficult to resolve. Disagreements occur nowadays within each side, some men urging compromise and others remaining intransigent. This was the implication of a remark which a Maliyaw speaker made during the second Manggalaman debate:

Nowadays, all men know mythology, and are able to name their children themselves. But in the past they had to work for their simbuk, and in return he would name them. But these days everyone thinks he is a simbuk, and keeps giving the wrong names to his children and causing arguments.

Men often disparage their opponents in this way, claiming that the easier access to myth has lowered standards of expertise. But my own evidence is that younger, aspiring orators sometimes provoke name-disputes in an attempt to displace established leaders of their subclans, and pre-empt their control over their groups' involvement in name-disputes. Not surprisingly, these attempts by younger orators to engage their subclans in debates often meet with opposition from their seniors. If, as older men suggest, more men nowadays become or hope to become orators, perhaps this kind of rivalry within the subclan has become more common. With the status of orator no longer so exclusive as it once was, co-leaders of the same descent group tend to bid for authority against each other by proposing alternative courses of action in name-disputes. I am not suggesting that competition for leadership has intensified, as I see no reason for that to be so, but rather that the focus of the rivalry may have shifted. If access to knowledge was more restricted in the

---

[1] See Forge (1972a: 534–5) for a similar observation concerning ceremonial exchange partnerships between Big Men in Melanesian societies.

past, competition within the subclan or lineage would have centred mainly on the inheritance of knowledge. In other words, it would have tended to take the form of succession disputes, from which one man would be likely to emerge as more or less undisputed leader. This was very probably the reason for the now largely defunct practice of younger men soliciting their teachers with food-gifts and labour. They would have stood as potential heirs of a monopoly of their groups' hereditary lore. But nowadays, it is not so much access to knowledge that tends to be the contentious issue between agnates, so much as the strategies they are to follow in name-disputes.

Other related factors too may contribute to the high incidence of name-disputes of which older men complain. Disputes would presumably have been settled more easily if leaders formed a smaller, more closely-knit, circle of affines and uterine kin. The increase in the modern tempo of the initiatory cycle has had some effects as well, as initiations have become smaller-scale but more frequent. In the past, there would have been long periods when no rituals were pending, and during those periods name-disputes perhaps tended to subside, arising episodically with the long phases of the ritual cycle. A number of factors seem therefore to have combined in the modern period both to 'democratise' men's access to cosmological knowledge, and to lead to a growth or expansion of the debating system. Modern conditions seem to have thereby had two apparently contradictory effects. On the one hand, the traditional privileges of senior men have weakened as larger numbers of aspiring orators have come into the debating system. On the other hand, what these increased numbers of competitors are nevertheless still seeking are the traditional goals of hereditary privileges in ritual and cosmology. At one level, the system has become more open and egalitarian; at another, the ideology of ascribed status in ritual and cosmology has actually become reinforced, as a wider range of actors seek access to important 'hereditary' positions in it.

Elsewhere in Melanesia, modern conditions – especially the imposition of peace and the greater accessibility of wealth – seem to have led, in rather analogous ways, to expansions of the ceremonial gift exchange systems (Gregory 1982; A.J. Strathern 1971; Young 1971), drawing larger numbers of actors into these systems and increasing the scale and frequency of the prestations. The debating system at Avatip is actually quite a close structural analogue of these competitive feasting or gift exchange systems. Like ceremonial gift exchanges in many other Melanesian societies, debates are the main political arena of Avatip society, and the forum in which leaders arise and ambitious men compete for influence and reputation. An obvious difference, of course, between an Avatip debate and a competitive exchange of wealth is that, in the latter, material goods are transacted, while all that is exchanged in a debate are words. A competitive feast or wealth exchange is a test of each side's capacity to produce or mobilise economic resources, while a debate is simply a test of their knowledge and oratorical skills. Defeat in ceremonial exchange can entail quite severe economic or political costs. A.J. Strathern, for example, notes that a group losing badly in a sequence of Moka exchanges 'could become politically dependent on the victor' (1971: 129). Young, similarly, observes that the loser in a bout of *abutu* competitive food exchange can incur debts which take years of work to repay (1971: 205). In an Avatip debate, on the other hand, there are no apparently material rewards to be won or penalties to be suffered. The medium of the exchange, and the losses and gains, seem essentially intangible or symbolic.

But there are some important similarities. First of all, the pattern of social ties by which the two sides in a debate are recruited, the physical layout of the event, the participation of women, the self-decoration, the lengthy and elaborate oratory, and the whole atmosphere of ceremonial display and self-aggrandisement, have some close parallels: with the *abutu* system of the Goodenough Islanders, for instance (Young 1971), with the Moka exchanges of the Highland Melpa people (A.J. Strathern 1971, 1975; Strathern and Strathern 1971) and with many other wealth-exchange systems both in the Highlands and elsewhere in Melanesia (Goldman 1983; Kaberry 1971; Oliver 1955; Malinowski 1935: 124; Rappaport 1968; Serpenti 1965; Tuzin 1976). The competitive exchange of esoteric names that forms the final stage of a debate could quite easily be replaced by a competitive exchange of yams or pigs: few other changes to it as an institutionalised event would be needed to convert it into a quite typical Melanesian exchange contest.[2]

In other words, the kinds of political relations being expressed are formally similar. To regard a debate as a 'symbolic' contest and a ceremonial exchange as an 'economic' one risks obscuring some important points. Firstly, every study of a Melanesian exchange system has shown that the material objects transacted are more than simply physical matter but are as much symbolic objects as are magical names or well-turned speeches in Avatip debates (see for instance Schieffelin 1980; Schwimmer 1979; Weiner 1977). In all these cases the relationships among political actors are being symbolised in the objects or tokens they transact, and those objects, whether they are pigs or words, may therefore be described as symbols. But the political relations themselves, of course, simply exist: it would be meaningless to suppose they might be more material or more impalpable in some societies than in others. Avatip men are simply establishing among themselves, by means of immaterial signs, the same kinds of real political relationships that, in some other societies, men create by means of material objects.

Secondly, both at Avatip and elsewhere in Melanesia, those relations among political actors concern an entire range of intangible and tangible rewards. Groups successful in the debating system do not only gain status, but attract affines: men wish to bestow wives on groups of high ceremonial status,

---

[2] I am indebted to Anthony Forge for having first pointed this out to me in relation to the long-yam exchanges of the Abelam.

and to become allies prepared to support those groups' claims, both within the immediate forum of politics and outside it, to a host of values including land and productive resources. The rewards of political success are essentially similar. Directly or indirectly, the actors are pursuing a complete range, in Weber's (1947: 280) phrase, of ideal and material interests simultaneously: from reputation, at the most incorporeal extreme of the continuum, to their means of physical reproduction at the most concrete. What primarily differ are the media of their transactions, and the surrounding sociocultural context that gives those media value and meaning.

One important difference is that, at Avatip, the political arena is less immediately engaged with relations of production. In comparison with a competitive food exchange or a Highland pig festival, it does not require major productive outlays and preparations to stage a debate. It does not for instance, involve extra land being brought under cultivation (Feil 1985), or the difficulties of obtaining a synchronised repayment of debts from a wide network of exchange partners (A.J. Strathern 1971). The logistics are relatively simple, and the economic costs are rather small even by Avatip standards. Groups organising a competitive feast are working within quite proximate productive constraints. The main material-world constraints on a group's effectiveness in the debating-system are probably its size and rate of reproduction. These are no less of a constraint but their effects on a group's capacity for political action are longer-term and more indirect.

It is this less immediate engagement of debating with economy that poses a problem. In the case of the Highland societies, it is easy to see what makes valuables, pigs, and other prestige items a limited good. There are real material determinants of the scale and frequency with which a group can mount its prestations, and what maintains the scarcity of wealth are by and large its own or its exchange-partners' limitations of manpower, land and productive capacity (Modjeska 1982). It is rather less easy to see what at Avatip keeps magic a limited good. What needs explaining, in fact, is why the ceremonial contests in this society should exist at all, given that the values for which men compete are not, as they are in the Highlands, inherently a scarce resource. Avatip cosmology functions as a type of prestige economy, and men are treating names and ritual powers as objects they can own, steal from one another, hoard, exchange, buy, destroy and so forth. They are operating a kind of reified economy of meaning. Those values are a focus of intense competition for status: and presumably, there is nothing to keep any subclan from manufacturing magical powers and ritual knowledge for itself *ad infinitum*, except the ambition and imagination of its leaders. The question then is what, given these intense competitive pressures on men, keeps the false coin of their dream, as Mauss and Hubert (1950: 119) called magic, from limitless inflation.

The first point I should like to make is that, in the public forum, names and magical spells are in some respects thing-like, in that they count as objective properties of the world, neither created by human beings nor dependent on them for their reality.[3] It is not, I should say, that men are incapable of distinguishing things and the contents of their own minds (cf. Hallpike 1979). Their conceptual realism is not a cognitive deficiency but a mode of representing, and in fact of constituting, their own political order. The kinds of arguments used in debates show that men are perfectly capable of conceptual reasoning. And, in any case, Avatip political life involves men constantly and quite consciously fabricating names and totemic ancestors in the disingenuous hope of getting them recognised as real entities in the debating forum. It is simply that, for the purposes of public political action, they draw the boundary between words and things at a different point, or in different ways, from ourselves.

To return to the problem of a semiotic prestige-economy: there is also of course the perceived necessity of preserving the scarcity value of ritual knowledge (Barth 1975; Lindstrom 1984: 301), because it is on the control of that knowledge that what Allen (1984) calls the 'gerontocratic' authority of senior men depends. This is important, but it can account only for the restrictions on the distribution of knowledge, not for the restrictions on its production. It explains why ritual powers are monopolised by senior men, but not what sets a limit on the ritual powers those competing men are able to claim.

The answer to that has to do with the basic assumption men make of an 'organic' ritual interdependence between their groups. If a subclan were to introduce a new power into the system, out of nothing as it were, it would change, however slightly, the existing balance of cosmological powers throughout the total society and challenge the status of every other group. Ambitious would-be innovators of cosmology in this society face difficulties, I suspect, in having their claims accepted, because it would require that the entire political community comply with and recognise a new and – to all groups except the innovators themselves – unfavourable political *status quo*. Because all ritual powers are assumed to form an interrelated totality, any entirely new gain in status by one group would be perceived to entail a loss to all others. The strong tendencies of every Avatip subclan toward a kind of cosmic self-aggrandisement, which would certainly flourish unchecked otherwise, are kept under control by all its rivals.

I should say that this system is by no means closed in actuality. I explained earlier that groups often imported magic and ritual from neighbouring societies in the past (see Harrison 1987), and perhaps they have also invented new ceremonial powers for themselves now and then. But my point is that men

---

[3] A number of ethnographers have commented on the 'thing'-like qualities ascribed, in some contexts, to words and especially to magical spells in Melanesian societies. See for instance Leenhardt 1979: 127–44; Malinowski 1923; Weiner 1983.

act politically on the basic assumption that their society is, so to speak, a global, relational whole, and so, in the great majority of cases, a subclan which acquires some new ritual prerogative does so by taking an existing one away from another group. Its aim, in other words, is not simply to demonstrate a claim to a particular power but at the same time to demolish some rival subclan's claim to it; and the competition is, as A.J. Strathern (1971: 10–14) describes the Moka exchange system, a zero-sum game, and takes place within the framework of the existing cosmology. When it is successful this process of course entails a readjustment of the balance of ritual functions between groups. But the change does not pose a threat to all uninvolved groups, since all that happens is that an existing power migrates from one subclan to another. The only group whose status is diminished is the previous holder of the prerogative; and so the change does not provoke a total, community-wide resistance to it.

When descent groups compete for some magical power, the question at issue in their debates is never whether that power exists, but simply which group is its owner. It would in fact be impossible in a debate for one side to challenge the actual existence of a magical power claimed by the other side. There are no means by which opposing claims of that sort could be compared and such a dispute resolved. A group can disprove that another one has a particular power only by claiming that power for itself. The only kinds of conflicts which a debate is capable of settling are conflicts sharing the same assumptions about cosmology. All that debating is intended to resolve is the allocation of ceremonial powers among groups, and within that framework, men can expend much productive effort and ingenuity and reach conclusive settlements. But there is no institutional context in which the reality of those powers can be called into question (see Lindstrom 1984: 294).

In short, while debating is the only context in which cosmology is opened up to public dispute, the conventions of debating make possible only certain types of arguments about cosmology, and preclude examining the assumptions on which those arguments rest. The cosmology itself is not a subject of argument but is the precondition of the arguments. It is part of what Bourdieu (1977: 159–71) calls doxa: the universe of the undisputed, as opposed to the universe within which conflicts of opinion are possible. The most basic implicit message of Avatip political discourse is that the totemic cosmology and all powers deriving from it are real. That assumption cannot be contested within the framework of the discourse. All the conflicting arguments put forward in debates, and all the legitimate or underhand tactics men use to win, unanimously reiterate it.

In effect, in acting out their rivalries men are also acting to reproduce the system of meaning that, in turn, gives rise to the rivalries themselves. On average, two or three debates take place each year at Avatip, and, to the villagers, it is part of the definition of subclans that they are groups that

174

constantly challenge and test each other's capabilities in the debating-arena. In an area of Melanesia in which 'clans essentially consist of a series of names' (Forge 1972a: 531), at Avatip they are also inherently organisations for defending names and must struggle to preserve and augment the political identities the names confer.

In a discussion of the language of traditional politics in Oceania, Brenneis and Myers have made the important suggestion that a polity 'is as much the creation of meaning as of sanctions or coercion' (1984: 11) and that in the politics of egalitarian societies speech is a crucial constitutive activity by which to accomplish or sustain 'polity' as a shared framework of understandings. Avatip groups do not compete for status by exchanging wealth but by exchanging words, and they are not simply arguing with each other but acting to ensure that their arguments shall continue to be possible. In their debates they work constantly with and against each other to recreate a shared universe of meaning and that universe, for as long as it is reproduced, 'is' their polity.

8

The rise of the subclan Maliyaw

Introduction

By far the largest of the sixteen subclans at Avatip is Maliyaw of Wuluwi-Nyawi clan-pair. With 246 members in 1978 it represented nearly a fifth of the population of Avatip, and was almost half as large again as its nearest rival in size, the subclan Yimal. Maliyaw is the most powerful and aggressive group in the debating system, and has been involved in more name-disputes over the past forty years or so than any other group. Many weaker subclans are dependent on its orators for support in debates; particularly the small but ritually senior Nggəla'angkw subclan Makəm, as I described in Chapter 6, in its long-standing disputes with its powerful junior subclan, Yimal. Maliyaw had six highly expert orators in 1978, a number equalled only by one other subclan. And these men, who ranged in age from about forty to seventy were notorious – as their predecessors seem to have been before them – for 'always stealing people's names'.

The growth of Maliyaw to its present size occurred fairly rapidly and within the past three generations or so. It is genealogically the most junior of the seven Wuluwi-Nyawi subclans, and in the course of its expansion it has engaged, with many successes, in a long-term bid to improve its ceremonial status. This process is still continuing; and what I wish to examine here are the strategies its leaders are using and, so far as I can reconstruct them, the strategies their predecessors used in the past, to gain important ceremonial powers for their subclan. I shall then make some inferences about their long-term political goals.

Of all the name-disputes in which Maliyaw has been involved in recent times, three particularly important ones have been continuing for between two and three generations. At the risk of overburdening the reader with case-material, I wish to describe these three disputes in some detail in this chapter, because they reveal important long-term processes at work. By outlining their historical development up to 1979, I show that Maliyaw has over this period been in the process of redefining itself as higher in ceremonial rank than several subclans genealogically senior to it, and that its leaders have been trying to acquire for it the highest ceremonial rank in Wuluwi-Nyawi clan-pair. Of all

176

subclans at Avatip, it is Maliyaw whose ceremonial rank bears the least correspondence to its genealogical seniority. It has been able to redefine its rank purely through its own political effectiveness in name-disputes.

But the most important dispute I discuss is a struggle between Maliyaw and the Nggəla'angkw subclan Yimal. In this dispute, Maliyaw have been trying to dispossess Yimal of its ritual control of the fishing lagoons and of its status as the community's founding subclan. What the Maliyaw leaders have been trying to acquire for their subclan are powers over all the community's main economic resources; and ritual precedence, not only over its own agnates, but over its marriageables as well. In other words, the long-term political goal of these men seems to be ritual dominance of the whole community.

Maliyaw, it will be remembered, owns a simbukship. The simbuk at the time of my fieldwork, Nəmandimi, was old and senile and his juniors did not allow him to speak in debates, though he had been a powerful orator in his time. He died in 1979 and his elderly successor, Yuambangk, who was a competent orator though not a major political figure, had still not been installed in the office by the time I left the field. But second in line of succession was a middle-aged and ambitious orator, Nyəngkaiwəs, who was also the Councillor for Yentshanggai, the elected representative of that village on the Local Government Council. Ever since the first colonial administration in the 1920s, Maliyaw has tended to monopolise these sorts of administrative roles, which have become almost its quasi-hereditary prerogative (see Chapter 4). Although the present Councillor is still, as an orator, subordinate to the older and more prominent orators of his subclan, he seems likely to become a major figure in the debating system, as well as a simbuk in time, and perhaps also an important figure in local government politics as well (see Figure 3).

Maliyaw has tended to attract powerful allies. Ambitious men of other subclans seek marriage alliances with its leaders, and many of the community's major orators are its leaders' close affines and sisters' sons. But the orators of Maliyaw are not, if I can so put it, well liked or popular men. To Avatip men, an 'ideal' leader is someone who can 'laugh and joke' (*wandjən rək kwurna*) with them in ordinary situations and act as their equal. Many important orators and ritual leaders have reputations of that sort, but not those of Maliyaw. They have a manner that disturbs many men, because it suggests that they do not acknowledge an ethic of egalitarianism, and have no need to because the dominant position of their subclan is so secure.

Maliyaw treads the subclan Nanggwundaw underfoot

The most important part of the ceremonial estate of Wuluwi-Nyawi is the yam harvest ritual. This is organisationally the most complex of all Avatip rituals, because it is performed simultaneously by three separate ceremonial associations. Each association is under the authority of an hereditary office, one held

The rise of the subclan Maliyaw

Table 17. *Composition of the yam harvest ritual associations*

Association	Member groups in order of seniority
Meipərnəmbər	1 Nyakaw (Kamei lineage) [Core group] 2 Nanggwundaw (Mawiyanggən lineage) 3 Maliyaw (Wapikas lineage) 4 Wanəkaw (Wainəmbuk lineage)
Yanggəlimbaw[a]	1 Ambasarak [Core group] 2 Sarambusarak[b] 3 Nawik
Awiwa'anggw	1 Maliyaw (Malikəmban lineage) [Core group] 2 Nyakaw (Mbwindimi lineage) 3 Nanggwundaw (Mamiandimi lineage) 4 Sarambusarak[b] 5 Wanəkaw (Kambanawur lineage)

[a]The lineage Ndjəmalwan of the Nggəla'angkw subclan Valik, and the lineage Makapangkw of the Nambul-Sambəlap subclan Sambəlap, also belong to the Yanggəlimbaw association (see Table 4).
[b]The subclan Sarambusarak provides men for both the Yanggəlimbaw and Awiwa'anggw associations.

by the Nyakaw lineage Kamei, one by the single-lineage subclan Ambasarak, and the third by the Maliyaw lineage Malikəmban. The latter two offices are particularly important ones since they are simultaneously simbukships. I refer to these three office-holding groups as the core groups of their respective ritual associations.

The mythical water-holes in which yams first came into being nowadays exist in the form of large water-filled pits alongside the ceremonial houses of these three subclans, and are the ritual foci of the three ceremonial associations. Although the associations are unnamed, men speak of themselves in the context of the yam harvest ritual as 'belonging' to one or other of these holes, and I will therefore refer to each association by the name of the water-hole identified with it.

The composition of the ritual associations is validated by each core group having a totemic relationship with each of the other groups in its association. Because all totemic ties take the form of senior/junior relationships, each core groups stands as senior to all the other members of its association. The core groups Kamei and Ambasarak are by agnation senior to the groups in their associations, so that their genealogical and totemic ties with their ritual associates are congruent. But the third core group, Malikəmban, is by genealogy the most junior lineage in the whole clan-pair, and all the groups in its association are its seniors by descent criteria. Here, totemism has taken precedence over descent, and the actual order of ceremonial seniority of the Wuluwi-Nyawi subclans, as it is reflected in kin term usage between agnates, is

The rise of the subclan Maliyaw

Table 18. *Genealogical and ceremonial ranking of the Wuluwi-Nyawi subclans*

Genealogical ranking	Ceremonial ranking
1 Nyakaw	Nyakaw
2 Ambasarak	Ambasarak
3 Sarambusarak	Nanggwundaw
4 Wanəkaw	Maliyaw
5 Nanggwundaw	Sarambusarak
6 Nawik	Wanəkaw
7 Maliyaw	Nawik

in fact based largely on their ceremonial ties and bears only a loose resemblance to the order of seniority implied in the clan-pair genealogy. In Table 18, the genealogical positions of these subclans are compared with their order of ceremonial rank.

Nanggwundaw and Maliyaw are treated, in short, as senior to two subclans senior to Nanggwundaw by genealogy, and I would now like to describe how this situation appears to have arisen. It seems to have been the result of a long-term – and still continuing – attempt on the part of the leaders of Maliyaw to raise the ceremonial rank of their subclan.

According to myth, the ritual office held by Maliyaw was not actually brought into existence by this subclan. It was created by the totemic ancestors of Nanggwundaw, the senior subclan of the same clan. These ancestors then ceded the office, and many of the names associated with it, to the totemic ancestors of Maliyaw. For at least two generations, Maliyaw leaders have been trying to suppress this myth, with the long-term aim of redefining the office as entirely the creation of their own ancestors, and there have been many debates between Maliyaw and Nanggwundaw over this issue. Although the two groups are close agnates, their dispute has long since escalated to the staging of full-scale debates.

Nanggwundaw has been a small group for several generations, with only thirty members at the time of my fieldwork. Its small size, and the nature of the disputed myth, together suggest that the office in question was originally held by Nanggwundaw and later escheated to Maliyaw. If this was so, Maliyaw thereby pre-empted the successorial rights of Nawik, the subclan intermediate between Nanggwundaw and Maliyaw in agnatic seniority. Why Nawik might have forfeited its claim to the office can best be explained by its tiny size: it is even smaller than Nanggwundaw itself, and has been so for as long as can be remembered.

It is probable then that three or four generations ago the core group of the Awiwa'anggw association was the subclan Nanggwundaw; and that Maliyaw and Nawik, as junior members of the same clan, were affiliates of this association. If this was the case, the ceremonial ranking of the Wuluwi-Nyawi subclans would have corresponded much more closely than it does now with their order of genealogical seniority. What I would suggest is that it was by taking over this office that Maliyaw was able to 'jump' several positions in the rank order of seniority within Wuluwi-Nyawi. And what its leaders have since been trying to do, is consolidate their title to the office and abolish the remaining mythological connections which the office still has with Nanggwundaw.

The disputed mythology is focussed on a mythical village called Ambianggai said to have been created by the totemic ancestors of Nanggwundaw. These ancestors built there a ceremonial house called Ambunyawərəmbi, and it was in this that they created the ritual office. But they later abandoned the village, and the totemic ancestors of Maliyaw took possession of it and everything in it. Nanggwundaw still own some of the names deriving from this myth, among them the names Ambianggai and Ambunyawərəmbi themselves. Many others are owned by Maliyaw. But there are five strategic names which both subclans claim, and it is around these that the whole extended dispute has revolved.

The earliest remembered phase of the dispute concerned the names Kwu-ta'akw and Kwusunəmbər. It is no longer known when the controversy over these two names first started, but Maliyaw and Nanggwundaw apparently reached an agreement to use the names in turns. At the time of my fieldwork they were borne by two elderly Maliyaw women. Nanggwundaw had begun to remind Maliyaw publicly that, when these women died, it would then be the turn of their own subclan to use the names. But the Maliyaw leaders made it clear that they would be unwilling to relinquish the names, and the two groups seem headed for a renewal of the dispute.

Kwusunəmbər is the totemic name of the ceremonial mound which stood in front of the mythical ceremonial house Ambunyawərəmbi. Such ceremonial mounds are important foci of Manambu ritual and, in the myth, the mound Kwusunəmbər plays a key role in the creation of the disputed office. Maliyaw claim that Kwusunəmbər now exists in their own ward in the material form of the ceremonial mound in front of their own ceremonial house. Kwuta'akw is the name of the third-stage initiates' hearth (*tanggayendjəmb*) of Ambunyawərəmbi. Maliyaw leaders say, similarly, that it nowadays physically exists as the senior hearth of their own subclan's ceremonial house. The senior hearth of a ceremonial house is ritually the most important part of the building. It is at his subclan's *tanggayendjəmb* that a new simbuk lights a fire as part of his installation ritual, and at which an hereditary head of a yam harvest ritual association performs his magic during the harvest ceremony.

Nanggwundaw has been in a weak position in all its debates with Maliyaw, because one of its two lineages belongs to the yam harvest ritual association which Maliyaw heads and thereby effectively accedes to the ritual authority of that subclan. In most of the debates between the two subclans, Nanggwundaw have conceded to their opponents' claims. They have argued merely that the disputed ancestors are still their own by genealogy, and that their subclan therefore still has a right to use their names now and then.

Some time in the 1920s, during the lead-up to the last performance of the Maiyir ritual, the two subclans held a full-scale debate over a third name, Marəngkayevinəmbər. In myth, this is the name of the *ndja'amb*, or sitting platform, inside Ambunyawərəmbi. Sitting platforms are another ritually significant part of Manambu cult-houses, since they may only be used by men of the highest initiatory grade. Marəngkayevinəmbər plays an important role in the origin-myth of the office now held by Maliyaw, and Maliyaw claim it as a totemic ancestor, saying it is nowadays embodied as the sitting platform in their own ceremonial house.

For this debate, Nanggwundaw actually built a sitting platform on the debating ground, the better to demonstrate its mythological claims. At the time, this subclan had one elderly but highly expert orator, and during the debate he climbed onto the platform to re-enact a scene from myth and make a speech. But in doing so he apparently collapsed, and died shortly afterwards, and the debate was abandoned in disarray. Afterwards, the men of Maliyaw let it be known that they had killed him by sorcery, claiming it a great coup to have finished off their opponents' main orator in the very middle of a debate. But because of its inauspicious associations, the Marəngkayevinəmbər dispute has never been reopened, and both sides continue to use and claim ownership of the name.

Nanggwundaw has a totemic-sibling tie with the Nggəla'angkw subclan Makəm, and these two groups, together with their allies, therefore support each other in debates. As part of their tie, they are linked together in the Ambianggai mythology. They claim that this village was created by a totemic ancestor of Nanggwundaw, called Yuananggərman; and that this figure was helped by a partner called Yuandanai, who belongs to Makəm.

In the early 1970s, as the plans to resurrect the Maiyir ritual were being laid, the leaders of Maliyaw began asserting that both of these figures were actually totemic ancestors of their own subclan, on the grounds that both names contain the word for the greensnail shell (*yua*), which is a Maliyaw totem. This claim had radical implications. Up to this stage, Maliyaw had been claiming that the ritual office was ceded to its totemic ancestors by those of Nanggwundaw; now it was claiming that its ancestors had actually *created* the office. The crucial issue here is that, if Maliyaw were to get this claim accepted, it would thereby make itself senior to the Nanggwundaw lineage affiliated to its ritual association. What the Maliyaw leaders seem to have been trying to do, in other words, is to create grounds for claiming higher ceremonial rank than Nanggwundaw, and for moving their subclan up a further step in seniority.

Maliyaw first laid claim to the name Yuandanai, holding a full-scale debate against Makəm and its Nanggwundaw supporters in 1973. There seem to have been two reasons why Maliyaw adopted the tactic of attacking the claims of Makəm first. Makəm is only tangentially involved in the Ambianggai mythology, and its ceremonial status rests elsewhere. It might therefore have been induced to part with the name Yuandanai more easily than Nanggwundaw would have been to relinquish Yuananngərman; and once in possession of Yuandanai, Maliyaw would then have been in a stronger position to claim the second name. Secondly, Maliyaw had largely monopolised the alliances of Makəm for two generations, and most of the adult sisters' sons of Makəm were Maliyaw men. Of these, four were the leading orators of Maliyaw, and all these men knew much of the secret mythology of their maternal subclan. They presumably felt that they therefore stood a good chance of defeating Makəm in debate, because Makəm is a small group with no orators of its own and in fact relies heavily on its Maliyaw sisters' sons for support in debating.

If the Maliyaw orators thought they knew the Makəm version of the secret name of Yuandanai, they were proved wrong when the debate took place. Makəm was defended by another of its sisters' sons, the leading orator of the subclan Nyakaw, who interrogated the Maliyaw leaders and found them ignorant of the relevant esoterica. The debate therefore ended inconclusively, the two sides arranging to debate the name again at some later stage.

Shortly after this debate, Maliyaw started laying claim to the name Yuananngərman. This issue was raised frequently over the next five years or so, whenever public gatherings gave Maliyaw and Nanggwundaw men an opportunity to voice their claims. When I left the field in late 1979, the name had not yet been formally debated, though the two groups had agreed in principle to a full-scale debate.

Like Makəm, Nanggwundaw had had no orators of its own for some time, relying in debates almost wholly on the support of sisters' sons and other allies. Both are senior but small subclans in the process of being 'trodden underfoot' by large and powerful subclans junior to them: Makəm by Yimal (see Chapter 6) and Nanggwundaw by Maliyaw. I have suggested that totemic-sibling ties develop out of the need which groups have for support, outside their own clan or clan-pair, in their chronic name-disputes with their own agnates. Both Makəm and Nanggwundaw have need of such support and their totemic-sibling tie seems to be a coalition between them in their shared predicament.

The dispute over the seniority of the yam harvest ritual effigies

In the previous chapter, I described a dispute between Maliyaw and another Wuluwi-Nyawi subclan, Sarambusarak, concerning the ownership of storm-magic and their relative seniority in the third-stage initiation ritual associated with this sorcery. I now describe another dispute between these two groups, this time concerning the seniority of Maliyaw in the yam harvest ritual.

The rise of the subclan Maliyaw

The three core groups are often in conflict with one another over their relative status in the ritual. For one thing, they are rivals for affiliates, and in recent decades there have been several cases in which they have been able to attract whole lineages away from each other. To some extent, affiliation with a yam harvest ritual association is political allegiance to its core group.

The most junior of the three core groups, the lineage Malikəmban of Maliyaw subclan, has in particular been trying to improve its status, its leaders claiming that the first yams in the world were disgorged from their own water-hole as well as from that of Ambasarak. Ambasarak men reject this claim, but so far the issue has not reached the stage of a formal name-dispute between the two groups. More importantly, Malikəmban – or rather, the whole of Maliyaw subclan – has been trying for some two generations to have itself reclassified as higher in ceremonial rank than Ambasarak and as senior to it in the ritual, staging some seven debates over this period in an attempt to challenge the seniority of the Ambasarak effigy to its own. The strategy of Maliyaw has been to attack, not Ambasarak itself but Sarambusarak, a subclan with which Ambasarak has very close mythological and totemic ties, and which owns a number of crucial names relating to the Ambasarak effigy.

The effigy is called Nggəleinwakən. According to myth this figure was born without a head, and was given one by totemic ancestors of Sarambusarak, who also decorated the infant Nggəleinwakən with yellow paint (*nyawər*) and incised designs (*ndjəmb*). In the myth, these latter two items of decoration carry the totemic names Manambunyawər and Manambundjəmbandu respectively, and these names are owned by Sarambusarak. When the effigy is built during the yam harvest ritual, Sarambusarak men accordingly have the right to carry out these parts of the effigy's construction.

Malikəmban has a virtually identical myth concerning the birth of its own effigy, which is called Kobavwi. Ambasarak and Sarambusarak claim that Kobavwi is the junior of the two ancestors, and was born, adorned, and equipped with a head after their own. It is this assertion which Malikəmban has been challenging for the past two generations and it has done so by trying to gain ownership of the names Manambunyawər and Manambund-jəmbandu.

Malikəmban seems to have started laying claim to the latter name in the 1930s, saying that it was the name of the designs incised on the infant Kobavwi, their own effigy, not on Nggəleinwakən. Moreover, Kobavwi was incised first, and is therefore the elder brother.

Maliyaw subclan held three full-scale debates against Sarambusarak over the ownership of the name, over a period of about a decade. During the last of these, Maliyaw seem to have shown themselves acquainted with some of the esoteric lore of Sarambusarak, and were able to impose a revision of the myth. According to this new version Nggəleinwakən's mother, Kukuleimbaw, had 'thrown him away' immediately after his birth. Kobavwi's mother, Səsəsakwi, had found him and fostered him together with her own son. Sitting together on her lap, the pair were incised simultaneously by Kobavwi's maternal uncles. To signalize this new version, it was agreed at the debate that Maliyaw would take the name Manambundjəmbandu while Sarambusarak would take the female form of the name, Manambundjəmbata'akw. This device was only a temporary truce, and both groups still say they will debate the name again. In the meantime, Sarambusarak leaders have begun to claim that Kobavwi's mother held Nggəleinwakən on the inner part of her lap and Kobavwi outermost; and that Nggəleinwakən remains, by this minimal criterion, still senior.

Maliyaw began trying to acquire the name Manambunyawər in the late 1950s, claiming similarly that it was the totemic name of the paint applied to its own effigy, Kobavwi, and that Kobavwi was ornamented in this way before Nggəleinwakən. Their own ancestor was therefore in myth the first of the two to be completed, and is therefore the senior. Four full-scale debates have taken place over the ownership of Manambunyawər, the last three in the late 1960s and early 1970s during the lead-up to the most recent performance of the initiatory version of the yam harvest ritual in the mid-1970s. The debates were inconclusive; Kobavwi remained the 'younger brother' of Nggəleinwakən, and was erected after it in that performance of the ritual.

In the whole of this extended dispute over the yam harvest ritual, the group with the most to lose has, of course, been Ambasarak. This is the subclan that actually 'owns' Nggəleinwakən as a totemic ancestor and leads the ceremonial association which constructs this effigy. In effect, Ambasarak is in the invidious position of having its ceremonial privileges the subject of a dispute between two other subclans. Its position has been made even weaker by the obligation it has had, for many generations, to provide Maliyaw with support in debates (see Chapter 7). In all the debates between Maliyaw and Sarambusarak, Ambasarak and its allies have mostly sided with Sarambusarak but have always assigned some of their men to support Maliyaw – even though it is Ambasarak itself whose ceremonial status would suffer most if Maliyaw won. A further complication in the debates has been that Sarambusarak provides men for both of the yam harvest ritual associations which Maliyaw and Ambasarak control (see Table 17); and this has been the cause of lengthy recriminations between Maliyaw and Sarambusarak in all their debates, since groups belonging to the same association are supposed to avoid conflict.

Maliyaw claims the status of founding subclan

For some two generations, Maliyaw has been involved in a dispute with the subclan Yimal of Nggəla'angkw clan-pair. This dispute is the only one to have taken place between these two subclans in living memory, but for several reasons it is a very important one. The protagonists are the two largest and, in the debating system, politically dominant subclans at Avatip. Secondly, they are marriageables, and the dispute between them has come closer than any other name-dispute in remembered history to jeopardising the whole ideology of mutually 'maternal' nurture between affines and uterine kin on which cosmology and the ritual system are based. Lastly, at stake in the dispute are the most important mythological issues involved in any known name-dispute, because what the two groups are each claiming is the ritual responsibility for the vital fishing-grounds on which the community depends for its livelihood, and the status of having founded Avatip.

Besides being the two largest subclans at Avatip, Yimal and Maliyaw are also unusual in that their component lineages act as independent alliance units. Both subclans consist of a pair of lineages, each of which makes bridewealth and mortuary payments separately and is a separate entity for reckoning uterine kinship. The significance of this is that both of these subclans allow, and in fact encourage, marriages between the members of each lineage and the sisters' children of the other lineage, in order to have allies who are doubly obligated to them as simultaneously sisters' sons and sisters' husbands. The explicit purpose of encouraging marriages of this sort is to make doubly certain the allegiance of allies in debating, and to make all secret lore imparted to those allies doubly secure. No other subclans at Avatip are able to permit this kind of intermarriage with sisters' children, because none have lineages large enough to finance their own bridewealth and mortuary payments. It is an advantage that only these two very large subclans can afford, and it gives Maliyaw and Yimal some powerful allies with complete and undivided allegiance to them.

The myth of the foundation of Avatip is a complicated one, but its basic outline is as follows. At the very beginning of things, when water covered the whole of the present landscape, two ancestors existed at what is now the site of Avatip. One was the *kwa'as* bird, a totem of the subclan Makəm; the other was the domestic fowl (*tapuk*), a totem of the subclan Nambul (see Chapter 7). The two ancestors were unable to move, both being immobilised in mud, and were covered in ugly sores. They were discovered in that state by a figure called Təpəsawun, whom the subclan Yimal claim as a totemic ancestor, and Təpəsawun offered to extricate them and cure their sores. They refused, saying that others, who would come later, would help them. His task, they told him, was a more important one: to raise dry land out of the water for a village site, and to found Avatip.

The subclan Yimal owns magic for draining swamp and reclaiming land, and it was this magic that Təpəsawun used to create the village site. When he had done so, totemic ancestors of other subclans began to arrive, some of them rescuing the Makəm and Nambul ancestors as the latter had foretold. A settlement began to grow, Təpəsawun allocating to each subclan, as its ancestors arrived, a section of the site as its ward. The very last subclan to appear was Maliyaw, its ancestors coming from its mythical origin-village

The rise of the subclan Maliyaw

Ambianggai far to the north. Təpəsawun created with his magic a temporary causeway across the Sepik River, to enable the Maliyaw ancestors to cross into the village. He then swore a ritual oath (*sa'al*) of friendship with them, to the effect that his descendants and theirs would live and gain their livelihood together and share all the surrounding natural resources. Taking a fish, he put its head in the mouth of one of the Maliyaw ancestors, and the tail in his own, and then cut the fish in half. As a legacy of this oath, Maliyaw now owns the personal name Ambakami ('fish-head') and Yimal the name Ngginyakami ('fish-tail'). Təpəsawun then assigned Maliyaw its ward.

This is the most widely accepted version of the foundation myth, and on the basis of it Makəm and Nambul are considered the two founding subclans at Avatip, a status which gives them some prestigious, if somewhat nominal, ceremonial rights (see Chapter 7). But it is the subclan Yimal, although a later arrival, which plays the central role in the myth. For those who accept this myth, Yimal is the effective founder of Avatip and 'owns' the village and its environs.

Its status as 'owner' of Avatip gives Yimal a complex of powerful ritual sanctions. Three of these are particularly important. Firstly, Yimal has a highly senior role in the Ndumwi ritual of third-stage initiation, junior only to the subclan Makəm whose prerogatives in this ritual Yimal has for several generations been gradually appropriating (see Chapter 6). Secondly, Yimal controls the fertility of all the main lagoons on which the village depends for fish, and can ritually interdict the use of these lagoons. This, in fact, is precisely the significance of the scene with the fish, described above: what it implies is that it is only by permission of Yimal that other subclans use the village's fishing-grounds, and that Yimal has an hereditary ritual right to prohibit access to these resources. The third sanction Yimal holds has to do with its magic for creating dry land. This magic (and the foundation myth is the charter for it) has a potentially sinister use. It can be used to silt up fishing-lagoons, and by owning it Yimal is believed to have the highly feared power of destroying all of the village's fishing-grounds.

Much of the magical and ritual lore on which the powers of Yimal are based have also come to be known by the leaders of Maliyaw, because many of these men are, or were during their lives, sisters' husbands and sisters' sons of Makəm and so learned much of its hereditary lore. It will be recalled that these men have been crucial defenders of the hereditary prerogatives of Makəm against the encroachments being made by Yimal, and have often substituted for their Makəm maternal kinsmen in the Ndumwi ritual and acted as their proxies during periods when Makəm had no initiated men of its own. What is in effect happening in the Təpəsawun dispute is that Maliyaw are claiming all these powers as their own subclan's hereditary property, and the dispute is in effect a conflict between Yimal and Maliyaw to take over all the key prerogatives in the ceremonial complex of Nggəla'angkw clan-pair.

The rise of the subclan Maliyaw

To back up its claims, the subclan Maliyaw have a rival version of the foundation myth, and in this version Təpəsawun is a Maliyaw ancestor. There are two main protagonists in this version of the myth: Təpəsawun and another figure called Apasawun, a totemic ancestor of the Sambəlap lineage Makapangkw. Maliyaw and Makapangkw, who have a totemic-sibling relationship, claim that these were the two very first ancestors to arrive at the village site, appearing there even before the ancestors of Makəm and Nambul. An island of floating grass ran aground against them and took root to form a plot of dry land, and this was therefore the first part of the village site to come into being. After this spot had been formed, the Makəm and Nambul ancestors appeared and, after them, the ancestor of Yimal. But Maliyaw and Makapangkw deny that this figure was called Təpəsawun and say that he must have borne some other name. From this point on, the myth follows the Yimal version in its essentials, but with one fundamental difference. The Maliyaw and Yimal ancestors made a compact, just as Yimal claim; the head of the fish being put in the mouth of the Maliyaw ancestor and its tail in the Yimal ancestor's mouth. But it was the Maliyaw ancestor who was called Təpəsawun, he who offered the fish, and he who performed the oath and cut the fish in two. It was, in short, Maliyaw that invited Yimal to settle in the village and use its resources, not the reverse. Yimal may have later settled the other subclans at Avatip, as it claims; but Yimal itself had been allowed to settle there in the first place by Maliyaw.

The dispute revolved, in other words, around three contested elements in the myth: which of the two ancestors was called Təpəsawun; which of them was the first to arrive at the village site and create dry land; and, in the scene with the fish, who was in fact giving the fish to whom.

The foundation myth, and the ownership of the name Təpəsawun, have been debated by Yimal and Maliyaw without result several times. The last two debates took place in 1972 and, just before my arrival at Avatip, in 1977. Both sides used etymological arguments, among other sorts. Maliyaw and Makapangkw claimed that Təpəsawun and Apasawun were egrets (*sawun*), a persuasive point since the egret is a joint totem of theirs but not a totem of Yimal. Yimal countered by claiming that while the name does contain the word *sawun*, *their* Təpəsawun was not an egret but their own totem, the cormorant (*tambul*). What they stressed was the element *Təpə-*, from the word *təp*, or 'village'. Any name containing this word must belong to Yimal, they argued, since Yimal founded and owns the village (this seems to me a *petitio principii*, but I do not know if it was pointed out by Maliyaw).

When these debates took place, relations between the Yimal leaders (particularly Kamiapan of Silikindu lineage – see Chapter 7) and the leaders of Maliyaw, had been embittered for many years and they had had innumerable private disputes. These had been aggravated by the fact that Kamiapan was married into the Maliyaw lineage Malikəmban, and was a sister's son of

Wapikas, the other Maliyaw lineage. In other words, he was himself one of the double-allies of Maliyaw and should therefore have been a very close ally and supporter of that subclan. He had learned much of Maliyaw myth from his classificatory mother's brother, Nggawindu, the leader of the Maliyaw lineage Wapikas. But having done so, he poured scorn on this lore, claiming publicly that it was all lies. Nggawindu was so enraged that he swore an oath never to teach his subclan's myths to his allies again. But this only advantaged Kamiapan, because it made him one of the few men in the community from whom these myths could still be learned.

A few months before the second debate took place, Kamiapan asserted his subclan's rights by putting a total interdiction on Walɔmaw, the largest of the community's lagoons and its main source of fish. He said it was because the women were over-fishing the lagoon with their gill-nets. These nets are a European introduction, and are often criticised by the men of Nggɔla'angkw as wasteful and destructive, unlike the traditional dip-net the women also still use. Left tied to bamboo poles set in the lagoon-bed, a gill-net traps large amounts of fish, but if left unattended for long many of the fish die and have to be discarded. Kamiapan's interdiction applied to the whole community, including his own subclan, and for six or seven months nobody in the community used the lagoon until, in mid-1977, the other Nggɔla'angkw leaders persuaded him to lift the interdiction. They and he sacrificed fowls in the ceremonial house Kamandja'amb, and also at Walɔmaw itself, to suppli- cate the spirits and reopen the lagoon.

Late in the same year, ten months after the last debate, Kamiapan challenged Nggawindu, with rhetorical hyperbole, to debate the name with him singlehandedly in a verbal duel, with the loser's subclan to leave Avatip for ever. He boasted that would make Nggawindu and all his subclan uproot their ceremonial houses and domestic houses and carry them back to where they all came from (that is, to mythical origin-village of Maliyaw subclan). The two subclans agreed provisionally to hold a full-scale debate early in the new year. Nggawindu announced that he would take a Maiyir oath during this debate and swear that Tɔpɔsawun was a Maliyaw ancestor. People could judge whether he was lying, by whether or not the oath killed him.

As the time for the debate approached, Nggawindu grew increasingly reluctant to swear this oath. This seems to suggest that he knew the Maliyaw myth was an innovation and, perhaps, that he himself had been involved in creating it as a young man. If so, this would put the date of its invention at some time in the 1930s or 1940s. At any rate, Nggawindu told his subclansmen that the debate would have to be postponed indefinitely. He reminded them that they had recently had a full-scale debate against the subclan Sarambu- sarak over the name Manggalaman, and he did not want to strain their resources any further by holding another one so soon. As a result, the debate fell through, and Nggawindu evaded the oath without losing face; in fact his subclansmen were grateful to him for what they interpreted as his magnanimity toward them.

The debate had still not taken place by the time I left Avatip for the last time nearly two years later. In the meantime, Kamiapan found other outlets for his hostility to Maliyaw: the dispute with Makəm, the maternal subclan of most of the Maliyaw leaders, over the ownership of the name Yanggənmawai (see Chapter 6); a dispute with his mother's lineage over the ownership of a stand of palms; and, just as I was leaving late in 1979, a spectacularly public divorce of his Maliyaw wife amid bitter recriminations and mutual threats and accusations of sorcery between himself and his affines.

History, politics and cosmology

It is clear that the leaders of Maliyaw have had, probably since the beginning of this century, the long-term aim of gaining a monopoly of all the major ritual powers in the society. They have been trying to acquire for their subclan the highest ceremonial rank within their own clan-pair, Wuluwi-Nyawi, and control of its whole ritual complex. Secondly, they have been trying, since at least the 1940s, to acquire the status of founding subclan, and the ritual control of the fishing-grounds, held by the clan-pair Nggəla'angkw. The goal these men have had is to make their subclan superior in status to all other groups, marriageable and otherwise, in the community. This is not a goal they admit to, in public at least. But it is evident, from the consistent political strategies they have been following, that their aim has been to make the whole community ritually dependent on their subclan.

What these men seem to be imagining, and trying to create, is a situation such as exists in the Trobriand Islands, and in the village of Kalauna on Goodenough Island, in which all the key magical powers are the prerogative of one, high-status descent group (Malinowski 1935; Powell 1960; Young 1971). They are seeking to abolish the basic principle on which ritual relations between Wuluwi-Nyawi and Nggəla'angkw are based – a mutually nurturant, 'maternal' reciprocity between equals – and to replace it with an asymmetry, a unilateral dependence of all groups in the community upon their own subclan.

As Avatip ritual and cosmology stand, agnates are ranked and unequal, while marriageable groups are represented as equals, 'giving mother's milk' to one another in a self-reciprocal uterine relationship of mutual succour and dependence. What the Maliyaw leaders seem implicitly to be trying to do is to widen the scope of ritual rank and inequality beyond relations between agnates, and extend it also to their relations with all their marriageables. This seems to me to imply a very basic change in the structure and meaning of Avatip ritual and cosmology.

But let me say first that it would require only the most minor modifications to the actual *details* of cosmology. It is clear that name-disputes usually involve only very slight changes to myth; and while new mythological claims are constantly being made by ambitious groups such as Maliyaw, it is likely that much of Avatip myth, ritual and cosmology has remained relatively unchanged over very long periods of time. What mainly changes is the *ownership* of the names, myths and associated powers: these elements itinerate from one group to another as time goes by, but in themselves are relatively fixed and enduring. If Maliyaw were to succeed in gaining a monopoly of all the key cosmological powers, then the myth of the founding of Avatip, the ritual power to control the fishing-lagoons, the initiation rituals of the men's cult, and so forth, would all presumably remain much as they are now because it is quite clear that the leaders of Maliyaw are making no attempts to alter their substantive content. The myths and ritual privileges themselves would be largely the same: what would have radically changed is their significance, their implications for political relations. It is simply the concentration of their ownership in one subclan, an alteration in the structure of their distribution, that would have fundamentally altered their *meaning*.

I would therefore agree with Bloch's (1986) conclusion, in his analysis of the history of the Merina circumcision ritual, that the content of symbolic systems is slow to change; it is the political interests they can be made to serve, that can alter rapidly over time. But it does not necessarily follow that their *meaning* is stable, because actors can attribute, according to their own perceived interests, quite variable interpretations to the same symbolic content. What is politically manipulated in Avatip cosmology, and therefore highly variable over history, is not so much the myths and ceremonial privileges themselves but the pattern of their social distribution; but as they become concentrated in the possession of one group, or dispersed again among many, so the grounds of their intelligibility are transformed. The idiom of 'giving mother's milk', in a context in which one single subclan was the sole source of all such symbolic nurture, would carry implications of dominance and superiority quite different from those it has in the present structure of ritual relations between groups, in which it expresses the mutually supportive equality of marriageables. Among the Murik people, near the mouth of the Sepik River, very similar idioms of maternal nurture and feeding form part of ideologies of rank, and refer to the superiority of high-ranking individuals and the dependence of their inferiors on them (Lipset 1984; Meeker *et al.* 1986). It is from the total context of inter-group relations formed by their distribution that the elements of cosmology draw their interpretability. And as this context of their distribution is manipulated, so their import can be made to alter in quite fundamental ways, even though the content of the cosmology itself is left relatively unaltered. The leaders of Maliyaw are not trying to create a new cosmology and ritual system, but to bring about a metamorphosis in the *meaning* of the existing cosmology through a reordering of the pattern of ritual responsibilities between groups.

The rise of the subclan Maliyaw

I see no reason to suppose that Maliyaw is unusual in the ambitions of its leaders. The leaders of many other subclans may have, and may have had in the past, similar ambitions for their groups. It is just that, at the present time, Maliyaw comes closer than any other subclan to being a political force effective enough to actually achieve such ambitions. Maliyaw is, *de facto*, politically the most powerful subclan at Avatip. What it lacks, as do all groups in this society, is a means of institutionalising its power, of having it transmitted by hereditary right across the generations. Its influence must constantly be recreated and earned anew by each generation. What the leaders of Maliyaw seem to be trying to exploit is a potentiality inherent in the organisation of ritual: that is, that the hereditary status-inequalities of ritual could be developed into political authority. If Maliyaw were to achieve ritual dominance of the community, that ceremonial pre-eminence could offer a way to give its actual power a religious validation and to guarantee its transgenerational continuity by representing it as immemorial and hereditary. Just as Maliyaw is not seeking to create a new symbolic order, neither is it seeking to bring wholly new kinds of influence into existence, nor a radically new political order. Maliyaw already *is* the dominant subclan in the community. All that its leaders are seeking is to change the way in which that dominance is represented and conceptualised.

The basic dialectic of Avatip history is between two spheres of action: a ritual system pervaded by notions of ascribed inequality, and an everyday world of relatively unrestricted and egalitarian competition between groups for important positions within that system. In these competitive processes, some groups are politically more adept or successful than others, and may, as Maliyaw does currently, temporarily come to dominate that arena of competition by their size, adroit use of marriage alliances, bribery and all the other innumerable strategems that make for political advantage and survival. The ritual system and the cosmology both motivate these conflicts, and also potentially offer a successful group the means to represent the provisional and 'contingent' dominance it won in the conflicts as a structural, institutionalised one. What the emergence of rank at Avatip would require, in short, is not so much a new ideological order, nor a new political one. The goal of powerful groups such as Maliyaw is rather a new synthesis of those two existing orders, in which cosmology and the existing distribution of power and influence are brought into correspondence with each other in such a way that a current and, in itself, unstable pattern of political relations in the community becomes legitimised in ritual and cosmology as perpetual, timeless and unchallengeable.

It may be that it is only in the modern era that such a strategy can have become feasible. It would not, for instance, be possible nowadays physically to assassinate a simbuk who used his ritual powers as a means to political power. That sanction of political equality has been removed, and cannot now be an effective threat with which to keep ritual authority confined to the ritual sphere. And introduced political institutions, such as the Local Government Council, offer new opportunities, which the leaders of Maliyaw have taken, for ambitious ritual leaders to acquire forms of power unavailable in the past. But most of the disputes I have described in this chapter, began before European contact. The predecessors of the present leaders of Maliyaw had, in other words, the same political goals as their successors have now, before the arrival of Europeans on the Sepik.

Large, flourishing subclans such as Maliyaw can marshal many allies and supporters in debates. They have the demographic resources with which to take personal names from other groups. And they are more able than small groups to maintain an unbroken transmission of their ritual functions, mythological lore and so forth, from one generation to the next. Reproductive success tends, in effect, to carry a group 'up' the ceremonial ranking system, displacing weak groups 'downwards'. This connection between the size of descent groups, and their status in the ceremonial system, seems in fact to work in both directions. Because high-status groups tend to attract bestowals of wives, high ceremonial rank is likely to give a reproductive advantage in the long run. There is probably a long-term trend for differentials between groups in their size, ceremonial rank, and their capacity to attract affines, to widen progressively. In other words, there is a kind of inherent instability, a tendency for any inequalities which develop between groups to amplify themselves. I doubt that this is itself a post-contact phenomenon. Because of the synergistic connection between reproduction and ceremonial rank, the society has had the potential to give rise to dominant groups such as Maliyaw in the past as well as in the modern era.

The intensity of competition for ceremonial privileges is partly owing to precisely this perceived danger inherent in the ceremonial system: that is, that the system could be used, by a powerful and successful group, to legitimise claims to hereditary political authority. This possibility is not particularly difficult for any adequately socialised actor within the system to see. Competing in the debating system is a perceived necessity for every group, because it is only by competing with others that a group can prevent others from gaining a predominant position in ritual. One of the reasons for the resilience of the debating system, amid the many changes now taking place in the society, is that the competition could not be abandoned without leaving in existence permanent status asymmetries between groups. Nor could any group withdraw unilaterally from the debating system without dropping to the lower end of the ceremonial status-hierarchy, because other groups would appropriate all its entitlements. In fact, such a group would quite possibly be driven into extinction. Avatip descent groups are 'locked' into their rivalries because those rivalries are understood to be capable of crystallising into hereditary social inequalities. All political actors must compete for status whether their aim is to bring that stratification into existence, or to prevent it from emerging.

The rise of the subclan Maliyaw

Although Avatip is not a ranked or chiefly polity, political action is motivated by an awareness, among some men at least, that the relations with one another which they act out in ritual are a potential form of political organisation. It is the organisation of ritual which provides men with their 'model' of hereditary inequality, and ascribed status is a powerful and compelling idea in the men's religious representations. The ultimate issue at stake, for them, is whether those ritual inequalities are to be expanded and transformed into political ones. Some groups, such as Maliyaw, are trying to make use of the ritual system as the basis of a claim to permanently high status. Other, less powerful, groups are trying to prevent them from doing so in the name of more 'secular' notions of egalitarianism. It is in the interests of strong groups to promote the idea of hereditary privilege, and in the interests of weak ones to uphold an ideal of equality, and it is the competition between groups which keeps alive that dynamic between the two ethics.

Conclusion

In the previous chapter, I referred to the suggestion by Brenneis and Myers (1984) that a characteristic dilemma of egalitarian social systems is the need for symbolic resources by which to constantly accomplish or sustain 'polity' as a shared world of significations. In much the same way as those societies discussed by Brenneis and Myers, the political integration of Avatip is fragile and exiguous, and seems to have been in the past as well, and relations between its descent groups are highly fractious and egalitarian in a characteristically Melanesian way. Each subclan has considerable political independence, and in the past these groups often made offensive warfare quite separately, though the village always combined for defence. Many subclans are large enough, and their members are aware that they are large enough, to be viable as autonomous single-segment villages, as indeed those groups are represented in myth and cosmology.

Yet, paradoxically, in ritual contexts men act out an image of their society as an organically cohesive whole in which all their descent groups cooperate to maintain the world order, each in accordance with its hereditary powers and rank. These ascribed ritual inequalities are therefore not in some sense an objective property of the society, or a reflex of its actual political structure, but a provisional system of meaning which men continually work in cooperation and competition with each other to recreate in oratory and ritual. It is almost as though that image were an ideological compensation by these groups and their leaders for their actually highly atomised political relations. There are periods, in the intervals between rituals or debates, when the villagers are primarily involved in their everyday domestic activities, and a polity hardly exists at all. The community acts simply as a collection of cooperating but essentially self-sufficient household economies. Polity is perhaps most real at the climax of initiatory rituals, and it is a hard-won, rare and momentary achievement. All the political conflicts I have discussed in this book are the preparations for those episodic accomplishments, when that image of the society as an organised totality is made briefly to materialise in collective action in the heightened ambience of ritual.

Conversely, that image is the source of bitter rivalries and divisions such as those I have discussed in this chapter. Ritual and religion do not so much seem to unify this society or maintain solidarity and consensus, as in Durkheim's (1976) conception. They seem rather to pit groups and their leaders against one another as competitors and create a superfluity of deep and long-lasting antagonisms. Ultimately, the issue at stake in these conflicts is how permanently and completely immanent in social action that conception of their polity, cyclically accomplished in ritual action, should become. So far as I can see, Avatip has in its men's cult the basic ideological and structural elements of a small-scale ranked society but simply does not use those resources for such purposes. If it were to do so, what would be necessary is not so much a qualitative transformation of the society, but rather an expansion of an already existing form of action out of the men's cult into secular domains of social life which that form does not as yet reach. The basic causes of conflict in the society are not simply ritual privileges, or rivalry over which subclan owns the hereditary right to impersonate this or that spirit, but the contested political implications of the principles of ritual action.

Writing of Iatmul debates, Bateson observed that '[t]he problems which seem most to exercise the Iatmul mind seem to us fundamentally unreal' (1958: 229). Indeed, the main analytical difficulties posed by Avatip politics are its apparently irreal goals. Fissions, succession disputes, sorcery feuds, competitive oratory and so forth are all familiar aspects of the politics of small-scale societies. The problem I have tried to solve is why at Avatip these sorts of competitive processes are aimed at gaining control of personal names and the ceremonial prerogatives connected with them. The strategies themselves are intelligible enough. It is the ends to which they are put that seem, to us, to call for explanation. What gives the goals for which Avatip men compete an appearance of unreality is that the ultimate concerns that motivate them are with the uses to which the ethic of ritual could or might be put, with future possibilities and not just the actualities of power, with foreshadowed or imagined forms of inequality rather than with existing ones. When men argue over mythology they are not disputing the present or, still less, the past, but competing images of the future.

I have shown that power in Avatip society is based on the control of religious knowledge. The most basic power which that knowledge gives to senior men, and denies to women and juniors, is access to possibilities of historical action. Behind what A.J. Strathern (1975) calls the 'veiled speech' of oratory men dispute their secret ritual prerogatives and, behind that again, confront one another as agents of historical change carrying out a deeper and longer-term controversy about the limits of inequality. The most valued and closely guarded privilege which ritual knowledge confers is access to that deeper dispute, and to roles in determining the outcome that it may, perhaps, eventually have.

The future of the community is, of course, nowadays highly uncertain and much less under the villagers' control than it was in the past. But a question which the argument of this book raises is whether, if European contact and the radical changes it brought had never occurred, Avatip society might eventually have developed fully-fledged institutions of rank, and what form these institutions might perhaps have taken.

A difficulty is that in the chiefly societies of Melanesia, aspirants to chieftainship have typically to prove themselves by mounting feasts and other forms of public largesse (Lipset 1984; Meeker *et al.* 1986; Powell 1960); that is, they must validate their claims to office by acts of economic 'achievement' actually quite similar to those of Melanesian Big Men. The problem here is that it is precisely these systems of material prestations that Avatip society lacks, and one is therefore inclined to suggest that the low level of surplus production could not easily have supported a 'restributive' economy of the sort associated with chieftainship. But if some form of hereditary stratification had ever emerged, it might have been underwritten by the control of external trading relations, rather than by the control of surplus production. If an Avatip subclan were to take over the total ritual patrimony of a rival group, it would automatically acquire that group's external totemic relationships, its trading partners, and its functions in the trading system. And were any descent group to gain an overall predominant position in cosmology, it would thereby gain monopolistic control over trade and over the community's total trade relations. In the past, when the regional trading system was still intact, an implicit competition for trading relationships may have been an important undercurrent in the rivalry for names and ritual powers. This cannot ever have been the ultimate goal, and cannot explain the competition, because the traditional trading system has largely disappeared and is certainly no longer essential for subsistence, yet the cosmological rivalries between Avatip groups still remain intense. But if, in the past, the existing differentials in ceremonial rank had ever developed past a certain point, they would almost certainly have led to inequalities of access to the material commodities, as well as to the ceremonial ones, circulating in the regional trading system. Perhaps there might eventually have come a time when high-ranking descent groups had some sort of privileged rights – in much the same way that Brunton (1975) argues in regard to Kula valuables in the Northern Trobriands – to shell valuables, which the Manambu obtained largely from the Iatmul and used in their bridewealth and other payments. There is perhaps no point in speculating further, except to say that the Manambu have for some generations been developing, in their ritual system and religious representations, the conceptual, symbolic or legitimising apparatus of a system of rank: and that these processes, if they had been taken to their final conclusion in the pre-contact era, would also have created material relations capable of underwriting such a system.

9

Symbolic economies in Melanesia

To Marx, the final determining force of change is change in economic relationships and in the material conditions of life. To imagine otherwise is to suppose, with Hegel, that sheer acts of thought and the interplay of ideas can produce history. But a problem is that cultures can be working with very different conceptions of 'economy'. Studies of the semiotic or communicative dimensions of consumption, of the role of commodities as signs, show wealth and meaning to be integrally interconnected even in western economies (Appadurai 1986; Baudrillard 1975, 1981; Douglas and Isherwood 1981). Sahlins (1976), for instance, argues that a modern economy, ostensibly oriented towards utility and material 'needs', is predicated on the existence of a specific scheme of values, and is a system for the production not only of things but of meaning. What I have examined in this book is, in a sense, an example of the converse of this: a society in which certain categories of ideas are treated as economic goods, not only standing in meaningful or logical relations but in relations of value. The nearest equivalent of Avatip cosmology in western society is perhaps not religion but the markets in stocks and shares. What is exchanged in these markets are pure signs or messages, yet these informational transactions yield real profit for successful players and can have major consequences for the distribution of economic and political power. The closest equivalents to Avatip cosmology in Melanesia itself are the prestige economies such as the Kula, Moka and Tee.

The characteristic structures of a Melanesian gift-economy appear in Avatip cosmology in two related nexuses. Firstly, all Avatip rituals and performances of magic are, conceptually, *prestations* in which men act to give nurture and sustenance to affines and uterine kin. They are not simply symbolic statements or vehicles of meaning, but concrete acts of reciprocity and exchanges of *values* with the structure of a Melanesian gift-exchange system, except that the structure is transposed into the medium of magic and ritual. Secondly, these ritual powers themselves and the names encapsulating them are not only religious symbols but *property*, and the subject of highly rivalrous transactions in the debating system as groups struggle for ownership of them. The first nexus is the locus of an ideology of ascribed inequality based

197

on the 'hereditary' ritual powers of descent groups. The second is an arena in which ambitious men earn influence and reputation by competing for these 'ascribed' patrimonial powers on behalf of the groups they represent

Marilyn Strathern has argued that a very basic assumption, which proper analysis of these Melanesian gift economies calls into question, is our own dichotomy between persons and things (M. Strathern 1983, 1987, 1988; see also Kopytoff 1986). Western folk models tend implicitly to represent individuals as indivisible subjects standing in controlling, possessing, transacting relationships to an inert world of objects; and these models, implicit in some anthropological analyses, distort our understanding of Melanesian economic life and gender relations. In Melanesia, she argues, gift items stand instead for partible aspects of the person, so that these gift economies are based on concepts, not only of wealth but also of the person, that differ in quite basic ways from our own. Many observers have noted the ways in which wealth in Melanesia may represent body substances and substitute for them symbolically: shell wealth may be equated with semen (Lindenbaum 1984), meat with human flesh or milk (Wagner 1967) and so forth. At Avatip, names and magical powers are intrinsic constituents of the identities of persons and groups. Ultimately, an Avatip subclan simply *is* whatever quantity of names and ritual powers it has been able to draw to itself and keep, and when men give away these patrimonial powers to their successors, or have them stolen by other groups, it is a real diminution of their social identities and of their powers of political action.

There seems, in fact, to be no rigid dichotomy between material wealth and ritual knowledge in Melanesia, but rather a continuum, because material wealth itself is often thought to have magical powers: shell valuables are believed to magically attract brides, or more wealth (Strathern and Strathern 1971: 20, 84, 140). And, of course, a very strong preoccupation of Melanesian religions is with the creation of wealth by means of magic and ritual (Keesing 1982a: 146–7; Lawrence and Meggitt 1965), a notion manifesting itself notably in the cargo cults of the region. This attribution of magical efficacy to wealth objects cannot be explained as simply commodity fetishism, a mystification of underlying economic relations, because there are societies such as Avatip in which the exact converse of this also occurs: ritual knowledge is commoditised and magic bought and sold, so that an imaginary economy of magical signs is constructed and economic relations brought into existence that operate above the sphere of material production and independently of it. This quite literally *metaphysical* economy then functions as a prestige nexus of a thoroughly familiar sort, a universe of high-status wealth-items distinct from the exchange and production of subsistence goods.

In some Melanesian ceremonial exchange systems, notably the Kula, important and prestigious valuables carry personal names and have their own legendary 'biographies' (Campbell 1983; Malinowksi 1922: 89; Munn 1983;

A.J. Strathern 1971: 236). At Avatip, it is the names and their associated mythical biographies by themselves that are the prestigious valuables that circulate. But in both cases, their value depends on culturally highly specific canons of connoisseurship and knowledge, and on properly socialised transactors operating within a common informational universe. In a sense, a famous Kula armshell or necklace 'is' the name and history associated with it, and it derives its identity and integrity as a circulating piece of information from the physical token to which it is bound. At Avatip, on the other hand, an ancestral name gains its identity and integrity as a unit of wealth not so much from its referent (a whole class of resources such as 'all yams') but from its relation to all other names in a global and putatively timeless structure of cosmology. But names and ritual powers at Avatip, and yams or pearlshells in other societies, all equally function as wealth because they represent the social identities of their transactors and their capacity to reproduce themselves and their social relations over time (see Weiner 1977). It is not that one is wealth while the other is not. It is simply that there is a whole spectrum of different instruments or media, ranging from pigs or yams, to magical names or spells, by means of which Melanesian societies create prestige economies.

A difficulty which an analytical division between economy and the cultural order can create is that some of these economies may 'look' to a Western observer like cosmologies or religions, while others seem interpretable more as primitive forms of capitalism or as markets (Epstein 1968; Finney 1973; Pospisil 1963). Thus some Melanesian societies, such as Avatip, appear to have highly elaborated systems of religious belief, while others give an impression of having thoroughly secular, transactional and pragmatic cultural attitudes, and this has resulted in some controversy over whether these apparently highly varied degrees of elaboration of religion in Melanesia are real or merely artefacts of analysis (Brunton 1980a, 1980b; Gell 1980; Johnson 1981; Jorgensen 1981; Juillerat 1980; Lawrence 1988; Morris 1982). My argument is that it is not so much the degree of systematisation of religion in itself that differs, but rather that these societies have elaborated the principle of gift exchange in different directions using different cultural definitions of wealth.

What these Melanesian gift economies therefore especially call into question is the opposition in anthropological theory (see Ortner 1984) between materialist explanations of social phenomena and those explanations that take meaning and the symbolic order as their starting points. The particular problem I have addressed in this book in this connection is the question, as Brunton has implicitly posed it, of whether the existence of rank and chieftainship in Melanesia is to be explained in terms of the economy, or in terms of religion and culture. I have argued that the basic issue is not whether religion or economy is the determining factor but the degree to which the prestige goods – whether these are material or immaterial, Kula valuables or magical spells – form a conceptually finite universe of values or an unbounded one. In some Melanesian societies, such as in those Highland areas where any ambitious man can, together with his wife, produce much or all of the wealth for his feasts and prestations (A.J. Strathern 1969), the political economy is a relatively open system because individual actors can easily create new wealth themselves, and their political success can therefore depend to a large extent on their own productive achievement. In other Melanesian societies, such as Avatip or, in a different way, in the Kula Ring, the items of key prestige value form a rather more closed system. Of course, there are ecosystemic and other constraints that Highland actors must work within and which put definite limits on their production of pigs and other wealth (Modjeska 1982; Rappaport 1968). And conversely, Avatip cosmology is partially permeable and open to incorporating foreign ritual powers. But an Avatip subclan that comes into possession of a new ritual power, or a Kula player who acquires a famous valuable, does not normally do so by creating it or in some other way acquiring it from outside the system, but by removing a pre-existing value from all rivals and other actors in the same political universe. Named valuables in the Kula system, or named totemic ancestors in Avatip cosmology, are conceived as perduring and unique values, and their existence may in actual fact transcend the lifespans of the actors who struggle for them. Men are tending in these systems to compete for shares of a comparatively fixed and immemorial fund of these 'singularised' (Kopytoff 1986: 73–7) wealth-items, rather than competing to bring homogeneous and transitory ones constantly into existence as Highland pig-producers must do. Only in these conceptually finite systems of putatively imperishable and unique values can a minority of men claim a special access to these values as their hereditary right in the way that Brunton suggests, and monopolise them as a basis of claims to rank. It is the degree and nature of the boundedness of the system that matters, rather than whether it can be classified as a religion or an economy.

What closes the universe of values within which Avatip men compete is an ideology of realism: the conception, enacted in ritual, of their society as a global, supra-individual reality. The basic assumption on which political actors operate is that the distribution of cosmological powers in their society forms a relational totality or system, a change in any of its parts having repercussions on the others. The changes to cosmology being fought over in debates are certainly small and piecemeal. But they are systemic in their *implications* because an attempt by one group to improve its status affects other groups directly and has immediate consequences for those groups' status. Potentially, every change has society-wide ramifications, and is necessarily an issue of concern to the political community as a whole and not just to the innovators themselves or their private associates. The debating system is the public forum in which all the senior men in the community gather to air these controversial changes in the esoteric language of oratory, argue them out and try to resolve them.

Symbolic economies in Melanesia

What political actors at Avatip are starting from is an assumption that their cosmology is a finite whole of which all their groups and the hereditary powers they own are the refractions. A group's names and cosmological powers represent its share, its hereditary ratio or portion of that system. Its names and powers therefore measure the group's significance or *value* in the system, a purely relational value yielded only by comparison with the value of others. The names and their associated privileges are a political currency, in that they can be transferred or transacted, and are an accepted standard or measure for establishing relative values, these values being the political status of groups. For a group to take over some prerogative from a rival, all it needs is sufficient real-life political influence to force the change through. In principle, there are no limits on the cosmological powers a group can appropriate from others in this way, thereby augmenting its own status at the expense of diminishing theirs, except its effectiveness at political action in competition with its rivals. What a system of this sort therefore offers is the possibility of quite radical redefinitions of the relative political status of the groups within it. But more importantly, a structural change of this sort, in which all the major ritual powers become a monopoly of one group, is a conceived possibility to the competitors themselves, an intentional goal, an envisaged end to which all their attempted innovations can be purposively directed.

For the observer, the significance of the debating system is that it is an institution for constantly producing or revising cosmology, so that these processes are, at Avatip, relatively visible and easy to examine. That is to say, these processes are institutionalised as the central arena of public politics. It is true that debates are represented by senior men, for the benefit of women and juniors, as a kind of elevated and abstruse verbal sport; but behind that easily penetrable camouflage, quite purposive processes of symbolic innovation are being fought out.

Let me contrast this with processes of endogenous innovation in some other Melanesian religions. Keesing (1982a: 210–16) suggests in his study of the Kwaio that changes in the religion of this Solomon Island people may arise in dreams, possession states, divination sessions, and sometimes simply through random errors in the transmission of ritual knowledge. Whether these changes are accepted depends on their consonance with existing symbolic forms, and also upon political considerations, such as whether or not they serve to confirm the privileges of senior men.

Barth (1987), in a slightly different vein, suggests that innovation in the Mountain Ok cosmologies of the West Sepik is shaped by a combination of psychological, cognitive and cultural determinants acting upon the ritual experts themselves. These custodians of religious lore revise their knowledge in small steps on each of the rare occasions when they teach or reveal it, in ways influenced by their own life-experiences, psychological needs or implicit notions of conceptual order.

Among these two Melanesian peoples, changes in religion and cosmology

201

seem to occur at a sub-institutional level, and perhaps not always consciously even to the innovators themselves. Comparing Avatip with these societies, one is tempted to suggest that the more that actors conceive of their cosmology as a finite and organic unity, the more they tend to act purposively within it as though it were an economy. A closed, putatively static cosmology may, as Bloch suggests, serve to make political authority unchallengeable. But also, it can make the elements of cosmology appear as thing-like, enduring tokens of status, indestructible units or stores of value. What is at issue among Avatip men in their disputes is not so much the meaning or symbolic content of the myths, rituals and so forth (these, as I showed, do not seem to be manipulated politically and seem in fact highly stable) but their value as limited goods. To Avatip men, their cosmology represents primarily a universe of possessions or resources in which they are competing for property-rights. My interpretation of Avatip history is that incipient forms of rank have come into being in religion and cosmology; but what I am arguing is that this nascent political order arose, not out of changes in the *content* of these symbolic systems, but out of changes in the social relations of property in the *existing* religion and cosmology.

I have suggested that Avatip society, as Gewertz (1983) showed with the nearby Chambri, needs to be understood in a regional context, and especially in the context of its relations with the neighbouring Iatmul. It is clear from Bateson's ethnography, and the more recent studies of the Iatmul by Stanek (1983) and Wassman (1982) that disputes over the ownership of names and ceremonial privileges are, or were, important features of political life in the Iatmul villages. Perhaps Avatip imported the institution of debating from the Iatmul, along with much of the rest of its cosmology and ritual. But leadership among the Iatmul seems to have involved other dimensions as well: in particular, elements of the Big Man pattern common in Melanesia, with its attendant focus on wealth and ceremonial exchange (see for instance Bateson 1932: 258). In these respects, the Manambu are a culturally and politically 'specialised' version of the Iatmul, having developed their political patterns around a single theme drawn from the more generalised political repertoire of the Iatmul.

The Iatmul are a large group and seem to have had relatively high rates of mobility and intermarriage between their villages. The Manambu, on the other hand, have always been in comparison a small, closed and insular society, having had for much of their history only a single village: first Asiti and, later, Old Avatip. A single, politically independent community, culturally dependent on a large and powerful neighbouring people yet also having its own identifiably distinct language, culture and social organisation, is perhaps conducive to the development of specialised and involuted cultural forms: and especially to the formation of a conceptually closed universe of significations such as Avatip politics has as its arena.

What underwrites this conceptual closure is the endogamy of the community, itself largely a response to the perceived threat to its existence posed by the Iatmul. Descent groups – in particular agnates – are therefore competing for a limited quantity of reproduction in a largely closed connubium, and the main physical resource men exchange and seek to control is not material wealth but women's fertility. At one level, names and magical powers represent hereditary status and prestige; but at another, they are shares in this finite fund of reproductive capital. They represent the capacity of groups to attract affines and so reproduce themselves physically and socially, and in this respect they are an analogue of the circulating prestige goods that function in some other societies as bridewealth. The political processes within the community since the early years of this century have revolved very largely around the attempts by the subclan Maliyaw to corner the market, so to speak, in these shares by trying to achieve dominant cosmological status in the community.

Because, at Avatip, it is specifically the ritual system and cosmology that function as a closed prestige economy, it is specifically in ritual contexts that notions of hereditary status are powerfully expressed, but not in the rivalrous business of everyday politics. Problems arise if one tries to classify whole Melanesian polities as ranked, chiefly, egalitarian and so forth, and one needs rather to specify the spheres of social life in which these sorts of ideologies are being put to work. The ritual system at Avatip, with its ideology of hereditary rank and status, is clearly dissonant with the highly competitive and egalitarian political relations of everyday life and does not directly reflect their structure. These different spheres of action in the society, mundane and religious, public and esoteric, are not homologous or congruent with each other but related dialectically, and generating historical change through the tensions and differentials between them.

This brings me finally to my main point concerning the role of religion in Avatip history. What has structured this dialectic at Avatip is the men's initiatory cult, with its hierarchy of grades and successively more secret levels of knowledge. Ritual and religion in this society cannot be interpreted simply in relation to the existing political *status quo*, as its symbolic reflection or ideological legitimation. The basic problem is that the goal harboured by the leaders of Maliyaw, in which the whole community is totally dependent on their subclan ritually, does not correspond to any 'observable' political relations at all, either in everyday life or indeed in ritual itself. Yet almost all of ritual politics in the society has been the outward repercussions of a submerged and secret conflict among initiated men over these covert ambitions of Maliyaw leaders to legitimise themselves and their subclan in some sort of 'chiefly' status. Real in other parts of Melanesia, rank is absent at Avatip, yet it is impossible to understand the political processes that have occurred at Avatip this century without also understanding the importance which this non-existent institution has had for political actors as a prefigured future –

envisioned as a goal by some, as a danger by others – because it has been the implicit construct driving those processes.

To put this slightly differently, it is quite likely that, to a small group of elderly men of Maliyaw subclan, their society already 'is' a ranked or chiefly one; it is simply that the society's existing political institutions have not yet caught up with their own private conceptions. In the secret, restricted ritual sphere of men, the society moves several steps ahead of itself and looks beyond its existing institutional arrangements; the secret sphere of male ritual has been an important arena of endogenous political and ideological innovation. It has given senior men a forum and a language in which to construct hypothetical or incipient institutional realities, and to dispute or rehearse these experimental conceptions of political order before they come into being.

The problem is that this may 'look' as though political changes in Avatip society were being led by changes in the cultural or religious system, and that this interpretation of Avatip history must therefore be idealism, the anodyne fallacy that ideas in themselves produce historical change. But idealism arises out of dichotomies – between object and subject, economy and religion, things and ideas – that Melanesian societies do not construct, or base their religious and everyday modes of action on, in the same way as ourselves. My view is rather that it is these sorts of oppositions of our own making that the peoples of this region implicitly call into question and invite us to reconsider. My aim has been to show that Avatip cosmology is the prestige economy of the society; and to explain why, in the higher grades of the men's cult, contested attempts are being made to restructure this economy and the political order which it signifies.

Bibliography

Allen, M. 1967. *Male Cults and Secret Initiations in Melanesia*. Melbourne: Melbourne University Press.
  1984. Elders, Chiefs and Big Men: Authority Legitimation and Political Evolution in Melanesia. *American Ethnologist* 11: 20–44.
  (ed.) 1981. Vanuatu: *Politics, Economics and Ritual in Island Melanesia*. Sydney: Academic Press.
Andreski, S. 1984. *Max Weber's Insights and Errors*. London: Routledge and Kegan Paul.
Appadurai, A. 1986. Introduction: Commodities and the Politics of Value. In A. Appadurai (ed.) *The Social Life of Things: Commodities in Cultural Perspective*. Cambridge: Cambridge University Press.
Asad, T. 1983. Anthropological Conceptions of Religion: Reflections on Geertz. *Man* (n.s.) 18: 237–59.
Babcock, B.A. (ed.)1978. *The Reversible World: Symbolic Inversion in Art and Society*. Ithaca, London: Cornell University Press.
Barnes, J.A. 1947. The Collection of Genealogies. Rhodes-Livingstone Journal 5: 48–55.
  1962. African Models in the New Guinea Highlands. *Man* 62: 5–9.
Barth, F. 1966. *Models of Social Organisation*. Royal Anthropological Institute Occasional Papers, no. 23. London: Royal Anthropological Institute.
  1975. *Ritual and Knowledge among the Baktaman of New Guinea*. New Haven: Yale University Press.
  1987. *Cosmologies in the Making: a Generative Approach to Cultural Variation in Inner New Guinea*. Cambridge: Cambridge University Press.
Bateson, G. 1932. Social Structure of the Iatmul People of the Sepik River. *Oceania* 2: 245–91, 401–53.
  1958. *Naven* (2nd edition). Stanford: Stanford University Press. (First published 1936).
Baudrillard, J. 1975. *The Mirror of Production*. St Louis, Mo.: Telos Press.
  1981. *For a Critique of the Political Economy of the Sign*. St Louis, Mo.: Telos Press.
Behrmann, W. 1922. *Im Stromgebiet des Sepik*. Berlin: A. Scherl.
Bloch, M. (ed.) 1973. *Political Language and Oratory in Traditional Society*. London: Academic Press.
  1974. Symbols, Song, Dance and Features of Articulation. *European Journal of Sociology* 15: 55–81.
  1977. The Past and the Present in the Present. *Man* (n.s.) 12: 278–92.
  1986. *From Blessing to Violence: History and Ideology in the Circumcision Ritual of the Merina of Madagascar*. Cambridge: Cambridge University Press.
Bourdieu, P. 1977. *Outline of a Theory of Practice*. (trans.) R. Nice. Cambridge: Cambridge University Press.

Bibliography

Bowden, R. 1977. The Kwoma: a Study of Terminology and Marriage Alliance in a Sepik River Society. Ph.D. Thesis, Monash University, Melbourne.

1983a. Kwoma Terminology and Marriage Alliance: the 'Omaha' problem revisited. *Man* (n.s.) 18: 745–65.

1983b. *Yena: Art and Ceremony in a Sepik Society.* Oxford: Pitt Rivers Museum.

1984. Art and Gender Ideology in the Sepik. *Man* (n.s.) 19: 445–58.

Bragge, L.W. 1984. The Japandai Migrations. Paper presented at Wenner-Gren Foundation Symposium, 'Sepik Research Today', Basel, August 1984.

Brenneis, D.L. and F. Myers (eds.). 1984. *Dangerous Words: Language and Politics in the Pacific.* New York: New York University Press.

Brunton, R. 1975. Why do the Trobriands have Chiefs? *Man* (n.s.) 10: 544–58.

1980a. Misconstrued Order in Melanesian Religion. *Man* (n.s.) 15: 112–28.

1980b. Correspondence. *Man* (n.s.) 15: 734–5.

Burridge, K. 1957. Disputing in Tangu. *American Anthropologist* 59: 763–80.

Campbell, S. 1983. Attaining Rank: a Classification of Shell Valuables. In J.W. Leach and E. Leach (eds.) *The Kula: New Perspectives on Massim Exchange.* Cambridge: Cambridge University Press.

Charbonnier, G. (ed.). 1969. *Conversations with Claude Lévi-Strauss.* (trans.) J. and D. Weigtman. London: Jonathan Cape.

Chowning, A. 1974. Disputing in Two West New Britain Societies: Similarities and Differences. In A.L. Epstein (ed.) *Contention and Dispute: Aspects of Law and Social Control in Melanesia.* Canberra: Australian National University Press.

1979. Leadership in Melanesia. *Journal of Pacific History* 14: 66–83.

Cohen, A.P. 1985. *The Symbolic Construction of Community.* London: Routledge and Kegan Paul.

Collier, J.F. and M.Z. Rosaldo. 1981. Politics and Gender in Simple Societies. In S.B. Ortner and H. Whitehead (eds.) *Sexual Meanings.* New York: Cambridge University Press.

Curtain, R. 1978. *The 1974/75 Rural Survey: a Study of Outmigration from Fourteen Villages in the East Sepik Province.* I.A.S.E.R. Discussion Paper no. 3. Port Moresby: Institute of Applied Social and Economic Research.

1980. Dual Dependence and Sepik Labour Migration. Ph.D. Thesis, The Australian National University, Canberra.

Douglas, B. 1979. Rank, Power, Authority: a Reassessment of Traditional Leadership in South Pacific Societies. *Journal of Pacific History* 14: 2–27.

Douglas, M. and Baron Isherwood. 1981. *The World of Goods.* New York: Basic Books.

Dumont, L. 1970. *Homo Hierarchicus.* London: Weidenfeld and Nicholson.

Durkheim, E. 1933. *The Division of Labour in Society.* New York: Free Press. (First published 1893).

1976. *The Elementary Forms of the Religious Life.* London: George Allen and Unwin. (First published 1912).

Dye, T.W. 1984. Economic Development and Local Politics: Wagu Village 1963–1983. Paper presented at Wenner-Gren Foundation Symposium, 'Sepik Research Today', Basel, August 1984.

Epstein, T.S. 1968. *Capitalism, Primitive and Modern: Some Aspects of Tolai Economic Growth.* Canberra: Australian National University Press.

Errington, F. and D. Gewertz. 1985. The Chief of the Chambri: Social Change and Cultural Permeability among a New Guinea People. *American Ethnologist* 12: 442–54.

1986. The Confluence of Powers: Entropy and Importation among the Chambri. *Oceania* 57: 99–113.

Bibliography

1987. *Cultural Alternatives and a Feminist Anthropology: an Analysis of Culturally Constructed Gender Interests in Papua New Guinea.* Cambridge: Cambridge University Press.

Evans-Pritchard, E.E. 1937. *Witchcraft, Oracles and Magic among the Azande.* Oxford: Clarendon Press.

Feil, D.K. 1978. Women and Men in the Enga Tee. *American Ethnologist* 5: 263–79.

1984. *Ways of Exchange: the Enga Tee of Papua New Guinea.* St Lucia: University of Queensland Press.

1985. Configurations of Intensity in the New Guinea Highlands. In D. Gardner and N. Modjeska (eds.) *Recent Studies in the Political Economy of Papua New Guinea Societies. Mankind* 15, Special Issue no. 4, pp. 87–100.

1987. *The Evolution of Highland Papua New Guinea Societies.* Cambridge: Cambridge University Press.

Finney, B.R. 1973. *Big-Men and Business: Entrepreneurship and Economic Growth in the New Guinea Highlands.* Honolulu: University Press of Hawaii.

Forge, A. 1966. Art and Environment in the Sepik. *Proceedings of the Royal Anthropological Institute of Great Britain and Ireland*, 1965, pp. 23–31.

1970 Prestige, Influence and Sorcery: a New Guinea Example. In M. Douglas (ed.) *Witchcraft Confessions and Accusations.* London: Tavistock.

1971. Marriage and Exchange in the Sepik. In R. Needham (ed.) *Rethinking Kinship and Marriage.* ASA Monographs 11. London: Tavistock.

1972a. The Golden Fleece. *Man* (n.s.) 7: 527–40.

1972b. Normative Factors in the Settlement Size of Neolithic Cultivators (New Guinea). In P.J. Ucko, R. Tringham and G.W. Dimbleby (eds.) *Man, Settlement and Urbanism.* London: Duckworth.

1972c. Tswamung: a Failed Big-Man. In J.B. Watson, (ed.) *Crossing Cultural Boundaries: The Anthropological Experience.* San Francisco: Chandler.

1984. The Power of Culture or Vice-Versa. Paper presented at Wenner-Gren Foundation Symposium, 'Sepik Research Today', Basel, August 1984.

Fortune, R.F. 1932. *Sorcerers of Dobu.* London: Routledge and Kegan Paul.

Freedman, M. 1958. *Lineage Organisation in Southeastern China.* London: Athlone.

Geary, P. 1986. Sacred Commodities: the Circulation of Medieval Relics. In A. Appadurai (ed.) *The Social Life of Things: Commodities in Cultural Perspective.* Cambridge: Cambridge University Press.

Geertz, C. 1957. Ritual and Social Change: a Javanese Example. *American Anthropologist* 59: 32–54.

1966. Religion as a Cultural System. In M. Banton (ed.) *Anthropological Approaches to the Study of Religion.* A.S.A. Monographs no. 3. London: Tavistock.

1972. Deep Play: Notes on the Balinese Cockfight. *Daedalus* 101: 1–37.

Gell, A.F. 1980. Correspondence. *Man* (n.s.) 15: 735–7.

1986. Newcomers to the World of Goods: Consumption among the Muria Gonds. In A. Appadurai (ed.) *The Social Life of Things: Commodities in Cultural Perspective.* Cambridge: Cambridge University Press.

Gellner, E. 1973. *Cause and Meaning in the Social Sciences.* London: Routledge and Kegan Paul.

Gerth, H. and Mills, C. Wright (eds. and trans.) 1946. *From Max Weber: Essays in Sociology.* Oxford University Press.

Gewertz, D.B. 1977a. The Politics of Affinal Exchange: Chambri as a Client Market. *Ethnology* 16: 285–98.

1977b. 'On Whom Depends The Action of the Elements': Debating Among The Chambri People of Papua New Guinea. *Journal of the Polynesian Society* 86: 339–53.

Bibliography

1978. Tit For Tat: Barter Markets in the Middle Sepik. *Anthropological Quarterly* 51: 37–44.

1983. *Sepik River Societies: A Historical Ethnography of the Chambri and their Neighbors*. New Haven and London: Yale University Press.

Gluckman, M. 1955a. *Custom and Conflict in Africa*. Oxford: Blackwell.

1955b. *The Judicial Process among the Barotse of Northern Rhodesia*. Manchester: Manchester University Press.

Godelier, M. 1986. *The Making of Great Men: Male Domination and Power among the New Guinea Baruya*. Cambridge: Cambridge University Press.

Goldman, L. 1983. *Talk Never Dies: the Language of Huli Disputes*. London: Tavistock.

Gregory, C. 1982. *Gifts and Commodities*. London: Academic Press.

Guiart, J. 1972. Multiple Levels of Meaning in Myth. In P. Maranda (ed.) *Mythology: Selected Readings*. Harmondsworth: Penguin.

Gulliver, P.H. 1963. *Social Control in an African Society*. London: Routledge and Kegan Paul.

Haantjens, H.A., P.C. Heyligers, J.R. McAlpine, J.C. Saunders, and R.H. Fagan. 1972. *Lands of the Aitape-Ambunti Area, Papua New Guinea* (Land Research Series no. 30). Melbourne: Commonwealth Scientific and Industrial Research Organisation.

Haiveta, C. 1984. Health Care Alternatives in Maindroin Village, Sissano, West Sepik Province. Paper presented at Wenner-Gren Foundation Symposium no. 95 Sepik Research Today, Basel, August 1984.

Hallpike, C.R. 1979. *The Foundations of Primitive Thought*. Oxford: Clarendon Press.

Harrison, S.J. 1982. Yams and the Symbolic Representation of Time in a Sepik River Village. *Oceania* 53: 141–61.

1983. *Laments for Foiled Marriages: Love-Songs from a Sepik River Village*. Port Moresby: Institute of Papua New Guinea Studies.

1984. New Guinea Highland Social Structure in a Lowland Totemic Mythology. *Man* (n.s.) 19: 389–403.

1985a. Concepts of the Person in Avatip Religious Thought. *Man* (n.s.) 20: 115–30.

1985b. Ritual Hierarchy and Secular Equality in a Sepik River Village. *American Ethnologist* 12: 413–26.

1985c. Names, Ghosts and Alliance in Two Sepik River Societies. *Oceania* 56(2): 138–46.

1987. Cultural Efflorescence and Political Evolution on the Sepik River. *American Ethnologist* 14(3): 491–507.

1988a. Armageddon in New Guinea. *Anthropology Today* 4(1): 5–7.

1988b. Magical Exchange of the Preconditions of Production in a Sepik River Village. *Man* (n.s.) 23(2): 319–33.

1989. Magical and Material Polities in Melanesia. *Man* (n.s.), 24(1): 1–20.

Hau'ofa, E. 1981. *Mekeo: Inequality and Ambivalence in a Village Society*. Canberra: Australian National University Press.

Hauser-Schäublin, B. 1977. *Frauen in Kararau. Zur Rolle der Frau bei den Iatmul am Mittelsepik, Papua New Guinea*. Basler Beiträge zur Ethnologie 18, Basel.

Herdt, G.H. 1981. *Guardians of the Flutes*. New York: McGraw-Hill.

(ed.). 1982. *Rituals of Manhood*. Berkeley: University of California Press.

Hogbin, I. 1970. *The Island of Menstruating Men*. Scranton: Chandler.

1978. *The Leaders and the Led*. Melbourne: University Press.

and Wedgwood, C. 1953–4. Local Grouping in Melanesia. *Oceania* 23: 241–276; 24: 58–76.

Huizinga, J. 1949. *Homo Ludens*. London: Routledge and Kegan Paul.

Bibliography

Irwin, G. 1983. Chieftainship, Kula and Trade in Massim Prehistory. In J.W. Leach and E. Leach (eds.) *The Kula: New Perspectives on Massim Exchange*. Cambridge: Cambridge University Press.

Johnson, R. 1981. Correspondence. *Man* (n.s.) 16: 472–4.

Jorgensen, D. 1981. Correspondence. *Man* (n.s.) 16: 471–2.

Josephides, L. 1985. *The Production of Inequality: Gender and Exchange among the Kewa*. London, New York: Tavistock.

Josephides, S. 1982. The Perception of the Past and the Notion of 'Business' in a Seventh Day Adventist Village in Madang, New Guinea. Ph.D. Thesis, University of London (L.S.E.).

1984. Seventh Day Adventism and the Image of the Past. Paper presented at Wenner-Gren Foundation Symposium, 'Sepik Research Today', Basel, August 1984.

Juillerat, B. 1980. Correspondence. *Man* (n.s.) 15: 732–4.

Kaberry, P.M. 1941. The Abelam Tribe, Sepik District, New Guinea: a Preliminary Report. *Oceania* 11: 233–58, 345–67.

1942. Law and Political Organisation in the Abelam Tribe. *Oceania* 12: 331–63.

1971. Political Organisation among the Northern Abelam. In R.M. Berndt and P. Lawrence (eds.) *Politics in New Guinea*. Nedlands: University of Western Australia Press.

Kahn, M. 1986. *Always Hungry, Never Greedy: Food and the Expression of Gender in a Melanesian Society*. Cambridge: Cambridge University Press.

Keesing, R.M. 1982a. *Kwaio Religion: the Living and the Dead in a Solomon Island Society*. New York: Columbia University Press.

1982b. Introduction. In G.H. Herdt (ed.) *Rituals of Manhood*. Berkeley: University of California Press.

Kelly, R.C. 1977. *Etoro Social Structure: a Study in Structural Contradiction*. Ann Arbor: University of Michigan Press.

Kopytoff, I. 1986. The Cultural Biography of Things: Commoditization as Process. In A. Appadurai (ed.) *The Social Life of Things: Commodities in Cultural Perspective*. Cambridge: Cambridge University Press.

Langness, L.L. 1967. Sexual Antagonism in the New Guinea Highlands: a Bena Bena Example. *Oceania* 37: 161–77.

Lawrence, P. 1984. *The Garia: an Ethnography of a Traditional Cosmic System in Papua New Guinea*. Carlton: University of Melbourne Press.

1988. Twenty Years After: A Reconsideration of Papua New Guinea Seaboard and Highlands Religions. *Oceania* 59(1): 7–27.

Lawrence, P. and M.J. Meggitt (eds.). 1965. *Gods, Ghosts and Men in Melanesia*. Oxford: University Press

Laycock, D.C. 1965. *The Ndu Language Family (Sepik District, New Guinea)*. Canberra: Linguistic Circle of Canberra.

Lea, D.A.M. 1964. Abelam Land and Sustenance: Swidden Horticulture in an Area of High Population Density, Maprik, New Guinea. Ph.D. Thesis, The Australian National University, Canberra.

Leach, E.R. 1954. *Political Systems of Highland Burma*. London: Athlone Press.

1961a. *Pul Eliya, a Village in Ceylon*. London: Cambridge University Press.

1961b. *Rethinking Anthropology*. London: Athlone Press.

Lederman, R. 1986. *What Gifts Engender: Social Relations and Politics in Mendi, Highland Papua New Guinea*. Cambridge: Cambridge University Press.

Leenhardt, M. 1979. *Do Kamo: Person and Myth in the Melanesian World*. (trans.) B.M. Gulati. Chicago: Chicago University Press.

Lévi-Strauss, C. 1966. *The Savage Mind*. Chicago: University of Chicago Press.

Bibliography

1969. *The Elementary Structures of Kinship*. (trans.) J. Bell, J. von Sturmer and R. Needham. London: Eyre and Spottiswoode.

1973. *Totemism*. (trans.) R. Needham. Harmondsworth: Penguin.

1978. *Structural Anthropology*. vol. II (trans.) M. Layton. Harmondsworth: Penguin.

Lindenbaum, S. 1984. Variations on a Sociosexual Theme in Melanesia. In G. Herdt (ed.) *Ritualised Homosexuality in Melanesia*. Berkeley: University of California Press.

Lindstrom, L. 1984. Doctor, Lawyer, Wise Man, Priest: Big-Men and Knowledge in Melanesia. *Man* (n.s.) 19: 291–301.

1985. Personal Names and Social Reproduction on Tanna, Vanuatu. *J. of the Polynesian Society* 94: 27–45.

Lipset, D.M. 1984. Boars' Tusks and Flying Foxes: Authority and Stratification in Murik Society. Paper presented at Wenner-Gren Foundation Symposium, 'Sepik Research Today', Basel, August 1984.

Losche, D. 1984. Utopian Visions and the Division of Labour in Abelam Society. Paper presented at Wenner-Gren Foundation Symposium, 'Sepik Research Today', Basel, August 1984.

Lutkehaus, N. 1984a. The Flutes of the Tanepoa: the Dynamics of Hierarchy and Equivalence in Manam Society. Ph.D Thesis, Columbia University.

1984b. The Flutes of the Tanepoa: Traditional and Modern forms of Leadership of Manam Island. Paper presented at Wenner-Gren Foundation Symposium, 'Sepik Research Today', Basel, August 1984.

MacCormack, C.P. and M. Strathern (eds.) 1980. *Nature, Culture and Gender*, Cambridge: Cambridge University Press.

Malinowski, B. 1922. *Argonauts of the Western Pacific*. London: Routledge and Kegan Paul.

1923. The Problem of Meaning in Primitive Languages. In C.K. Ogden and I.A. Richards *The Meaning of Meaning*. London: Routledge and Kegan Paul.

1935. *Coral Gardens and their Magic*. vol. II. London: Allen and Unwin.

1954. *Magic, Science and Religion, and Other Essays*. New York: Doubleday.

Mauss, M. 1966. *The Gift*. London: Cohen and West. (First published 1925).

Mauss, M. and H. Hubert. 1950. Esquisse d'une Théorie Générale de la Magie. In M. Mauss *Sociologie et Anthropologie*. Paris: Presses Universitaires de France. (First published 1902–3).

McDowell, N. 1975. Kinship and the Concept of Shame in a New Guinea Society. Ph.D. Thesis, Cornell University.

Mead, M. 1938. *The Mountain Arapesh: an Importing Culture*. American Museum of Natural History, Anthropological Papers no. 36: 139–349.

1963. *Sex and Temperament in Three Primitive Societies*. New York: William Morrow. (First published 1935).

Meeker, M.E., K. Barlow and D.M. Lipset. 1986. Culture, Exchange and Gender: Lessons from the Murik. *Cultural Anthropology* 1: 6–73.

Meiser, L. 1955. The 'Platform' Phenomenon along the Northern Coast of New Guinea. *Anthropos* 50: 265–72.

Metraux, R. 1978. Aristocracy and Meritocracy: Leadership among the Eastern Iatmul. *Anthropological Quarterly* 51: 47–58.

Mitchell, W.E. 1978. On Keeping Equal: Polity and Reciprocity among the New Guinea Wape. *Anthropological Quarterly* 51: 5–15.

Modjeska, N. 1982. Production and Inequality: Perspectives from Central New Guinea. In A.J. Strathern (ed.) *Inequality in New Guinea Highland Societies*. Cambridge: Cambridge University Press.

Morauta, L. 1973. Traditional Polity in Madang. *Oceania* 44: 127–55.

Bibliography

Morris, B. 1982. Correspondence. *Man* (n.s.) 17: 350.

Munn, N. 1983. Gawan Kula: Spatiotemporal Control and the Symbolism of Influence. In J.W. Leach and E. Leach (eds.) *The Kula: New Perspectives on Massim Exchange*. Cambridge: Cambridge University Press.

Nader, L. and Todd, H.F. (eds.) 1978. *The Disputing Process: Law in Ten Societies*. New York: Columbia University Press.

Needham, R. 1966. Age, Category and Descent. *Bijdragen tot der Taal-, Land-, en Volkenkunde* 122: 1–35.

Newton, D. 1971. *Crocodile and Cassowary: Religious Art of the Upper Sepik River, New Guinea*. New York: Museum of Primitive Art.

Oliver, D. 1955. *A Solomon Island Society*. Cambridge: Harvard University Press.

Ortner, S.B. 1984. Theory in Anthropology Since the Sixties. *Comparative Studies in Society and History* 26(1): 126–66.

Peel, J.D.Y. 1971. *Herbert Spencer: the Evolution of a Sociologist*. London: Heinemann.

Popper, K. 1957. *The Poverty of Historicism*. London: Routledge and Kegan Paul.

Pospisil, L. 1963. *The Kapauku Papuans of West New Guinea*. New York: Holt, Rinehart and Winston.

Powell, H.A. 1960. Competitive Leadership in Trobriand Political Organisation. *Journal of the Royal Anthropological Institute* 90: 118–45.

Rappaport, R.A. 1968. *Pigs for the Ancestors: Ritual in the Ecology of a New Guinea People*. New Haven: Yale University Press.

Read, K. 1959. Leadership and Consensus in a New Guinea Society. *American Anthropologist* 61: 425–36.

Roberts, S. 1979. *Order and Dispute: an Introduction to Legal Anthropology*. Harmondsworth: Penguin.

Rowley, C.D. 1958. *The Australians in German New Guinea, 1914–1921*. Melbourne: Melbourne University Press.

Rubel, P. and A. Rosman. 1978. *Your Own Pigs You May Not Eat: A Comparative Study of New Guinea Societies*. Chicago: University of Chicago Press.

Sahlins, M. 1963. Poor Man, Rich Man, Big-Man, Chief: Political Types in Melanesia and Polynesia. *Comparative Studies in Society and History* 5: 285–303.

1976. *Culture and Practical Reason*. Chicago: University of Chicago Press.

1985. *Islands of history*, Chicago, London: University of Chicago Press.

Salisbury, R.F. 1962. *From Stone to Steel*. Melbourne: Melbourne University Press.

Schieffelin, E. 1980. Reciprocity and the Construction of Reality. *Man* (n.s.) 15(3): 502–17.

Schwimmer, E. 1973. *Exchange in the Social Structure of the Orokaiva*. London: C. Hurst.

1979. Reciprocity and Structure: a Semiotic Reinterpretation of Some Orokaiva Exchange Data. *Man* (n.s.) 14(2): 271–85.

Scoditti, G. (with J.W. Leach). 1983. Kula on Kitava. In J.W. Leach and E. Leach (eds.) *The Kula: New Perspectives on Massim Exchange*. Cambridge: Cambridge University Press.

Serpenti, L.M. 1965. *Cultivators in the Swamps: Social Structure and Horticulture in a New Guinea Society*. Assen: Van Gorkum.

Sillitoe, P. 1979. *Give and Take*. Canberra: Australian National University Press.

Spencer, B. and F.J. Gillen. 1904. *The Northern Tribes of Central Australia*. London: Macmillan.

Spencer, H. 1876. *Principles of Sociology*. London: Williams and Norgate.

Staalsen, P. 1965. Brugnowi Origins: the Founding of a Village. *Man* 65: 184–88.

Stanek, M. 1983. *Sozialordnung und Mythik in Palimbei, Bausteine zur ganzheitlichen*

211

Bibliography

Beschreibung einer Dorfgemeinschaft der Iatmul, East Sepik Province, Papua New Guinea. Basel: Basler Beiträge zur Ethnologie 23.

Strathern, A.J. 1969. Finance and Production: Two Strategies in New Guinea Highland Exchange Systems. *Oceania* 40: 42–67.

1971. *The Rope of Moka: Big-Men and Ceremonial Exchange in Mount Hagen.* Cambridge: Cambridge University Press.

1975. Veiled speech in Mount Hagen. In M. Bloch (ed.) *Political Language and Oratory in Traditional Society.* London: Academic Press.

Strathern, A.J. and M. Strathern. 1971. *Self-Decoration in Mount Hagen.* London: Duckworth.

Strathern, M. 1972. *Women in Between.* New York: Seminar Press.

1983. Subject or Object? Women and the Circulation of Valuables in Highlands New Guinea. In Hirschon, R. (ed.) *Women and Property, Women as Property.* London: Croom Helm.

1984. Domesticity and the Denigration of Women. In D. O'Brien and S. Tiffany (eds.) *Rethinking Women's Roles: Perspectives from the Pacific.* Berkeley: University of California Press.

1987. Conclusion. In M. Strathern (ed.) *Dealing with Inequality: Analysing Gender Relations in Melanesia and Beyond.* Cambridge: Cambridge University Press.

1988. *The Gender of the Gift.* Berkeley: University of California Press.

Townsend, G.W.L. 1968. *District Officer: From Untamed New Guinea to Lake Success, 1921–46.* Sydney: Pacific Publication.

Townsend, P.K. 1978. The Politics of Mobility among the Sanio-Hiowe. *Anthropological Quarterly* 51: 26–35.

Turner, V.W. 1957. *Schism and Continuity in an African Society.* Manchester: Manchester University Press.

1967. *The Forest of Symbols: Aspects of Ndembu Ritual.* Ithaca and London: Cornell University Press.

1969. *The Ritual Process.* Harmondsworth: Penguin.

Tuzin, D.F. 1972. Yam Symbolism in the Sepik: an Interpretative Account. *Southwestern Journal of Anthropology* 28: 230–54.

1976. *The Ilahita Arapesh: Dimensions of Unity.* Berkeley: University of California Press.

1980. *The Voice of the Tambaran: Truth and Illusion in Ilahita Arapesh Religion.* Berkeley: University of California Press.

Van Velsen, J. 1967. The Extended Case Method and Situational Analysis. In A.L. Epstein (ed.) *The Craft of Social Anthropology.* London: Tavistock.

Wagner, R. 1967. *The Curse of Souw.* Chicago: University of Chicago Press.

1986. *Symbols That Stand for Themselves.* Chicago: University of Chicago Press.

Wassman, J. 1982. *Der Gesang an den Fliegenden Hund. Untersuchungen zu den Totemistischen Gesängen und Geheimen Namen des Dorfes Kandingei am Mittelsepik (Papua New Guinea) anhand der Kirugu-Knotenschnüre.* Basel: Basler Beiträge zur Ethnologie 22.

Wedgwood, C.H. 1934. Report on Research in Manam Island. *Oceania* 4: 373–403.

Weiner, A.B. 1977. *Women of Value, Men of Renown: New Perspectives on Trobriand Exchange.* St Lucia: University of Queensland Press.

1983. From Words to Objects to Magic: Hard Words and the Boundaries of Social Interaction. *Man* (n.s.) 18: 690–709.

Whitehead, H. 1986. The Varieties of Fertility Cultism in New Guinea. *American Ethnologist* 13: 80–99, 271–89.

Whiting, J.W.M. 1941. *Becoming a Kwoma: Teaching and Learning in a New Guinea*

Bibliography

Tribe. New Haven: Yale University Press.

1944. The Frustration Complex in Kwoma Society. *Man* 44: 140–4.

Whiting, J.W.M. and S.W. Reed. 1938–9. Kwoma Culture: Report on Field Work in the Mandated Territory of New Guinea. *Oceania* 9: 170–216.

Williams, F.E. 1936. *Papuans of the Trans-Fly*. Oxford: Clarendon Press.

Worsley, P. 1955. Totemism in a Changing Society. *American Anthropologist* 57: 851–61.

1967. Groote Eylandt Totemism and *Le Totemisme Aujourd'hui*. In E. Leach (ed.) *The Structural Study of Myth and Totemism*. London: Tavistock.

Young, M.W. 1971. *Fighting with Food: Leadership, Values and Social Control in a Massim Society*. Cambridge: Cambridge University Press.

1974. Private Sanctions and Public Ideology: Some Aspects of Self-Help in Kalauna, Goodenough Island. In A.L. Epstein (ed.) *Contention and Dispute: Aspects of Law and Social Control in Melanesia*. Canberra: Australian National University Press.

1985. Abutu in Kalauna: a Retrospect. In D. Gardner and N. Modjeska (eds.) *Recent Studies in the Political Economy of Papua New Guinea Societies. Mankind* 15, Special Issue no. 4.

Index

Index

Epstein, T.S. 199
Errington, F. 59, 66, 77, 78
Europeans 76, 77
Evans-Pritchard, E.E. 63
exogamy 32–3
extended-case method 6

Feil, D.K. 21, 36, 40, 42, 172
Finney, B.R. 199
fishing 15, 49, 132, 188
fission 38, 126–7, 147
flutes 91–2, 95, 97, 103, 118
Forge, A. 8, 15, 16, 20, 42, 63, 168, 171, 175
Fortune, R.F. 108
Frederik-Henrik Island 14
Freedman, M. 141

gardening 15
Geertz, C. 85–6
Gell, A.F. 23, 199
Gellner, E. 3
German Sepik River Expedition 16
Gewertz, D.B. 15, 18, 19, 20, 22, 38, 59, 66, 77, 78, 140, 202
ghosts 31–2, 46, 108
gift exchange 2, 52, 170–1, 198–9
Gillen, F.J. 7, 51
Gluckman, M. 87, 153, 156
Godelier, M. 8, 59, 66, 114–15, 139
Goldman, L. 168, 171
Goodenough Island 14, 66, 168, 189
Great Men 115
Gregory, C. 42, 52, 170
Guiart, J. 142
Gulliver, P.H. 153

Haantjens, H.A. 25
Haiveta, C. 66
Harrison, S.J. 15, 17, 20, 25, 37, 41, 51, 60, 61, 63, 64, 89, 90, 102, 108, 162, 173
Hau'ofa, E. 66
Hauser-Schäublin, B. 15, 16, 23
Hegel, G.W.F. 197
Herdt, G.H. 84
history 7–11, 73–6, 189–93, 201
Hogbin, I. 8, 18
holism 3
Hubert, H. 172
Huizinga, J. 140, 161

Iatmul 1, 8, 15–17, 19–23, 59, 66, 78–9, 82–3, 105–6, 140, 142, 194, 202–3
idealism 197, 204
Ilahita Arapesh 15, 59, 105
incest taboo 32–3
inequality 4, 88, 90
initiatory grades 15, 92, 94, 101–2, 105, 110, 118, 123, 134

Irwin, G. 81
Isherwood, B. 197

Japandai 19
Japanese occupation 16, 26
Johnson, R. 199
joking divisions 104–5
Jorgensen, D. 199
Josephides, L. 63
Josephides, S. 8
Juillerat, B. 199

Kaberry, P.M. 8, 16, 59, 63, 171
Kahn, M. 20
Kamandjaw 16
Kambuli subclan 78
Kaunga 18, 23, 25
Keesing, R.M. 20, 84, 87, 198, 201
Kelly, R.C. 38
Keraki 59
knowledge 3, 21, 63, 102, 114, 141–2
knowledge-based polities 114, 141
Kopytoff, I. 21, 198, 200
Kove 59
Kula 81, 140, 195, 197–200
Kwaio 87, 201
Kwoma 16, 18, 19, 20–3, 59, 79

laki 101, 105, 106, 108, 110, 144
land 49, 65, 88, 150
Langness, L.L. 84
Lapanggai 16, 26, 29
Lawrence, P. 20, 198, 199
Laycock, D.C. 16
Lea, D.A.M. 15
Leach, E.R. 3, 9, 85, 87
Lederman, R. 42
Leenhardt, M. 173
legend 50
Lévi-Strauss, C. 11, 51–3, 55, 59, 73–5
Lindendaum, S. 198
Lindstron, L. 59, 114, 141, 173–4
lineages 69, 127
Lipset, D.M. 8, 20, 80, 190, 195
Local Government Council 77, 79–81, 136, 161, 168, 177, 192
Losche, D. 16
Lutkehaus, N. 8
luxury goods 21

MacCormack, C.P. 52
Madang 59
magic 33, 44–5, 47, 50, 56, 64, 73, 96, 106, 139, 150, 152, 157, 162, 172–3, 182, 185–6, 197–8
magical division of labour 66
Maiyir ritual 99–100, 134, 152, 181

Index

Index

scarification ritual 78–9, 100
Schieffelin, E. 171
schooling 28
Schouten Islands 8
Schwimmer, E. 171
Scoditti, G. 20
Serpenti, L.M. 14, 42, 171
settlement patterns 29
shamans 45, 78
Sillitoe, P. 36, 42, 63
simbuks 84, 93, 99, 106–11, 117, 123–4, 144,
   150, 156, 177–8, 191
Sissano 66
sorcery 19, 20, 60, 108, 136, 181, 189
Spencer, B. 7, 51
Spencer, H. 3
'Spirit'; see person
Staalsen, P. 19
Stanek, M. 16, 59, 140, 202
Strathern, A.J. 21, 42, 131, 170, 171, 172,
   173, 194, 198, 199, 200
Strathern, M. 40–1, 52, 171, 198
structural functionalism 6, 85
structuralism 52
subclans 32–8, 57, 62, 150

Tanna 59
teaching 114–39
Tee 197
Todd, H.F. 153
Tombema Enga 40, 41
totemic ancestors 29, 46–9, 67–8, 91, 137,
   143, 159, 167
totemism 1, 17, 23, 42–65, 67–8, 76, 78, 79,
   82–3, 187
tournaments of value 140–1
Townsend, G.W.L. 16, 25, 28, 60
Townsend, P.K. 8
trade 18–23, 79–81, 83, 195
'treading underfoot' 132, 182, 186
Trobriand Islands 59, 66, 81, 82, 189

Turner, V.W. 6, 87
tutelary spirits 28, 143
Tuzin 3, 15, 42, 59, 61, 63, 84, 105, 171

'Understanding'; see person
uterine siblings 37–8

Valik subclan 143–5
Van Velsen, J. 6

Wagner, R. 88, 198
Waranggamb subclan 95, 145
wards 29, 32, 143
warfare 16–17, 19, 26, 89, 98, 99
Wassman, J. 16, 59, 140, 202
wealth 82, 115, 118–19, 122, 139, 160, 175,
   198–9
wealth-based polities 114, 141
Weber, M. 172
Wedgwood, C.H. 8, 18
Weiner, A.B. 20, 59, 171, 173, 199
Wewak 77
Whitehead, H. 84
Whiting, J.W.M. 16
Williams, F.E. 59
World War Two 26
Worsley, P. 78
Wuluwi-Nyawi clan-pair 43–5, 49–50, 54, 58,
   63, 69, 92–5, 97, 99, 108–9, 128, 151–2,
   156, 176, 178, 180, 182, 189

yam harvest ritual 93, 100, 178, 183–4
yams 14–16, 25, 63, 93
Yawmbak 16, 26, 28, 29
Yentshanggai 16, 26–9
Yerikai-Garamambu 19, 23, 79
Yesan-Mayo 23
Yimal subclan 95, 132–8, 145, 176–7, 184–7
Young, M.W. 14, 42, 64, 66, 108, 168, 170,
   171, 189
Yuanamb 16–17, 18, 19, 28, 60, 78

Cambridge Studies in Social and Cultural Anthropology

Editors: JACK GOODY, STEPHEN GUDEMAN,
MICHAEL HERZFELD, JONATHAN PARRY

218

219

221

Lightning Source UK Ltd.
Milton Keynes UK
UKHW01f0202070618
323870UK00001B/20/P